The Marketing Director's Handbook

THE

MARKETING DIRECTOR'S HANDBOOK

*The definitive guide to
superior marketing for
business and boardroom success*

Tim Arnold and Guy Tomlinson

The Marketing Directors Ltd

First published 2008
Copyright © 2008 by Tim Arnold and Guy Tomlinson. All rights reserved.

Published by The Marketing Directors Ltd,
The Old Barrel Store, Brewery Courtyard, Draymans Lane, Marlow,
Buckinghamshire, SL7 2FF, England
Visit our website at <www.themarketingdirectors.co.uk>

Ordering Information
To order additional copies contact your local bookstore, visit our website
<www.themarketingdirectors.co.uk>, email <handbook@themarketingdirectors.co.uk>
or telephone +44 (0) 1628 400 699

British Library Cataloguing in Publication Data
A catalogue record for this book is available from the British Library
Arnold, Tim and Tomlinson, Guy
The Marketing Director's Handbook
The definitive guide to superior marketing for business and boardroom success

ISBN 978-0-9558860-0-3

Typeset in Monotype Ehrhardt and Gill Sans by
John Saunders Design and Production, Abingdon, Oxfordshire.
Printed and bound in Great Britain by Biddles Ltd., King's Lynn, Norfolk
This book is printed on acid-free paper responsibly manufactured from sustainable forestry in
which at least two trees are planted for each one used for paper production.

To our families

Linda, Sam and *Ben*
Nicky, Joanna and *Imogen*

Contents

Acknowledgements

We want to thank many marketing directors, colleagues and friends for their help in producing this book. There were many times when we sought and appreciated the knowledge and experience of those who had trod similar boards beforehand.

A number of marketing and commercial directors gave their time to be interviewed for this book: Nick Smith at Accenture, Phil Smith at Budgens, Paul Valdez at GlaxoSmithKline, Simon Thompson at lastminute.com, Morwenna Angove at Alton Towers, Russ Shaw at O$_2$, Kenny Boyle at Visit Britain, Gary Hughes previously at Hays, and Sarah Deeks previously at Universal Studios. Others have commented on our text: Hugh Burkitt at the Marketing Society, Michael Bates at Morrisons, Stuart Wilson previously at Kraft General Foods, Mark Hutchinson at Leader Drilling and Professor David Warren. Others have worked with us during our professional careers including Angus Fraser, Nick Ringer, Tony Lahert, Joe Flynn and many more. All have influenced this book in some form or other.

Particular thanks go to Patrick le Joncour at GMB Publishing for encouraging us to just do it, and for introducing us to Jessica Rawlinson who provided diligent and thought-provoking editing. Last but not least, thanks to John Saunders for bringing our work to life and to Sally Parker for our final proofreading and indexing.

Introduction

The Times They are A-Changin' – Bob Dylan (1964)

Why read this book?

Marketing is the one business discipline that almost everyone thinks they know about. It is the only function aimed at the customer so that is why both friends and colleagues readily comment on ads, what's in the shops and on the Internet. Even the chairman's wife will get in on the act.

Yet when undertaken professionally more than observation and comment is required. Sound judgement, proper process and intellectual rigour are prerequisites. As well as dealing with your colleagues' comments, there is a lot to do, a lot to learn and a lot to remember. And boards are asked to take collective responsibility, so you also need to know how to work with other functions.

Stepping up to become marketing director will be your biggest challenge yet. The risks will be greater and the rewards will be greater. With the average tenure of a marketing director being around two years – significantly shorter than that of a CEO at around four years – the available time in which to deliver is short and the consequences of failure remain high. Success will mean your career will soar.

What is certain, now as ever, is that every business needs marketing to realise its aims through its customers. But with the challenge of new channels and new technology both the job, functions and direction of marketing are in need of re-affirmation and re-assertion.

To do this marketers must lead and champion – and be seen to lead and champion – marketing thinking within their organisation. In simple terms you must put the customer at the heart of the business and make decisions based on what the customer wants, thinks and feels about your products or services.

Despite the fact that some marketers have achieved the lofty heights of a board position, the bad news is that the marketing profession has not yet earned its place as *the* profession of influence. With only fourteen of the UK FTSE 100 companies having a marketing director on the board (1), the profession still has a long way to go.

This is largely a result of being seen by critics as fluffy and lacking in rigour. Many view marketers and marketing thinking as synonymous with the creative arts, particularly advertising. There is some recognition of marketers' creative contributions but due to the high expenditures that are associated with advertising, some equate this with profligacy. Whilst this is probably rarely the case – these perceptions remain another issue that marketers must address. The challenge, therefore, for the marketing profession as a collective and for all marketers as individuals is to provide more scrupulous justification for creative initiatives and to underpin intuition with logic. New strengths must be added to existing perceived strengths. These include being seen as having the best interests of the business at heart, driving profitable growth, being commercial, structured and balanced thinkers whilst remaining innovative and inspired.

Superior and successful marketing is usually a result of not one, but many things – many skills, many techniques, as well as considerable knowledge or expertise. Great technical, leadership, influencing and management skills are needed not just to lead the function but to make an impact in the boardroom and on the commercial well-being of the business as a whole.

Who should read this book?

This book is designed to contain all the things a marketing director has to consider and act upon. As all marketing directors have a mind of their own this book is written as a set of insights, ideas and guides rather than hectoring instruction. Those already in the job will find it useful as if getting the views from a friendly peer.

Those who aspire to career advancement will find it helpful in understanding the additional pressures faced by your boss. You might even be able to make some worthwhile proposals as a result of reading it.

CEOs, fellow directors and agency colleagues may also find it worthwhile understanding how a marketing function operates. The outcome will be more harmonious working relationships and a more energised and successful business.

The purpose of this book

There are good books on brand management, market research and sales promotion. Ones on presentation and strategy, creativity and how to write a marketing plan – but no one book has brought it all together. Our aim is to create a definitive practical guide for anyone leading or aspiring to lead a marketing function. One covering both the management as well as the functional issues. It is based on extensive research on the best practices and processes available as well as practical insights and ideas accumulated during our many years of professional experience.

This book's first function is as a reference work of marketing best practices, tools and processes to help you at both a strategic and operational level. The second is to help you be an effective leader, influencer and manager; what is the best way of operating in the organisation? How to relate to and work with your colleagues? How to understand and optimise the impact of the other functions on marketing itself?

As marketers we perceived an unsatisfied demand with a least two customers and an enormous need. Ourselves. On checking and shaping the content of this book (via research) we found others perceived the need too. So here it is – The Marketing Director's Handbook. Not a text book, more a working book, born of experience and education, developed to help all of those engaged in the job of marketing director to actually do the job.

It is the book we needed. We trust it is the book you want.

In a single reference source, the aim is to help you:

- champion the marketing function at board level and throughout the organisation

- align organisation or business objectives with marketing objectives and activities

- provide a range of simple tools and models that reflect the best practices in the marketplace and that can help structure and enhance the quality and rigour of your thinking and inspire new ways to improve the marketing effectiveness of your organisation

- improve your own personal effectiveness/brands as well as your own worth.

How to use this book

This book is an aide-mémoire, source of ideas and guide. Look upon it as a source of advice, reassurance and inspiration when you need them. It's a work to help you get things done and not just read on a rainy day. It should never leave your side.

It is designed to be easy-to-read and digest, to be picked up or put down when needed or to be read through from beginning to end. Throughout you will find signposts and cross-references to other parts of the book to help you understand what to do quickly.

 Where to start

 Best Practices

 Why Bother

 Ten Minute Exercise

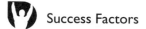 Pitfalls to Avoid

 Proformas

Key Questions

 Tools and Techniques

 Process Pointers

 Key Points to Remember

 Success Factors

Refer to Another Chapter (10)

The book has four parts. Each one is written differently, for you to use in different ways. Flick through the pages or refer to a chapter to get some fresh ideas or get started on a project you may not have done before! The sole aim of this book is to help you be a better marketing director – nothing else matters to us or indeed to you.

Part 1 Marketing Essentials (Chapters 1 and 2)

- Explains how the function of marketing fits into the business or organisation as a whole and provides insights and ideas to help you get to grips with your role.

Part 2 The Marketing Year (Chapters 3–10)

- Covers all of the key strategy and planning activities that you are likely to undertake in a financial year.

Part 3 Operational Leadership (Chapters 11–19)

- Provides insight and ideas to help manage your team and work with your boardroom colleagues as well as suppliers and agencies. It covers all the key tasks you are likely to undertake on a day-to-day basis.

Part 4 Major Project Planner (Chapters 20–30)

- Provides insight and ideas to deal with a range of possible challenges.

For those with a greater thirst for knowledge beyond the scope of each chapter, Appendix 1 contains references and suggestions for further reading. Appendix 2 summarises acronyms that are used throughout the book.

What you will learn in each chapter

1 Starting Out
- Seven essentials to be an effective marketing director right from the start
- How the reality may vary from your expectations
- The key elements of strategic planning
- What to do in your first quarter in the role

2 The Role of Marketing in the Business
- Seven essentials to be a superior marketing director
- How to help your colleagues understand marketing and the benefits it can offer

3 Strategy Development
- The importance, nature and benefits of strategic planning
- What makes a successful strategy
- How to create and get 'buy-in' for a strategic plan
- Strategic planning tools
- Strategic plan contents

4 Competitive Analysis
- The role, nature and benefits of competitive analysis
- Competitive analysis tools
- Useful research sources

5 Setting Objectives and Measuring Marketing Performance
- The purpose and benefits of setting objectives and measuring marketing performance
- Success factors for setting objectives
- How to devise useful marketing performance measures

6 Customer Strategy
- The purpose and benefits of understanding customers
- Different ways to segment and target customers

- Responsibilities of the board
- How to work with the CEO and fellow directors

14 Managing Market or Customer Research
- What customer insight is
- How to create a market research brief to get the best results
- Selecting and managing research agencies
- Ideas on qualitative and quantitative methods

15 Managing Agencies
- The agency landscape; different agency types and how they work
- The role that the marketing director should play
- How to brief agencies to get the best results

16 Brand Management and Positioning
- Common brand problems
- Types and benefits of brands
- How to position or reposition a product or corporate brand
- Brand architecture and options for managing a portfolio of brands
- Options for valuing brands
- Brand positioning tools

17 Optimising Customer Communications
- How to ensure communications meet your marketing objectives
- How to assess a creative idea
- How to create a compelling message
- Media options
- Pitfalls to avoid

18 Customer Relationship Management (CRM) and Database Marketing
- What CRM is
- The role and benefits of CRM and how data can help improve the performance of your marketing
- How to introduce CRM to your marketing
- How to build stronger customer relationships using CRM

19 Customer Channel Management
- What channels or routes to market are available
- How to improve customer channel effectiveness
- How to measure and optimise channel effectiveness

27 Culture Change and Brand Delivery
- What organisational culture is
- Types of organisational culture
- How to increase economic value
- How to change a corporate culture
- Culture change models

28 Crisis Planning and Management
- How to create a disaster management plan
- How to conduct a risk assessment
- What to do if and when a crisis occurs

29 Communicating with Other Audiences
- The benefits of communicating with different audiences
- Who are potential audiences and their needs
- The importance of corporate social responsibility and key messages
- How to create an effective communications plan

30 Marketing and the Law
- Key laws that govern the marketing profession
  - Consumer protection
  - Competition
  - Environment
  - Copyright and patents

Appendix 1 References and Recommended Reading
- Books, white papers and websites that expand on the subject matter covered in each chapter

Appendix 2 Acronyms
- Marketing acronyms

Marketing Essentials

1 Starting Out

Rise and Shine – The Cardigans (1996)

In this chapter you will learn:

- *Seven essentials to be an effective marketing director right from the start*
- *How the reality may vary from your expectations*
- *The key elements of strategic planning*
- *What to do in your first quarter in the role*

In the beginning...

You've made it. You have the office, the position on the board, the desk, the team and the budget. However, you now have to think beyond the roles of marketing manager and brand manager in the planning and implementation of marketing activity. So where to start? This chapter is designed to help you focus your energies and rise to the new challenge.

The role of a marketing director is unique: no other job or function is so widely known yet so universally misunderstood.

Being a marketing director involves engaging in strategy at the highest level. It also means understanding the ever-changing attitudes and behaviour of the customer and the market place and developing communications through a myriad of channels, while helping the board steer the organisation in the right direction.

The other functional directors will be used to using precise measures to set and monitor performance. It is the marketing director who has responsibility for communication and its associated need of creativity – both can defy measurement. (The notable exception will be the HR director, whose role is to interact with and understand employees but today, is primarily concerned with personnel practice and legislation.)

You will know that in marketing, while the sales data may be empirical, most decisions are inevitably leaps of faith, borne of value judgments reached by, at best, a combination of information, intuition and experience: your experience – that's why you are now a marketing director. Get it emphatically right and your brands and the business will soar; get it dramatically wrong and they will sink.

Be prepared to be misunderstood. Accept the fact that you will be scrutinised and aim to be measured but do not let the spark that lights the flame to enthrall and engage the customer ever be dampened. Always keep everyone informed and do everything you can to stay within budget – be prepared to defend it in its entirety at all times!

Success factors for starting out

The good place to start is to go back to the origins of your marketing training, when we were all taught the 'four Ps' – product, price, promotion and place. Let us now introduce you to the 'seven Ps' – the success factors that will help you be as effective as you can be, right from the start.

Figure 1.1 *Success factors for starting out*

Prepare	Be ready for your most important job yet
Purpose	Decide what you are setting out to do
People	Decide who you will be working for you and with you
Positive	Be positive and patient
Participate	Get involved and get to know the people
Pragmatic	Concentrate on what can be achieved
Plan	Above all, have a plan for everything!

Prepare: be ready for your most important job yet…

As soon as you have accepted the job you should start thinking as though you were already in it. Do some informal research to help you understand the potential issues and opportunities you will face. Ask for a copy of the budget and any key research reports. If possible ask to attend key meetings and try to shadow your predecessor.

Customer experience

Most important of all, this is the time when you can behave as a customer. Try every product, service and channel and make notes of the results. Of course do the same for the main competitors.

Research

Get hold of all the research from the organisation and if possible have it presented by whoever carried it out. However, the web is awash with other useful information – information for shareholders, on competitor organisations (there is usually the most interesting information under 'Press Releases'), product comparisons or review websites, and individual or 'customer' blogs. Trade Associations can also have very useful background information and industry data. Take time to look up agencies that you are inheriting, together with the agencies of your competitors; useful information lurks in 'Case Histories'.

Systems

Ask about the systems the company uses and get some training on them beforehand. Many a Microsoft user languishes in the face of Lotus Notes without some simple yet necessary training. The same goes for email protocols and the main IT systems used, particularly the databases. At the same time find out what reports are already regularly generated.

Personal

If you want to change your appearance – for example, shave off the moustache or indulge in a new hairstyle – now is the time to do it. More seriously, this is the time to get things done on a personal level as you may not have time when in post. Better to get as much done while you have the time. Also spend time with your partner so that the stresses and successes of the new job can be shared between you. Above all, this is time to get fit, both in body and mind, so don't waste the opportunity.

Purpose: decide what you are setting out to do

Just what sort of marketing director do you want to be? Is your mission to re-launch a set of faded brands, to maintain the steady successful growth or to look for insights that will help the company move forward? The role of a marketing director can be seen as one or a combination of several different manifestations.

Figure 1.2 *The role of a marketing director*

Architect	Helping design the overall structure and supervise the building works
Builder	The plans are completed but the building work must continue apace
Navigator	Everything is constructed but direction is needed
Philosopher	Where are we, what are we doing and where should we be going?

Ten minute exercise

At any one time, you will have to be all of the above – but which one should you be right now? Think about the big picture and use the list as inspiration to determine what you want to do against each type.

You will probably already know the answer to this but do take a considered look. The best starting point is the advertisement for the job itself, as that is what the business wants you to do. Set yourself a list of priorities – around the job but also around what your management style and approach will be.

You will need leadership skills like never before. Building trust and the art of delegation are paramount. This is the time to shed the so-called 'fuzzy image' of marketing; be direct, be knowledgeable but above all be approachable. In your dealings with the board and the company at large, resist the temptation to fall into 'marketing-speak' – talk in plain language (you will soon realise the importance of this when you start to communicate with your colleagues in IT). Be ready to make the complex simple and easy to understand.

If you now start to think of your role in the wider context, you will see that two themes emerge as the most important. First, and this is no surprise to anyone in marketing, you as the marketing director are the champion of the customer. No one else oversees the customer experience as a whole – make it your job, as your job depends on it. Second, you are the director for growth. Simply consider; while every other function responds to growth, only one creates it. Even sales needs marketing to put everything in place for them to be able to sell.

Start by championing projects to help ensure commercial success, like setting up a customer service ethos, new channels and the technology associated with changing customer contact or internal communications. It will not be long before you have to wrestle with the entanglement of brand and company.

If more marketing directors had taken this approach then the vagaries of call centre performance and many an IT system would have been avoided.

Revel in the wider business exposure – it will be your passport to the top job when you are ready.

Finally, be single-mindedly proactive. Work with the rest of the board but above all support the CEO. Help him/her as much as you can with your experience and back him/her up with presentations, market data, research findings and good public relations – anything, in fact that boosts his/her status. His/her success is your success.

People: decide who will be working for you and with you

People are important – better to have them as colleagues, friends and collaborators than enemies. Take a simple and honest approach and always open your conversations empathetically and democratically. Even if you get a less than positive response, always ensure your reaction is balanced and equally empathetic. After all, we all have off days!

However, if you get a negative response, don't continue the discussion. It is better to direct your energies where you will make an impact. Of course do not ignore the 'less than responsive person' simply accept that your positive energy may be not as effective as with others. Often their disaffection is with others rather than you. More often than not, the 'less than responsive person' will come around in the end.

Your team

You will inherit a group of people – some good and some bad – and some who thought they should have got your job! Quickly decide who will be your 'front runners'. This may not necessarily be the most senior or experienced members of the team but those who combine ability with enthusiasm and energy. You will be able to give them the benefit of your own experience and clear direction.

At the same time, review the organisation and suitability of the people to the tasks.

Inevitably, you will inherit a situation that is likely to be less than perfect; eCommerce, the embracing of Customer Relationship Management (CRM) and new channels and routes to market may have all added functions and led to many a dysfunctional marketing department.

In your first days, have 'one-to-ones' with as many people as you can manage. Try to understand each person and their current role but also try to get behind their initial reserve, perhaps by asking them what effect they feel they have on the business or what training would they like to have. Make some notes after each meeting – they will be useful later on.

Your fellow directors

Your induction process will be in the hands of HR – if not then arrange this yourself. With fellow directors, remember that you are among equals and your status as a director will affect everyone's attitude towards you. Figure 1.3 shows the key aims in working with your fellow directors.

Figure 1.3 *Key aims in working with fellow directors*

Function	Key aim	Relationship	Action
CEO	Support	Provide analyses and articulation of ideas	Presentations; speeches; information
Finance	Provide	Make sure your numbers stack up	Work within budget – aim to give some back
IT	Understand	What systems are you working with?	Be specific about you data needs
Sales	Encourage	Their performance is your performance too!	Be flexible – especially around key accounts
HR	Provide	Understand the culture	Embrace and influence the communications
Production	Inform	Understand the limitations	Match the timings

Other functions

Your first months are not the time for a 'land grab' of functions but a time to understand which functions and departments are critical to your needs. Start by deciding what you are going to need – resources, data, new packaging, faster distribution and so forth. At the same time, counterbalance this with understanding who will be most affected by your role. A clear picture of these aspects will help you interact with the rest of the company.

Positive: be positive and patient

Make the most of your early weeks in the role to be at your most positive. Yes, things may frustrate you, but do not be discouraged and remain upbeat. Here is a short checklist:

- You will need to shape the way you work into the established ways of the company.
- You will have to accept a new regime of accountability – most, if not all, will be quantifiable (or in the future made so by your own planning).
- You will need to embrace unfamiliar technology and systems.
- You will need to plan how you want to get things done – from listening to talking; from consulting to implementing.

Be positive in the eyes of your colleagues by embracing cross-company projects. These could range from new approaches to innovation to competitor information and, of course, the customer but perhaps also the organisation's culture.

Balance your positivity with patience. Wait until you have spoken to everyone and avoid the temptation to launch into any major initiatives. Remember that your early weeks will be spent listening, gathering information and understanding the implications and effects on others of your future action. Spend a great deal of time letting others get things off their chest!

Also be positive towards your suppliers, especially those with an intellectual commitment to your business, for example the advertising agency. Your aim in time will be to improve the creativity and the sharpness of communication and take back the reins of marketing strategy development. For now, take time out to reassure your colleagues and ask them for a fresh commitment to support you.

Courtesy counts

After every meeting and every request responded to, say 'thank you'.

Participate: get involved and get to know the people

This principle is more important than the detail. Don't wait for Christmas to get to know people – people act differently in social situations so make sure you run a 'get to know you' session for your team as soon as you can.

If there are any opportunities to join company social events then go along, and if there are social clubs, then seek them out and see what they do. You don't have to join but do accept invitations while you are able.

Every group will have its own pub, bar or regular social event. Seek them out, buy a drink and participate. You will be surprised at how much you can learn about the culture of the company and where the real power lies – valuable insights for you.

Pragmatic: concentrate on what can be achieved

There are three questions that you should ask yourself:

1. What can be achieved?
2. How long have I got?
3. What is the budget?

Above all, avoid the temptation to ride off in all directions. Take a long look at everything and reflect before you act. Decide where you can achieve the greatest effect in the shortest time. Everything else you are doing will help you as you formulate plans. Now is the time to understand what will affect your ability to be a success.

Culture

Understanding the culture of the company is vital. How open are people? Culture types range from sociable to competitive. What drives and affects people is important for you to understand. Is networking encouraged or is the organisation fragmented into fiefdoms or silos? Perhaps it is communal, with team working prevalent yet counterbalanced by limited decision making. Or it could be more mercenary, where everyone does things for a reason. By seeking to work within the prevalent culture you will achieve more – much more – than trying to break it down, initially at least. If you feel that the culture is not working to the best aims of the business, you should share your feelings with HR and then the CEO.

Budget

How much you've got to spend is not always as simple a calculation as you might at first think.

Here are some factors that could affect the budget:
- overspend claw-back
- currency fluctuations
- excess sales discounts
- supplier contributions
- sections held by other departments
- previously agreed fixed price contracts
- pricing fluctuations
- reduction through other departments overspending

Be prudent and make sure that your previously held views on what things actually cost and how they are valued are the same for this organisation. Each one of these factors represents an opportunity for you to operate more efficiently after you have dealt with issues in the budget. And in doing so, you will undoubtedly find more!

There is, of course, at least one more issue, and in marketing it seems always to be in play…
- business fluctuations

Marketing budgets are often seen to be less immutable and more flexible than any other budget. So at the outset it is worth raising this with the financial director and, as you're being pragmatic, find out what has gone on before and how you can best work together.

Workload

You will want to get lots of things done. Beware of your own workload tarnishing your performance or putting too much pressure on your own people. In working with your own staff or external departments, the well-tested management skill of asking people to set their own deadlines is the key.

Resource

Just what have you got to work with? How can you improve productivity? You may find that much time has been taken up with over-reportage, redundant information gathering and – inevitably – meetings. A re-evaluation of the use, format and need for these will enable you to release greater productivity from your team.

Consider the viability of using external resources at this time. If you have inherited fee-based relationships then ask for more within the fees – everyone you deal with will be keen to help you succeed.

Plan: plan for everything

First, you must ask yourself how long a 'getting started' period you'll need. This must be your decision and not one forced upon you. Many people talk around 100- or 90-day plans but in practice everything revolves around the board meeting. So set your plans to reach fruition by board meeting dates. Introduce yourself at the first one and present your plan for the next three months. When the three months has elapsed you will then be able to give a positive report by showing that you have achieved what you said you would. Always a good starting point!

This should culminate in an overall plan outlining your longer term objectives and how these will be achieved. You will then be able to gain board approval and a commitment from those departments involved to cooperate.

At this stage we should assume that you have prepared a marketing plan or two, or at least have been involved in the process. However, you may not have been involved in the type of planning that gets things done in a cross functional environment. This is the time for some project management knowledge. You may be lucky that your company has an established process and set of protocols to follow. In any case, you must bring yourself up to speed with the key practices. In doing so, you will be ensuring that your plans will reach successful fruition. Chapter 20 Project Management will get you started. **20**▸

Strategic planning

Planning and its precursor strategy are universally seen as being very important and are often complicated by this theorem or that formula. Yet the process is simplicity itself. All you need to do is answer three questions:

1. What is the business situation now?

2. Where does the business want to be?

3 What needs to be done to bridge the gap?

Unfortunately, this is where the simplicity ends and complexity begins. Understanding the current situation needs observation and research. 'Where you want to be' means listening to the business aims and seeing the opportunities. The most important of all is how you're going to get there. Philosophically, this means a combination of marrying the feasible with the practical then adding a leap of faith. Practically, it means laying out the milestones then detailing what has to be done, while at the same time understanding the implication on both performance and behaviour. These three headings should be those of your report to the board at the end of your 'starter period'.

There is no absolute guarantee of success in the planning process. You will need to bring together the elements of the business overall as well as your marketing specifics. This you can do in three ways.

First, you must embrace the company mission and where the business is aiming to be. Second, you must align your marketing planning to the business planning overall. Your marketing objectives must relate directly to the business forecast. Third, you must assess what external factors will impinge on and affect what is feasible; from the economy to the law, from competitive threats to demographic shifts. This will give you the foundations for an overall strategy, which can then be turned into actual plans.

Plan at two levels. Start with the broad sweep such as 're-launch this'; start a new channel; or reorganise the department. Don't give yourself too many. Start with, say, three or four – do them successfully and quickly. You can always add more later. Then break it down into the details – action specifics costed and allocated to individual people and departments for each of the broad plans. Then, as part of the process, ensure that you align the activity to the budget allocated.

This process is illustrated in Figure 1.4 and covered in more detail in Chapter 3 Strategy Development and Chapter 8 From Strategy to Delivery.   **3**   **8**

Figure 1.4 *Strategic planning process*

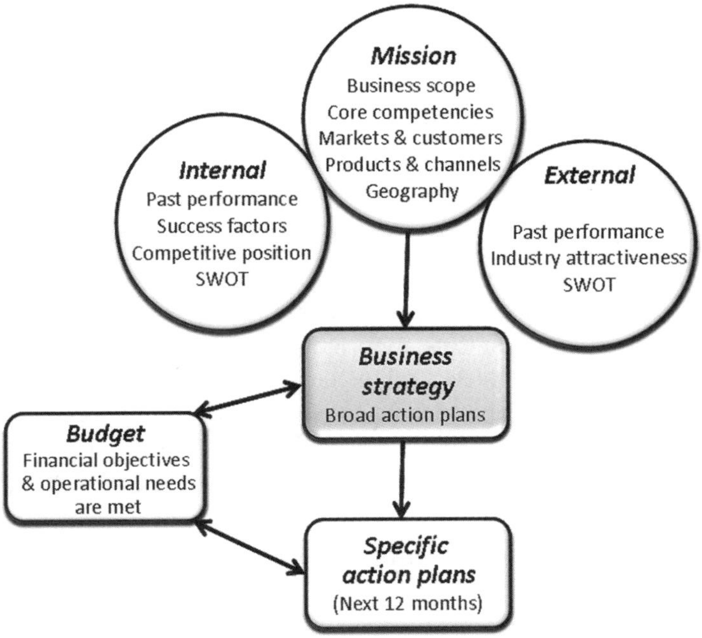

Make your first quarter count

Everybody comes under scrutiny in a new position but this is especially the case as a marketing director. There seems to be a universal expectation that YOU will do something. Perhaps there has been a pent-up frustration or a series of setbacks and disappointments that preceded your arrival. In any case, your first three months are key to your long-term success.

Here are some factors to help you succeed.

Start early and start fast

While you will already have started looking at your new company and its products and brands before you joined, it is vital to manage expectations at an early stage and agree what you propose to achieve or deliver in your first three months. Looking at and preparing a report on products or services, positionings and communications effectiveness, as well as what media and channels are used will be useful both for the short and long term. Try and spot the issues and opportunities. Find out what agencies and suppliers are used and compare this to ones you favour. This is a good background to discuss with your fellow directors, and of course, vital for your strategy development.

You cannot be held responsible for what happened before you arrived but you can readily assume that many of the other directors and managers do not like everything that is now being done. So, provide some quick wins – a presentation here, a trade campaign there and a new design or two. It is surprising how far a little early positive co-operation goes.

Talk the organisation's way

Learn the language of the company. Everyone is slightly different – titles describe different functions and three letter acronyms will be used that you will not have a clue about! Ask what they mean. It might be helpful both to you and the whole organisation to prepare a lexicon in your first three months and publish it. HR could even incorporate it in their staff induction pack. And of course, do not err on the other side. Keep your marketing lingo to a minimum too. At the same time, don't do too *much of 'the way I do it…'* or '*at my previous company we always did it this way*'. Your new colleagues will be proud of the way they do things and may not take your comments positively.

Build the status of marketing across the board

Not everyone sees the importance of marketing; this can especially be the case the closer to the customer the business operates. Help everyone to see the business as a customer sees it. For instance, a business is never seen in isolation but always as part of a 'basket' of offerings.

Sales and production will feel they are paramount, yet it is your role to be the champion of the customer in the business. Demonstrating what a difference a marketing approach can do is important, while at the same time agreeing realistic deliverables. Set Key Performance Indicators (KPIs) in the same format as the rest of the organisation uses or create your own. Issue a status report of your activities and plans.

Align marketing to the overall business

The CEO will have set business goals and overall performance targets, so the starting point for you is to understand exactly what these aims are and to realign all your marketing activity to support their achievement. Then start to work as positively and supportively as you can with the sales director. This person will be your most important ally and the owner of the function that can deliver the success you both seek.

Who's who and who's for you

In your first quarter you have to decide who the best is, who you can trust and who is not up to the task.

A starting point is to ask everyone for their status report and ask them to write down their own job description. Then, having made sure you've talked to them all, give each of them a specific task to deliver back directly to you, respecting of course any managerial levels.

With these responses, pick your lieutenants as quickly as possible and get behind them, as well as reinforcing and encouraging the working ways of the entire department. Finally, host a team event outside work after a month or so to say *'thank you for all the hard work'*. In Chapter 10 Structuring the Function you will learn of a number of categories into which you can fit your colleagues and your team.

Your supply chain

The temptation is to consider new agencies and to accept at least some of the flurry of new business approaches you will get. Resist them all, then reassure all the incumbents that your aim is to work with them. The quickest wins will be realised from asking your agencies what they want to do, so spend time getting to know them all. After a while, you can add a new one or de-select some but all in good time – professionally and fairly.

🦶 Key points to remember

1. First impressions count. Prepare as much as you can before you start work and then create and publish a plan outlining what you intend to do and what you expect to achieve in your first three months.

2. Make time to get to know your own people, their capabilities, motivations and personalities. Deciding on your lieutenants will be an important early task.

3. Get to know your fellow directors, their hopes, fears and needs as well as where resources lie that may be of assistance to you.

4. Be pragmatic, proactive and personable in your dealings with others. Now is the time to understand and learn so don't take anything personally. Be realistic about what you hope to achieve and allocate your time accordingly. Try and identify quick wins for the organisation as a whole, particularly your fellow directors.

Finally...

The three months or so are up. Time for you to stand up and be counted. Be confident and don't worry – if you have followed the process and put it into practice. You are about to become a truly successful marketing director.

The board is waiting for your presentation... good luck!

2 The Role of Marketing in the Business

What's It All About Alfie? – Cilla Black (1966)

In this chapter you will learn:

- *Seven essentials to be a superior marketing director*
- *How to help your colleagues understand marketing and the benefits it can offer*

It is an unfortunate truth that some chief executives bring in marketers with little clarity about the role that they will be undertaking. Some also have a deep distrust and misunderstanding of marketing, especially when the product or service is complex. Accepting that there are many who misunderstand what marketing is truly about, a major challenge is for marketers to explain, influence and add value to an organisation. A key objective of this book is to equip marketing directors with the know-how and skills to maximise the role and impact that marketing can play in the boardroom and throughout the organisation or business as a whole. The knowledge, skills and competencies you will need are summarised in Figure 2.1. These themes are developed in this chapter and throughout the book.

Figure 2.1 *The marketing director's 'Superior Performance Model'*

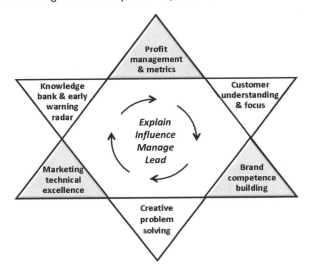

Profit management and metrics

The marketing director's responsibilities are no longer confined to the promotion of products and services to customers or the development of products and services. Together with your boardroom colleagues, you are responsible for shaping a stronger future for the organisation as a whole. You must enable the board to make investment decisions that deliver the best possible returns and ensure sustained profitable growth. Shareholders require better returns than they would otherwise be able to get from putting their money in a building society. Total shareholders' return (TSR) is the combination of capital growth in the value of the share, plus the dividend yield (the amount of profit paid back to shareholders in return for lending their capital to a business). As a benchmark and target to aim for, the most successful organisations deliver returns in excess of 20%.

In 1890, British economist Alfred Marshall invented the concept of economic profit (EP). This is profit after tax, less a charge for the capital tied up in the business. According to a survey conducted by PA Consulting in 2002 (1), the vast majority of companies do not use this measure. Unlike the conventional accounting view of profit (operating profit and profit after tax), this measure helps understand whether a company is creating or destroying value. The most successful companies use these measures and are the ones that sustain long-term positive growth in market capitalisation.

Measuring, making decisions on and delivering economic profit should be at the forefront of what you do. To achieve this, you will need to be financially literate and understand how sales and costs translate into profitability. You will need to demonstrate to the organisation at large, and the board in particular, that investments in marketing will deliver the desired returns, ie are economically profitable. You will also need to make investment recommendations and decisions based on what works best across the organisation as a whole. If appropriate measures don't already exist you will need to institute them.

Successful profit management also requires a highly developed commercial awareness and commercial leadership skills. You need to be a crystal ball gazer, and streetwise to where profitable opportunities lie in the marketplace and how to realise them.

Successful profit management also requires a close relationship with the chief executive and the financial director. To ensure influence, that relationship must be based on respect and speaking the same commercial and financial language.

Explaining, influencing, managing and leading

The marketing director can and should play a pivotal role in explaining, influencing and managing the effective delivery of the commercial strategy through the organisation at large.

Communicating and setting the tempo for the business can have a big influence on the motivation or drive of staff, in other words, how well the strategy is executed. As Jack Welch (2) once wrote in a letter to shareholders: *"In the old culture, managers got their power from secret knowledge: profit margins, market share, and all that... In the new culture, the role of the leader is to express a vision, get buy-in, and implement it. That calls for open, caring relations with every employee, and face-to-face communication. People who can't convincingly articulate a vision won't be successful. But those who can will become even more open — because success breeds self-confidence."*

Welch believed that great business leaders must:

- possess large doses of energy
- know how to use that energy to energise others

Marketing is still finding its feet in many organisations, especially service organisations and those outside the packaged goods sector. In these organisations, it is less clear where the remit of marketing begins and ends and the marketing director is less able to call the shots. Often the marketing remit is owned by the chief executive or managing director, as it is only at senior level that the various strands of responsibility come together. In these organisations, there may also be senior managers with overlapping roles and responsibilities. Thus the influencing and management challenges will be greater and more complex. You must expect to face difficulties that will test all of your technical and personal skills. Warring is more likely to dissipate rather than build influence. A charm offensive backed by strong commercial arguments is more likely to assuage and persuade. Keep reminding yourself that the harder the challenge, the greater the reward will be in terms of personal fulfilment and growth!

Customer understanding and focus

Having worked with many organisations, no matter how sophisticated they might seem on the outside, it's amazing how many lack a customer orientation. It's also amazing how so many people in so many organisations fail to grasp the basic concept of marketing. They don't understand and put the needs of customers first. Whether some of these people are in your own team, on the board or in different functions, the marketing director should never underestimate the need be a 'disciple' of marketing.

It is vital to advocate thinking from a customer point of view and put the customer at the heart of your decision making. Part of the job will involve helping others in an organisation grasp the concept and benefits of marketing and help them realise that it simply involves understanding customers and optimising products or services to meet customers' needs. Another part of the job will involve helping them understand your own customers and embrace and act on what they have learned.

You will need excellent communication and influencing skills to dispel many of the myths that surround marketing. You may need to convince them that marketing is not smoke and mirrors and is much, much more than communications. You should also bear in mind that telling them about the benefits of marketing is not the same as convincing them. By helping them discover the benefits of marketing for themselves they are more likely to appreciate what you mean.

So, right at the start, let us remind ourselves what marketing is all about. For often your colleagues will only see the output from the function not what underpins the delivery. In simple terms, marketing is about two things: customers and products. Marketing involves understanding a customer's needs and creating products or services to fulfil those needs. Of course, while this is very easy to say, it is less easy to do, especially when you are a #2 product or brand trying to catch up with the category leader! Figure 2.2 below helps bring the concept of marketing to life. View marketing as a matching process – that involves matching or meeting customer's needs with product or service benefits. Remember the graphic and you may find it useful when others struggle to understand.

Figure 2.2 What is marketing?

Oxford English Dictionary

Role-playing an encounter between a customer and sales person is a powerful way to help others start to embrace the concept of marketing and what it is all about. By having to think how a customer thinks and overcoming objections – often to the entertainment of others, people can genuinely discover for themselves what marketing is all about. There are also many applications of role plays – informal training or working sessions with disparate groups, as well as informal one-on-ones with senior managers.

Ten minute role play

What you need for the role play:
- At least two people; one to play the customer, one to play the salesman. Others are observers.

- A few cards, each describing a different object, for example, a pencil, a lipstick, a garden spade etc.

Objective of the role play:
- The objective of the role play is to help your colleagues to discover some of the benefits of marketing and how it works.

Guidelines for the role play:
- The objective of the salesman is to 'sell' the object described on the card to the person playing the customer. Five minutes is allowed for the task.

- The objective of the customer is to play him or herself and react naturally to what the salesman says or does. The customer is allowed to ask questions and the ultimate decision of whether to buy or not from the salesman is entirely in the customer's hands.

- The objective of the observers is to watch and listen and make notes on what they think is working or not during the role play. At the end, both the customer and salesman should be asked how they felt about the experience and the observers should contribute their insights on what worked and what didn't.

Lessons learned
This exercise tends to highlight at least three key lessons including:
- The importance of understanding or establishing a need before attempting to market or sell something to a consumer.

- The need for a product to offer demonstrable and differentiating benefits vs a range of possible alternatives.

- The need to communicate in an engaging style and tone in order to build rather than inhibit a relationship.

Benefits of marketing

Building on the insights revealed by the role play, six other benefits of encouraging a greater customer or marketing orientation in organisations are listed below:

- ensuring customer satisfaction, loyalty and advocacy
- building awareness and credibility

- reaching and attracting new customers
- providing insights on which to base continual product or service improvement, and differentiation vs. competition
- providing insights to optimise product cost, value/pricing and thus profitability
- providing a basis to align the activities of the organisation towards a common goal

All these points are generally recognised by the most successful organisations, many of whom enshrine a customer doctrine in their mission statements or corporate philosophies. For example, Sam Walton, the founder of Wal-Mart, the world's largest retailer, puts it very simply: "*The secret of successful retailing is to give your customers what they want.*" (3)

Unfortunately, the voice of the customer, or genuine customer insight or knowledge is sadly lacking in many boardrooms. The trouble with marketing is that everyone in the boardroom (rightly) has a personal view on what the customer wants, and they aren't always right. Seldom are misconceptions challenged until competition causes a wheel to fall off the corporate wagon. For example, in the late 1990s, after nearly 100 years of successful trading, sales and profits at Marks and Spencer nose-dived. In this instance, the CEO was famously responsible for product selection, even down to the chocolate puddings and underwear. At the time, Marks and Spencer did not have a marketing department so no one was truly responsible for ensuring the customer was heard in the boardroom. This is where the marketing director has a crucial role to play. The marketing director must bring the customer point of view to the boardroom in a way that it is credible and can be acted on. This is where research can be helpful. When members of the senior management team at Marks and Spencer were personally confronted by their customers in a research facility, this sparked a realisation that they had lost touch, and it marked a turning point in their fortunes. Among other things, it helped catalyse the recruitment of a marketing team that had not previously existed.

Brand competence building and delivery

The role of the marketing director and his/her department is also to create and define what it is about an organisation and its products and services that is distinctive and appealing to customers. It is about creating distinctive value propositions for which customers will shell out more of their hard-earned money. It is about creating and building brands. Underlying this challenge is a need to understand and nurture the strengths ie assets or skills of the organisation – to reinforce a positive and distinctive impression in the customers' minds. This requires rigorous examination, insight and analysis to understand what strengths can set the organisation apart and can be nurtured to deliver extra value.

In service organisations in particular, the marketing director must help the organisation as a whole communicate consistently and project a distinctive and appealing face to the customer. This requires effective management of the customer or brand experience, the touch-points or encounters that the organisation has with its customers. In some businesses, the range of touch-points or brand encounters (4) can be vast (Figure 2.3) and putting service at the heart of the experience can help achieve standout.

Figure 2.3 *Customer or brand touch-points or encounters*

Each of these touch-points needs to be managed so as to exert a positive and distinctive impression on customers. Exerting influence over these touch-points usually requires influence over many areas in the organisation that are not controlled by the marketing department. These areas may be customer facing, such as customer services, or internal such as HR or finance. To affect change through these areas will also require strong communication, influencing and managing skills. You will need to build strong relationships with colleagues to influence and motivate them to help you. For example, through the HR team, you will be able to influence employee communications, and influence the content of job objectives, job performance reviews and reward and remuneration packages.

Exerting influence over other customer-facing functions is unlikely to be an easy task. The marketing graveyard is littered with the remains of marketers who tried and failed. As well as using your persuasion you should use your marketing technical skills to obtain hard data to support your arguments. Use research to understand how consumers perceive the touch-points, what their expectations are and whether there is a shortfall between expectation and delivery. Also understand what drives or inhibits demand and loyalty, and would ensure an excellent customer experience.

Marketing technical excellence

In highly competitive markets, finely tuned marketing strategies and executional ideas can make a difference. A misplaced or poorly articulated word in a strategy could be misinterpreted and cause internal confusion. There is also a need for excellence in execution, especially in those markets where companies follow similar strategies. A misplaced or poorly articulated word in an advertisement could inhibit response and waste a lot of money. Conversely, a well-placed or well-chosen word could help cut-through and connection, thereby accelerating demand. The devil is in both the strategic *and* executional detail. You will need to establish processes, tools and techniques to ensure that both your strategic and executional decisions are of the highest order.

Overcoming perceptions that marketing is 'fluffy' is another key challenge that you may have to address. Mastering and using a few analytical tools and techniques can help you marshal and present your arguments in a simple and easy-to-understand manner. Not only can these distil complexity into simple messages but also give added rigour and impact to your arguments. A spreadsheet model will also be helpful. A number of useful tools and techniques are described throughout this book.

Creative problem solving

If the CEO's role is to manage the big picture and the financial director's is to manage the numbers, then the task of generating creative ideas to solve the organisation's problems lies with the marketing director. Creative problem solving is an area where you can carve out a truly distinctive role versus your peers. This is entirely consistent and justifiable in context of the marketer's main challenge: to ensure that products and services stand out and appeal in the market place.

To establish credibility as a creative problem-solver requires skill, tools and bravery. Skills and tools can be acquired, and there will be many agencies willing to support you in this cause. However, bravery is a state of mind that comes naturally to some and less so to others. Of course, what may seem brave to some, may not to others. For example, when the marketing director of a major retailer became frustrated at the unsuccessful attempts of his agency to develop new advertising, he set about developing new creative work himself. While this was highly unconventional and may seem risky to some, it led to a successful advertising campaign that has helped transform customer perceptions of the store. That store was Marks and Spencer.

So to solve problems in your business, don't shy away from demanding and creating genuinely differentiating solutions to build your business. Trust your instincts. What is wrong is probably wrong and what's right is probably right. With the experience you've gained in your career so far, you can be pretty sure that your gut instinct is as reliable as they come.

Knowledge bank and early warning radar

The final role that the marketing director can and should play is to be the eyes, ears and knowledge bank of the organisation. This fits perfectly with helping the organisation understand and focus on customers. However, it should go beyond this, to embrace all other dynamics that impact on current and future demand, such as competitors' dynamics and political, economic, sociological and technological (PEST) factors.

Knowledge is power. Those organisations that hold the most facts, insight and understanding about customers and environments in which they compete should be able to make better decisions and have the greatest advantage over their competitors. Within the organisation, there should also be benefits for the marketing department in terms of respect and profile. The marketing director and his/her team potentially have a very significant role to help ensure colleagues are familiar with the market place and customers. There will be almost unlimited opportunities to communicate and influence through board updates and briefings, presentations, exhibitions, open days and so on.

Monitoring and staying abreast of changing external dynamics is also important to enable you to remain alert to threats and be able to capitalise on emerging opportunities. Understanding these dynamics will also provide a valuable input into your future planning. At present, very few organisations are particularly good at monitoring external dynamics, or have well-established procedures to do so. Given the rapidly changing external environment, and competitive advantages to be gained, it is a role that sits comfortably with the marketing director and the marketing department.

 Where to start?

How businesses are driven, and the degree to which they are marketing- or customer-led in relation to others provides an initial indication of where and how marketers can add value to their organisations. As you become marketing director, or join a new organisation, a good place to start is to consider what the key drivers of the business are.

Identifying and understanding each of the drivers and then thinking through how marketing can help enable or support the different drivers is an important first step in deciding what to do and where to focus. In addition, understanding the degree to which the organisation is currently customer- or brand-driven will provide huge insights on the scale and scope of the challenge that lies ahead of you. Here's a short exercise to start you thinking:

Ten minute exercise

Objective of the exercise:

• To help define the role you could and should play in the business.

Guidelines for the exercise:

• Work through each of these steps in turn to generate and prioritise ideas to help you add value to the business.

  1. Make a list of the key drivers in your business.

  2. For each of the drivers, consider how more customer-driven or brand thinking could add value.

  3. Determine the degree to which your organisation is driven by customers relative to your competitors or benchmarks in other industries.

  4. What opportunities does this present to you? Assess each of the opportunities in terms of impact (high to low) and ease of do-ability (high to low) to help prioritise the ideas you have generated.

Figure 2.4 summarises some of the key drivers across a selection of industries.

Figure 2.4 *Examples of key drivers*

Industry sector	Key drivers
Agriculture, hunting and forestry	Land utilisation ie yield
Mining and quarrying	Land utilisation, resources eg mineral supply
Manufacturing – consumer goods	Consumer understanding/ promotion, distribution, relationships eg trade customers
Manufacturing – other products	Operations eg manufacturing; relationships eg trade sales, distribution
Electricity, gas and water supplies	Operations, resources eg water
Construction	Operations, land utilisation
Retail	Operations, purchasing, land utilisation
Transport	Operations eg resource utilisation
Post/telecommunications	Operations, resources eg people flexibility/cost
Financial services	Operations, risk management, resources eg IT systems
Business services	Relationships, operations eg service systems
Media/publishing	Resources eg creative skills, distribution
Consumer/leisure services	Operations eg service systems, resources eg people
Charities/not for profit	Operations, resource eg people
Public sectors	Government legislation

Manufacturing or fast-moving consumer goods (FMCGs) companies tend to be very customer driven. The marketing ethic is also critical and has been defined these companies. Barring disaster, nothing changes unless the customer or marketer says so. Typically, marketers in these companies can also enjoy career progression from product management to the board. In predominantly customer-driven companies, such as Procter & Gamble and Unilever, other functions are encouraged to be equally, if not more, customer-centric than the marketers. In some, the R&D teams even commission their own customer research. This leads to a healthy focus on customers. Use this list as a start-point to determine the key drivers in your organisation.

Figure 2.5 highlights the relative importance of a handful of key drivers across a range of industries. It highlights the difference in importance of customer marketing or customer centricity between companies in consumer goods or packaged products in comparison with other sectors. While customer marketing has relatively high importance in just two sectors, experience suggests that marketing is taking on greater importance in all.

Figure 2.5 *Relative importance of some drivers across sectors*

Industry Sector	Marketing	Operations	Purchasing	Distribution	R & D	Relationships	Risk management
Manufacturing – FMCG	H	M	H	H	H	M	M
Manufacturing-other	M	M	H	M	M	H	L
Energy	M	H	H	H	L	M	H
Construction	M	M	H	M	L	H	H
Retail	M	H	H	H	L	H	M
Transport	M	H	M	H	H	M	H
Post & telecoms	M	H	M	H	H	H	H
Financial services	M	H	M	H	M	H	H
Business services	M	M	M	M	L	H	M
Media & publishing	M	M	M	H	H	H	L
Leisure services	H	M	M	H	H	H	H
Not for profit / public sector	M	H	H	L	L	L	H

Key	High	Medium	Low

Key points to remember

1. As a key member of the leadership team, you are responsible for the commercial leadership of the business. This means taking joint responsibility with the other directors for making money ie investing shareholders' money and maximising the return on their investments. You need to be aware of where the profitable opportunities lie in the market and demonstrate beyond doubt that the investments the business makes, and in particular those made by the marketing department, deliver appropriate returns. This theme will be developed in Chapter 5 on Setting Objectives and Measuring Marketing Performance and Chapter 9 on Financial Management and Pricing. **5** **9**

2. You are the only member of the board with responsibility for marketing, so make sure your technical skills are first class. Set the standard and lead by example. Communicate and influence your colleagues by using language they understand and use your marketing skills and tools to help you. Always strive for strategic and implementation excellence. Keep abreast of the latest thinking.

3. The businesses that put the most focus on customers are usually those that are most successful. The marketing director must champion the voice of the customer, truly understand customer's needs and wants. Use the customer as a sword of truth to cut to the heart of issues and solve business problems. Don't underestimate the need to be a disciple of marketing. Expect your colleagues to misunderstand what marketing is about and be prepared to go back to basics to help them understand. Help them discover the benefits of marketing for themselves.

4. Get to know and build bridges with your colleagues, and work with them to influence and manage the customer or brand experience through all encounters (rather than through ownership). Concentrate on winning friends and advocates inside the business in order to win customers and advocates on the outside.

5. The marketing department is unique in having a creative reputation. Use the full range of creative skills and tools at your disposal to help solve problems throughout the organisation at large. Take confidence in your ability to judge a good idea.

6. Understand and make a point of nurturing key brand strengths to help your business, products and services stand out as brands in the market place.

7. Build superior customer knowledge, and be the early warning radar and knowledge bank for the organisation to help you make better decisions and set your organisation apart. This will also provide unlimited opportunities to communicate with and influence your colleagues, and build respect and credibility for your department.

8. In starting out, understand the key drivers of the business and determine what role a marketing or a customer or brand viewpoint can play to support or enhance each of these drivers.

PART 2

The Marketing Year

3   Strategy Development

Road to Our Dream – T'Pau (1988)

In this chapter you will learn:

- *The importance, nature and benefits of strategic planning*
- *What makes a successful strategy*
- *How to create and get 'buy-in' for a strategic plan*
- *Strategic planning tools*
- *Strategic plan contents*

While you will be familiar with leading a marketing strategy development process for a group of products, services or brands, you may not have led the process for an entire business group or organisation. Often this responsibility lies with the chief executive or strategic or business planning specialists in the business, but if the opportunity comes your way, it is one to grab.

An important aspect of your role

Dealing with the strategic development of the business is one of the most important tasks that you will ever undertake. It involves determining where the entire business should be, or what it should become, in the future. It involves making choices on markets and products, on profitability, growth, new revenue streams, brands, skills and assets for the business. It can involve defining a vision and purpose for the business. This is often better approached with a creative, as well as an analytical, mindset.

The purpose of this chapter is to provide a basic understanding of how to develop a strategy for an organisation or business, (and we have assumed that this most likely comprises a group of products, services or brands). We also highlight some alternative strategy development approaches, best practices, tools and techniques and their respective pros and cons to help to challenge and improve the planning processes in your organisation.

You should be reassured that you've probably acquired more business strategy development skills than you imagine in your previous roles, and there really is a very fine line between leading a strategy development process for a group of products or services and the entire organisation and business. The key difference is that the responsibility and perspective that you had previously now has to be much broader. To get this breadth of perspective a stint on the agency or consultancy side can be valuable. The acquisition of strategic skills and experience can also be a good reason to obtain professional qualifications, such as an MBA or mini MBA, read widely or work with external advisors or consultants.

It is likely that your organisation will have a tried and tested process or annual sequence of activities or events to create a strategic plan. Every company does it slightly differently and there is no fundamentally right or wrong way. Whatever your process, it will have its own strengths and weaknesses. If your organisation is performing well, then your processes are probably fine, but if it is not doing so well, then there is a case for casting a more critical eye and potentially making improvements. Some possible business strategy setting processes include:

- Bottom-up strategy setting and financial planning (as happens in many direct marketing organisations). Typically this generates a huge amount of detail. However, the process can be too rigid and lead to 'tunnel vision'. It can also leave an organisation vulnerable to threats from outside the traditional field of view.

- Separate strategic planning and tactical or financial planning, or when strategy is considered well ahead of the tactical and financial planning, provides more time for a thorough business review and can lead to a more visionary strategy setting. Conversely, it can lead to disconnections between strategy development and execution.

- Top-down strategy and financial target setting is a version of the above. In this instance the chief executive's wishes are cascaded down through the organisation into everyone else's strategies and targets. The downside may be that good ideas generated at the 'bottom' of the organisation may not be noticed or are difficult to get onto the agenda.

- Concertinaed or interlinked strategy setting and financial planning processes are probably the most common. These can feel a little rushed and process oriented. There is a risk in going through the motions for the sake of the process, and failing to step back and take a fresh view of the business. This can lead to tinkering, missed strategic opportunities and small incremental change rather than a fundamental review and significant change.

In the US, quoted companies must prepare quarterly financial reports for shareholders. This has prompted some to move to a more continuous, rolling 12-monthly means of strategic and financial planning. Arguments for this include forcing a continuous forward outlook and against include a lack of commitment to longer-term business strategies, investment in employees, and an extra burden on planning and reporting.

Objectives or goals versus strategies versus tactics

Before going any further, let's cover some basic definitions and frequently confused terms. To aid understanding, the original usage of the terms is also explained.

Figure 3.1 *Useful strategic planning terminology*

	Definition/original use of the term	Application in business strategy
Objectives or goals	Point to which the advance of troops is directed.	Sets out where the organisation, group of products, services or brands is aiming, or what it wants to achieve.
Strategy	Art or science of the planning and conduct of a war; command or movement of forces as to impose on the enemy the place and time and conditions of fighting preferred by oneself. Originates from the Greek word 'strategia' meaning 'generalship'.	Sets out how to achieve the objective; describes the key principles to guide the organisation over the long term.
Tactics	Art and science of the detailed direction and control of movement of forces in actual contact with the enemy; originates from the Greek word 'taktos' meaning 'ordered'.	Sets out what to do to achieve the objective and implement the strategy; sets out the plans that must be enacted to achieve short-term aim.
Mission	A defined combination of tactics designed to accomplish a specific objective; missions traditionally were of short duration with very specific engagement, assessment and troop disengagement procedures.	A corporate or departmental ethos or philosophy.

So to be clear, strategic planning involves setting business objectives, defining where your business is going and then laying out *how* to achieve those goals – *over years and months*. It is not about creating tactical plans for the year ahead as part of the annual budget process but the two activities often follow on from each other. The process of strategic planning should include an assessment of the success or failure of the enacted strategy or activities supporting that strategy to date.

It is also useful to distinguish three levels of decision making:

1. Corporate strategy decisions – are primarily concerned with determining what portfolio of businesses an organisation should hold and what its core purpose is;

2. Marketing (or business strategy decisions) – are primarily concerned with the allocation of resources at the business unit level (typically a subsidiary of a major division of a PLC) to achieve sustainable advantage in selected markets;

4. Tactical decisions – are concerned with the implementation of a marketing programme, based on the direction outlined in the marketing strategy.

When starting to develop a strategic plan, you'll first need to decide at which level you need to make decisions. If you already have a 'corporate' strategy and it is working well, then you can start at level 2.

Why bother developing a strategy or strategic plan?

Strategic planning was adopted by businesses in the 1950s at a time when markets started to become more concentrated and competitive. John Kay, the first director of the Said Business School, argues that business strategy "*is concerned with the match between a company's internal capabilities and its external environment – and that strategy is a set of analytical techniques for understanding and influencing a company's position in the market place.*" (1)

Let's look at some of the benefits of strategic planning in more detail. You may be able to think of specific ones to your organisation:

- provides a mechanism to align the needs of the business with the needs of the senior team

- encourages a focus on the future not just the here and now

- encourages more considered and rigorous thinking to business development, a distillation of ideas, and a ranking of priorities

- helps ensure market understanding and that there are sufficient customers to whom you can sell your products

- provides a focus on business strengths and weaknesses, portfolio gaps and actions that may be necessary to improve performance

- sets out a clear goal, aim or direction for the business to go in

- facilitates strategic (investment) choices, helps ensure that the resources and contingencies are in place with which to achieve agreed goals

- provides content that can be shared with potential or existing investors to secure or maintain their support (both financially and otherwise)

- provides content that can be shared with potential employees to encourage them to join, and with existing employees to provide confidence in the direction of the business and assist in retention

- provides a route map to facilitate internal alignment and to marshal and motivate employees

- provides a benchmark, allowing regular progress checking

Content for a strategic plan

There is no 'right' way to organise a strategic plan. What is important though is that the plan covers the topics and issues relevant to your company, and that the plan is arranged in a way that is relevant to your company. What goes into the plan, as much as how it is written, must be owned and agreed by those who contribute to its creation. So if you are starting for the first time, consulting with others is a good place to start.

At the end of this chapter, you will find a proforma with a list of headings to help structure a strategic plan. There are also many books and papers, business planning templates and software that you may find useful too. Some of these sources are listed in Appendix 1.

The starting point for setting objectives and strategies is usually at the highest level in an organisation or business. Figure 3.2 illustrates a potential hierarchy of strategies for a manufacturing business. Of course, the key strategic pillars will be different for every organisation, and reflect the key drivers of the business. You may be in the fortunate position of inheriting a corporate strategy from your CEO, if not, it may need to be created. Equally if your business is not performing well, this may suggest that your corporate strategy needs to be reviewed.

Figure 3.2 *Hierarchy of strategies*

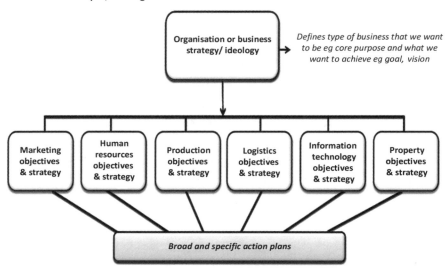

The translation of marketing strategies into plans is described in more detail in Chapter 8 Strategy to Delivery.

Success factors for creating a strategic plan

Be inclusive

A strategic plan is really a way of aligning the needs of the business with those of the top team. In time it will become your contract with your colleagues. You are agreeing to work with these people to achieve the same goals. We suggest that you lead from the front and put forward the people who should be involved. A survey of executives conducted at the beginning of 2005 showed that over 70% of directors wanted to be more involved in the process of setting a strategy, so don't underestimate the desires and feelings of fellow directors (2). A collaborative approach involving a combination of informal and formal meetings – offline working and research will probably work best. The implication with the former is that less emphasis is given to formal inputs and more to a free-flow of ideas. Some alternative forums are discussed below, together with brief pros and cons.

At the outset of the process, it will be motivating to signal an inclusive way of working. We also suggest briefing all of the participants both in writing and face–to–face, as this will avoid confusion and extra complexity later.

Figure 3.3 *Some alternative strategic forums*

Option	Pros	Cons	Success factors
Directors' or team away-day(s)	Team building; free flow of ideas; kick-start process; consider 'big picture'	Key player absent; perceived risk of bias (opportunity for facilitator?)	Clear agenda and objectives ensure comfort with the flow; techniques for generating relevant inputs (see below)
Marketing team away-day(s)	Prepare marketing director for wider meetings; means to cascade business strategy to the marketing team; engage, empower and generate team commitment and ownership.	No real cons.	Clarity on the nature and sufficiency of the current business strategy into the output from this meeting are needed in context of the whole process.
Business unit, country, product/ service/brand planning meetings (common in more hierarchical companies and multi-nationals)	Efficient use of senior management time.	'Show-piece' events can lead to 'all-or-nothing' decision-making (on products/ services/brands and people).	A consistent presentation of analyses so as to facilitate the absorption of necessary data, opportunities and key opportunities and key issues, thus enabling contributions to the debate.

Be clear who does what and when

The challenge to prepare a strategic plan can appear very daunting. While it is a complex task, it is easier if broken into small steps with clear outcomes at each stage and feeds from each stage to the next. Appoint a manager to co-ordinate the preparation of the plan and manage the logistics. This can be a good career development task for a senior marketer or financial manager. Having spreadsheet and word-processing templates that are used by all will help ensure a consistent look and feel of the output and facilitate comparison of business units or activities. With the highly sophisticated software packages now available, it isn't too difficult to create your own plan structure and proformas to help others think through and generate content. This will ensure the plan meets the needs of your business, and that the individual components can be easily 'rolled–up' or integrated.

A recommended sequence of events and example timetable is shown at the end of this chapter (Proforma 3A).

Winning hearts and minds

Setting the tone and nature of the strategy development process is a critical task for the leader as this can have a profound bearing on the outcome. Winning and aligning hearts and minds is essential to the process itself (how the end result is achieved), as well as the strategic solutions generated (what the result is). This is where the approach you choose and the nature of your personality can come to the fore!

In our experience, strategy development processes in some organisations are really dull. Conceiving the whole exercise as an event can make it more exciting, inspire better ideas as well as help motivate and ensure greater commitment to the outputs.

Away-days are a good place to start. Take a leaf out of the books of the teams responsible for some 'famous' world firsts – the first animated movie (Disney's *Snow White and the Seven Dwarfs)* or the first atomic bomb. Convene a small team and lock yourselves away in an inspirational environment! Taking the team out of the office can signal an escape from the everyday, and facilitate a more creative mindset. Choose somewhere complementary to the nature of what you are trying to do. Just put a few key words into a web-search engine and you'll be inundated with ideas. How about paying a visit to a lighthouse that has been converted into a hotel?

 Best practice

In the fast-moving mobile phone market O_2 kick-started their planning process with a *Dr Who* themed away day. The members of the marketing team 'travelled' into the future in a Tardis (a police box look-alike time machine) wearing fancy dress. This helped fuel ideas on what the future, and O_2's future, could and should look like.

Remember too that research suggests that groups operate more efficiently with less than ten people.

Whatever the event, eating and playing together is a good way to have fun and bond with colleagues. While it is fabulous to wine and dine in fantastic surroundings and be waited on hand and foot, why not select a venue where you can cook for yourselves? This could help with team bonding all the more.

Strategic planning process

Most strategic planning methods rely on a three step process:

- Step 1: Business situation analysis – where are you now?
- Step 2: Define the goal – where do you want to be?
- Step 3: Determine the strategy ie road map to bridge the gap

The process for analysing the current business situation and generating future ideas can be as simple or detailed, formal or informal and involving as you wish.

Reviewing and understanding the current performance of the business provides a robust foundation on which to build a future plan. Typically this should involve understanding the strengths and weaknesses of your business relative to competition and customers, both in the present day and into the foreseeable future. It is also important to look at the changing world about you to make sure your corporate radar is tuned into emerging opportunities and threats. The process of reviewing current business strengths, weaknesses and threats can be a powerful tool to crystallise issues that need to be addressed as well as help identify future opportunities. As well as the overall business, the thinking process can also be applied to each and every facet of the business, for example, individual products, services and brands, functions, resources and business units.

Another approach is to start with the end in mind and imagine an ideal finished state. Then work backwards to assess what the current situation is. This is usually a more creative approach and can be powerful in generating more future focussed and stretching goals in comparison with analytical methods. Ultimately a combination of both analytical and creative methods may produce a more robust and practical output.

Once you have a clear idea of both where you are now and where you want to be, you can identify the gaps that need to be bridged or issues that need to be addressed to realise the ideal finished state. The journey or 'how to's' to reach your goals are the strategies you employ. Strategies can also be viewed as a means of balancing the company's risks and achieving its goals. In addressing issues, it helps to frame them in the format 'how to…' '…reach the moon', '…jump over a cow', etc. It can then be easier to work out the options that enable your goals to be reached with least risk. The strategic alternatives can then be assessed and, if needed, researched in terms of their potential pros and cons, and eventually refined.

Figure 3.4 shows a simplified strategic planning process. While this is pictured as a sequential exercise, in reality the generation and evaluation of objectives and strategies is usually a creative and iterative process rather than a linear logical thinking one.

Figure 3.4 *Simplified strategic planning process*

```
┌─────────────┐        ┌─────────────┐
│  What is    │        │ Where does  │
│ the business│        │ the business│
│ situation   │        │ want to be? │
│ now?        │        │             │
└─────────────┘        └─────────────┘
```

```
┌───────────────────────────────────┐
│           Gap Analysis             │
│       What are the key issues?     │
│    What needs to be done to bridge gap │
│    ie what strategies should be employed? │
└───────────────────────────────────┘
```

```
┌──────────────┐   No   ┌──────────────┐
│ Are all issues│ ────► │    Revise    │
│  solvable?   │        │  objectives  │
└──────────────┘        └──────────────┘
        │ Yes
        ▼
┌──────────────┐
│ Objectives are│
│  achievable! │
└──────────────┘
```

 Strategic planning exercise

To get you started use either of the first two strategic forums discussed above to work through this simple exercise with your colleagues.

What you need for the exercise:
• at least four and up to around ten colleagues and a moderator
• at least half a day to a day of time
• lots of flipchart paper, wall space and a few marker pens

Objective of the exercise:
• To engage your colleagues and work with them to produce a high level strategic plan

There are three steps to the exercise:
• Step 1: to determine what the business situation is now
• Step 2: to determine where the business wants to be in the future
• Step 3: to determine the strategies to enable the business to go from where it is now to a desirable future state

Step 1: determine what the business situation is now

- A 'SWOT' analysis (strengths, weaknesses, opportunities and threats) analysis is a useful tool to start conducting a strategic review. (See Figure 3.5). This involves assessing the truly differentiating and distinctive strengths (and weaknesses) that the organisation, product group or brand group has, as well as opportunities and threats facing the business.

- Start by drawing a line down the middle of the page and then list all the strengths and then weaknesses of the business from top to bottom on the left hand side of the page.

- Strengths and weaknesses are hard to describe clearly; they must be expressed relative to competition so be sure to define them clearly and specifically. For example, all organisations say they have great staff – therefore this is not a sufficiently specific relative strength.

- To ensure objectivity, ask what words a customer would use to describe your strengths and weaknesses. Sometimes this may reveal latent or potential strengths that could be developed and exploited.

- Then consider all the external forces affecting the business, such as political, economic, social and technological (PEST), as well as competitive. Some will be threats, and should be listed underneath the weaknesses. Opportunities should be placed in the right hand column.

Figure 3.5 *SWOT analysis*

Step 2: determine where the business wants to be in the future

- Determining where the business wants to be in the future can be either an analytical or creative challenge. The process can be driven largely by the current business situation or the internal ambitions of the business. Usually a balance of both works best.

- A more analytical method is to review each of the strengths, weaknesses and threats in turn and generate a long list of associated opportunities. Write the opportunities on the right hand side of the page. This will naturally reveal ways to leverage or exploit strengths (ie assets and resources of the organisation) or address weaknesses. All should result in opportunities to improve competitiveness.

- Considering external forces may also reveal new market opportunities although these are unlikely to be unique to your organisation.

- A more creative approach is to brainstorm how you would like the future to look and feel. Consider using some of the techniques outlined in Chapter 21 Creativity and Problem Solving. For example, viewing the world through the eyes of Richard Branson might help reveal opportunities that your business might not naturally consider. **21▶**

Step 3: determine the strategies to enable the business to go from where it is now to a desirable future state

- Once a list of opportunities has been identified, they can be assessed and prioritised in terms of attractiveness, and strategies can be devised to help you realise them.

- Once a clear picture of the future has been agreed then the gaps that the business must bridge can be defined. Articulating challenges as key issues, expressed as 'how to...'s can be useful to generate alternative strategic options to bridge the gaps or address the issues.

- Aim for 3–5 issues; too many may result in spreading the organisation's resources too thinly and too few may be leave you vulnerable to competitive pre-emption or threats.

- For each issue, crystallise one or more than one way to address the issue.

- Split the group into small teams to address one or more of the issues. This will help generate richer and more considered content, as well as encourage ownership. Teams can then present their ideas to the full group who can then contribute additional builds.

- Aim to generate a number of options, and ask the various teams to present their ideas back to the group. You can then agree which are the favourites, and what more needs to be done to ensure that the option makes sense. This is likely to require more detailed analysis of both the upsides and downsides of the idea. It will also require time which will be better found outside a single working session.

- Figure 3.6 provides a visual representation of how this process should work.

Figure 3.6 *Setting objectives and strategies*

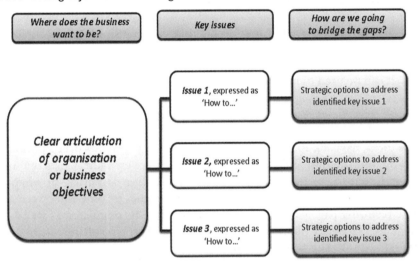

Tools and techniques to assess strategic options

There are two key ways to assess the attractiveness of alternative strategic options. The first is to determine the relative pros and cons or benefits and costs of the options. The second is to conduct a risk assessment and determine how to mitigate any potential risks.

Pros and cons analysis

This involves assessing and then listing, usually in two columns, the pros or advantages of an idea or option, alongside the cons or disadvantages. Assessing pros and cons is usually a qualitative exercise and the nature and length of the contents of the two can provide a quick visual gauge on the relative attractiveness of the ideas.

Cost/benefit or profit pool analysis

A more robust way to assess the attractiveness of the options is to calculate the costs and benefits or profit potential. Here the simple aim is to add up the potential revenues arising from a particular scenario and subtract any potential costs.

To assess the relative attractiveness of alternative market entry or growth scenarios, market profit pools can be calculated. First convert consumer market sales values to trade sales equivalents and then deduct amounts for manufacturing, distribution and promotion costs, as well as corporate overheads. Some assumptions may need to be based on market observations and experience.

This type of analysis can also be used to identify competitor brands or segments that may be particularly profitable and worth targeting. At a company level, together with a comparative assessment of financial strengths and weaknesses from corporate accounts, it can be used to help identify attractive acquisition candidates.

Payback analysis

In simple form, payback analysis involves assessing cost/benefits over a period of time and working out the time period to repay the initial investment. Costs will be either one-off or fixed, for example in plant and production facilities, or ongoing and variable, such as raw materials and labour. Benefits ie sales income will be accrued over time. The resulting payback period (PP) can therefore be calculated as well as the net present value (NPV) at a point in time. NPV discounts the resulting return on investment by taking into the time value of money, for example, by deducting costs for interest on capital borrowed and inflation effects.

In more sophisticated form, an attempt should be made to place a monetary value on more intangible benefits such as time savings, or value added to a brand.

Your company is very likely to have its own preferred methods for assessing investment alternatives and your financial department should be best placed to help you.

Risk management

The risks associated with a particular scenario (what can go wrong), and your ability to mitigate any risks, may significantly influence the attractiveness of a particular option.

There are two key steps to effective risk management:

- To assess the risks; what the risks are, the potential magnitude of the risk, and the probability that they will occur

- To devise plans to mitigate the risks (or deal with them should they occur)

A risk assessment should involve representatives from relevant functional areas and finance as well as the marketing department. External risk management experts could also be involved in unusual or complex circumstances. The outcome of a risk assessment should be a list of potential risks, together with an assessment of their potential magnitude and probability of occurrence.

Once the risks are identified, then plans to mitigate any risks can also be devised, and mechanisms to offset risks employed. For example, financial services organisations have historically focused on return on investment and financial risk management to make strategic and investment decisions.

 Best practice

Helping a major financial services organisation make better investment decisions and build a stronger, more appealing and differentiating customer proposition led to the creation of a tool that required the effect on customer satisfaction and the brand to be factored into the equation. While choices could still be made that offered no customer benefits, any potentially adverse effects on customers must now be recognised and mitigated – for example, to avoid adverse publicity and damage to the reputation of the brand.

Setting objectives

Objectives that are vivid tend to be more memorable, engaging and motivating to the people that have to implement them. Equally clear and specific objectives help keep a team grounded and allows performance to be measured (usually fixed over a time period).

The timeframes that you apply to the objectives and strategies set will depend on the nature of your business and nature of the goal. Five to ten years is reasonable for high-level business goals – this ensures that they are stretching, but achievable. Three to five years is reasonable for high-level strategies – this is as long as, if not longer than, the average tenure of the chief executive and marketing director! It is also a timeframe that is understandable and meaningful to most employees. However, the judgment is yours as even these may be too long in rapidly changing technology markets, or too short in industries where long lead times are required to tool up and set up production lines.

When you are ready to implement your strategic plan, the only thing that is certain is that the future is uncertain. It is therefore virtually guaranteed that your plan won't go exactly as projected. Make a point of building in measures and mechanisms to monitor performance continually and understand the reasons for any variances. When you write your plan build in flexibility to adapt your strategies and plans when the need arises and as you accumulate new knowledge update your strategic plan.

Chapter 5 on Setting Objectives and Measuring Marketing Performance covers these aspects in more detail.   **5**

Tools and techniques

This section describes some tools and techniques that are useful for conducting business situation analyses and strategic planning.

Figure 3.7 *Business or product/service life cycle analysis*

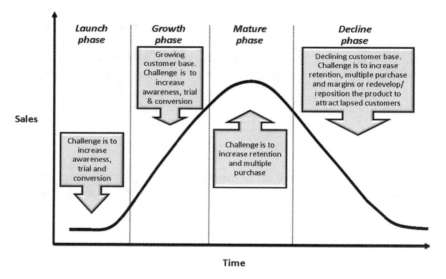

Most will be familiar with the concept of a product lifecycle (Figure 3.7). By analysing product sales over the life of a product, a clear picture can be formed of where the business or group of products or services is now in context of its recent history. Combined with understanding the trend in numbers of customers that a business or product has, as well as average purchases per customer, it helps provide an objective view of the strength of a business or group of products. Analyses of this nature also help reveal what needs to be done to restore growth or maximise profitability.

Most businesses will already track year-on-year sales trends for their products through their financial reporting systems. Reviewing this data in terms of a moving annual total trend can be more useful as it provides an early warning of an upward or downward trend that needs to be understood and managed. Various strategies can be employed to sustain sales. For example, in computing and toiletries, continual innovation is common-place. In food and entertainment, products are sometimes only available for a limited time period. Examples include the confectionery *Space Dust*, which has appeared a handful of times in the last forty years and *Walt Disney* DVDs, which have historically been released on a seven-year cycle.

Figure 3.8 *Product portfolio analysis – BCG Growth-share Matrix*

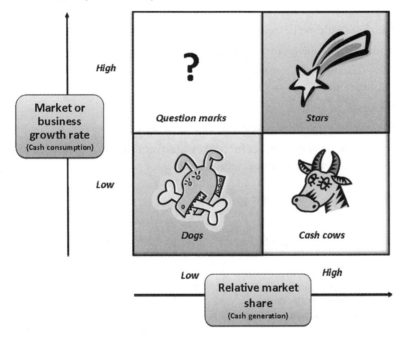

The Boston Consulting Group Growth-share Matrix (Figure 3.8) also helps analyse and understand the current state of the business (3). Invented by Bruce Henderson, who ran the Boston Consulting Group in the late 1960s and early 1970s, this model is useful for managing a group of business units or product and service lines, and for helping to determine what priorities they should be given ie hold, divest or grow. The BCG Matrix plots market share versus growth rate relative to competitors. Market share serves as a proxy for competitive advantage, and growth for sector attractiveness. This model assumes that an increase in market share will be cash generative (as production costs will be driven lower). It also assumes that growing markets will consume cash (as extra investment in assets will be needed to increase supply). Thus the larger an organisation's market share and slower the growth, the better.

The BCG Matrix segments business units or products into four groups. These are:

Stars (high growth and market share)

- use and generate large amounts of cash
- attractive to hold share because this will lead to the star becoming a cash cow when the industry matures

Cash Cows (low growth, high market share)

- profit and cash generation should be high
- the foundation of a company; provide funds for investment in other businesses or products

Dogs (low growth and low market share)

- tie up cash that could be better deployed elsewhere
- aim to minimise the number of dogs in a company
- unless a dog has another strategic purpose, or can grow share, it should be liquidated to deliver cash

Question Marks (high growth, low market share)

- poor cash generation yet demanding of cash
- some may have potential to increase market share and become stars, others may have no potential and merit divestment (to generate cash)

Figure 3.9 *Organisation or business strategy/ideology*

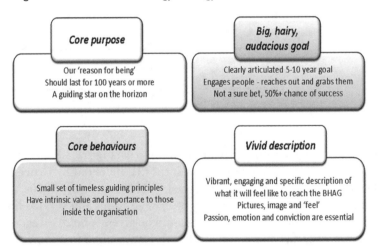

The strategy framework described in Figure 3.9 is inspired by the findings of research conducted by Jerry Porras and James Collins (4) and explained in their book *Built to Last*. The framework helps organisations think through and articulate where they want their business to be or what they want it to become in the future. It is particularly useful as a visioning tool to shape and cement the appetite or ambition of senior management teams. It is also powerful in providing a blueprint that can be discussed, refined and eventually nailed to the corporate flagpole and used to rally the wider team.

Over a period of six years, the authors of *Built to Last* identified 18 'visionary' companies and set out to determine what's special about them. To get on the list, a company had to be world famous, have a stellar brand image and be at least 50 years old. Each was compared with a control group of 'successful-but-second-rank' companies (based on stock market performance) to highlight what made them perform better than their competitors. Thus The Walt Disney Company is compared to Columbia Pictures, Ford to GM, Hewlett Packard to Texas Instruments, and so on.

The visionary companies were found to have a number of common characteristics – for instance, almost all had some type of core ideology that guided the company in times of upheaval and served as a constant benchmark. There are four elements to this ideology, as described in Figure 3.9.

Figure 3.10 shows a completed strategic framework (for Sony in the 1950s).

Figure 3.10 *Sony's vision (1950s)*

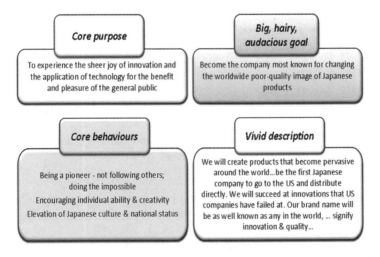

Ansoff's Matrix (3.11) helps crystallise strategic business development options and helps managers think creatively (5). This model covers the two key marketing variables (customers and products) and sets out four options to enable the business to grow.

Figure 3.11 *Marketing strategy options (Ansoff's Matrix)*

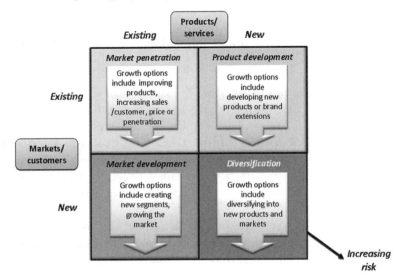

The four options are:

- **Market penetration** – developing the existing core business in existing market(s). This will be easiest if there is plenty of market share to be had at the expense of your competitors and if products are purchased infrequently. Using promotion or price may be a quick way to increase penetration. A strong market share may suggest that better returns may be obtained by extending your range of products/services or to expand by appealing to new customer segments.

- **Product development** – introducing a new product to your existing market(s). This is an attractive strategy if you have strong market share in a particular market and there is little upside potential to grow the market. In developing new products you may need to consider 'cannibalisation' risks and rewards. Chapter 23 on New Product and Service Development provides many insights and ideas on how to develop successful new products and services.   **㉓**

- **Market development** – developing new markets or customer segments for your existing products. This could be achieved by repositioning your products to attract customers in other segments or by bringing new customers into the market.

- **Diversification** – launching new products into new markets unrelated to the core is the highest risk option – not only do you not know the products but you will be less familiar with the market(s). This sort of activity should generally be regarded as additional and supplementary to the core business activity, and should be considered only after thorough analysis and testing. This option is commonly realised through acquisition. Expansion opportunities through merger or acquisition are covered in Chapter 25 Mergers and Acquisitions.   **㉕**

Whichever option you choose, you should be able to generate a list of pros and cons. You should also evaluate each in more detail and ensure that your assessment is robust.

Some additional strategic analysis tools are also described in Chapter 25.

 Proforma 3A: Content for a strategic plan

Executive summary

- Summary of plan
- Statement of key issues and opportunities
- Organisation/business strategy/ideology
- Statement of sales and profit potential
- Investment highlights

Current business status

- Results to date vs previous plan
- Lessons learned
- Strengths, weaknesses, opportunities and threats

Marketing objectives

- Market opportunities/potential
- Market projections and segments (sizes and growth)
- Market share projections
- Description of customers (including unfulfilled needs) and penetration projections
- Products/services offered and key differentiators/benefits
- Competition/competitive analysis

Marketing plans by product/service category, line or brand

- Projections eg by product/service line
- Strategies, plans and key assumptions/measures:
  - product/service development
  - promotion and selling
  - pricing and risk
  - distribution/delivery
- Key issues
- Plan risks and opportunities
- Priority projects and action plans

Resources and operational support

- Human resources (who does what?)
- Facilities (offices, plant, equipment and physical assets)
- Information systems
- Production
- details on how the product is to be produced or sourced
- research and development activities (if applicable)
- logistics/distribution

Financial

- Discussion of assumptions made in preparing financial statements
- Summary profit and loss statement(s)
- Summary balance sheet
- Summary cash flow forecasts (include sensitivity analysis)
- Break-even analysis (for any key initiatives/capital investments)
- Funding requirements (worst case, best case)
- Sources of funding
- Uses and applications of funding

Risk management

- identification of risks
- potential problems
- contingency plans
- protection of intellectual property

Appendices

- Relevant company details
  - history (background) of company
  - ownership structure
  - board of directors and/or advisors
  - other key people (management) involved (relevant experience)
- Product specifications
- Financial spreadsheets
- Historical information (if applicable)

Proforma 3B: Timetable for preparing a strategic plan

Event	Who	When
Meeting(s) to agree/ outline corporate/ business strategy.	Board	Week 1-4
Cascade strategy to all plan contributors.	Board/planning team leader	Week 5
Issue planning costs/other assumptions to marketing team.	Finance	Week 5
Prepare marketing strategies and outline P&Ls for each product line.	Marketing product groups	Week 7
Prepare departmental strategies and outline budgets.	Department managers	Week 7
Meetings to review product group strategies and departmental plans.	All/ board	Week 7
Prepare high level consolidated P&L.	Finance/planning team	Week 8
Review high level consolidated P&L.	Board	Week 8
Brief contributors on required revisions.	Board/planning team leader	Week 8
Refine and write up marketing strategies.	Marketing product groups	Week 8/9
Refine and write up departmental strategies and plans.	Department managers	Week 8/9
Prepare revised consolidated P&L.	Finance/planning team	Week 10
Prepare business, marketing and financial summaries.	Planning team leader + CEO, marketing and finance director	Week 10
Submit plan to head office.	Planning team leader	Week 11
Q&A with head office.	Board	Week 12

Key points to remember

1. Strategy development is really a means of aligning the needs of the business with the needs of the managers. That means the emphasis should be on the process as well as the strategy outputs. Involve the wider management team.

2. Both the nature of the planning process and the nature and personality of the leader can influence how the management team feels about the planning process as well as the strategy outputs generated. This is an opportunity to inject as much vision, ambition, analysis, creativity, drive and enthusiasm into the business as you think is needed.

3. Strategy development is about balancing risk and rewards. There are rarely 100% right or wrong strategies to develop any business. Build in flexibility to your process, strategies and plans, include mechanisms to learn how to improve your plans and manage any downside risks.

4 Competitive Analysis

Leader of the Pack – Shangri-Las (1964)

In this chapter you will learn:

- *The role, nature and benefits of competitive analysis*
- *Competitive analysis tools*
- *Useful research sources*

Competitive analysis can be seen as a menial task and is often delegated to the lowest ranks in a department. This, however, can be very dangerous! In some parts of the world, particularly East Asia, competitive analysis is a cultural preoccupation! This is evident in the rate with which companies copy each others' products. It leads to continuous product innovation and a steady lowering of costs as companies make changes to their products, having found new ways of making them cheaper. Copycat product development has become so widespread and effective in this region that it has provided those countries with an inbuilt competitive advantage when compared to others in the world.

In rapidly growing or fast-changing markets or markets containing products with short lifecycles, such as information technology and mobile telephony, even relatively modest innovations could present new threats and cause significant shifts in sales and market share. Marketing directors operating in these sectors therefore need to remain particularly aware of changing competition and market dynamics.

Why bother?

The purpose of competitive analysis is to determine the strengths and weaknesses of the competitors within your market as well as help alert you to potential opportunities and threats. It can help you to:

- identify attractive new market segments or opportunities to add more value by re-engineering your business processes
- reveal ways to improve the strategic marketing of your products and provide competititive advantage, for example, by creating better products and services
- anticipate the intentions of your competitors and thus pre-empt any emerging threats, for example, by erecting barriers to entry, or roadblocks to growth

- identify opportunities to improve the tactical marketing and selling of your products, for example, by using new sales promotion devices.

Ten minute exercise

This exercise is a useful starting-point to understand competitor's strengths and weaknesses or 'competitive edges' as well as related threats to, and opportunities for, your business. It works well in a small meeting forum and can be undertaken quickly. It can be then be built upon to focus and enable more detailed and robust research and analysis.

What you need for the exercise:
- At least a handful of colleagues; one to be moderator.
- A few pages of flipchart paper, wall space and a few marker pens.

Objective of the exercise:
- To start to reveal strengths and weaknesses of competitors.
- To start to generate threats to, and opportunities for, your business.

There are five steps to the exercise:
- Step 1: to determine current and potential competitors
- Step 2: to prioritise competitors or cluster competitors in groups
- Step 3: to brainstorm competitor strengths and weaknesses
- Step 4: to determine the threats to, and opportunities to improve, the competitiveness of your business, product, service or brand
- Step 5: to determine key questions/areas for further research

Step 1: determine current and potential competitors

- Start by drawing a line down the middle of the page.
- Encourage the team to see through the eyes of customers to create a long list of existing and potential competitors – write them in the left-hand column.
- All of the organisations, products or brands in your defined market or niche will provide an initial list.
- Emerging as well as potential competitors should be considered to help ensure your analysis is as 'future-proofed' as possible.
- Potential alternatives or substitutes for your products as seen through the eyes of customers should also be considered. This will help reveal new insights on the competitiveness of your products.

Step 2: prioritise competitors or cluster competitors in groups

- Important competitors or dominant players in a market merit greater attention as they are likely to be doing more things right.

- Consider clustering similar types of smaller competitors into groups eg price fighters. This helps provide better 'big picture' perspective and lead to a more insightful analysis.

- Mark each of the important individual competitors or competitor groups in the corners of one or more sheets of paper.

- An example 'competitive edges' analysis for the National Geographic Channel is illustrated in Figure 4.1.

Figure 4.1 *National Geographic competitive edges (2001)*

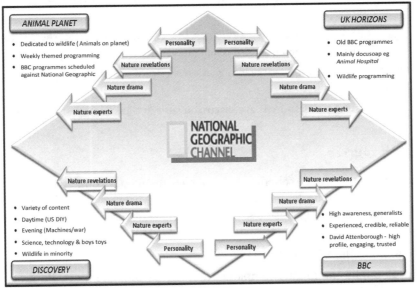

Step 3: brainstorm competitor strengths and weaknesses

- For each of the individual competitors or groups of competitors, write notes on the strengths and weaknesses in the respective corners of the page.

- Consider the questions outlined in Chapter 3 Strategy Development.

- The quality of analysis will depend on both the quality of research as well as the commercial experience of the analyst or team – this is why a good supervisor is important.

Step 4: determine threats to, and opportunities to improve, the competitiveness of your business, product, service or brand

- Information on new competitors as well as what competitors are doing, or plan to do, will provide insights on potential threats.
- For each of the competitive groups, consider what your business could or should do to improve your competitive position, mitigate potential threats and either catch up or overtake your competitors.
- The best opportunities will usually involve leveraging, strengthening one or more of the unique strengths of your business rather than simply being a 'copy-cat'.

Step 5: determine key questions/areas for further research

- It is highly likely that your discussion will have raised many questions, hypotheses and ideas that require detailed exploration. Make a note of them so they can influence your next steps.
- Make sure you research a wide range of sources, not just the Internet, as corroborating insights will provide more confidence in your findings.
- Analysis of company financial information is critical to determining relativities that need to be understood.
- A list of start-point sources are discussed later in this chapter.

Research sources

Use a variety of sources to obtain a holistic picture on your competitors, what they are doing, what their strengths and weaknesses are and what this means in terms of threats and opportunities to your business. The following research sources all merit review.

Company annual or financial reports

By law, all public and private companies must file an annual report. Public companies tend to publish very glossy and informative documents and they can usually be downloaded from their websites or obtained from the company secretary's department. These are useful to find out what companies say about themselves.

Private companies are not obliged to file much more than financial and ownership details but you may get lucky. In the UK, this information can be obtained from Companies House (www.companies–house.gov.uk) for a modest fee.

Analysts' reports

Some market research companies and a number of major investment and stockbrokers which also have their own in-house research departments produce regular research papers, for example, on particular industry sectors or individual companies. The analysts themselves can also be a useful source of information as they are in regular contact with industry experts and opinion leaders. Their reports can also be found on some share dealing websites.

The worldwide web

The worldwide web is a boon to researchers and business analysts everywhere. Just plugging in a few key words to your favourite search engine may take you to a competitor's corporate website or product site.

Most companies listed on the stock exchange tend to include an 'investor relations' section, where you should also be able to find the latest company annual or financial reports. You may also find press releases highlighting new products and management changes as well as performance and strategy updates. Companies listed on the US stock exchange or following US accounting regulations also tend to disclose business risks or potential threats in their reports.

If you are an online business, it is likely you will be able to experience your competitors' products and services online. The 'print screen' function on most computers enables easy recording of web pages. The images can then be pasted into a presentation package and be saved or printed for review. Web offers can also change very quickly and it is worthwhile monitoring them on a regular basis.

But don't stop there! There are an increasing number of sites, such as ciao.co.uk and tripadvisor.com where consumers post reviews on products, services and businesses. Some provide star ratings as well as insights on product quality. You can also tap into the information and comments of those who are openly on social and business networking sites such as My Space and LinkedIn and on a variety of individual blogs and forums.

News media

Recent company news can be found via news search engines such as Google, as well as the sites of the media owners, financial investment and share-dealing websites.

Shopping expeditions or trade research

Shopping for your competitors' products and services in-store can provide rich insights on product or service quality, positioning, pricing and promotion, as well as selection and purchasing issues and opportunities. Look out for literature and talk to staff as you explore.

Where, and the ease with which you find your competitors, will provide clues on distribution strategy and levels. The nature of promotion activity and the physical environment in which you find the product or service will also provide insights on the brand positioning and experience.

Ask your sales team what they think about different products and their competitive relativities.

Telephone research

Telephone research is invaluable for products and services marketed, delivered or serviced via the telephone. Prepare a list of standard questions so you can make direct comparisons from one provider to another. Research the experience from beginning to end and what drives or inhibits your relationship with the brand at each stage.

Professional and industry or trade associations

Trade or industry associations, or professional organisations such as the Marketing Society may also be able to contribute insights. Some will be worth calling and some may be worth joining so you can attend events.

Competitors

Most organisations tend to employ someone who has worked for a competitor so give them a call and find out what they know. You may be amazed at the first-hand knowledge and insights you can gain.

Equally consider calling the marketing directors at your nearest competitor and taking him or her for lunch. This may be easiest to do before you start in your role. You never know when the contact may be of assistance in your career.

Libraries

Libraries are not quite the stuffy places that they used to be and most of us are fortunate to live near one. The British Library in Marylebone Road, London, for example, is particularly useful. This houses a range of unusual and free market research reports as well as providing access to a range of online sources. Some of this knowledge can also be accessed online or by telephone.

Competitor analysis

Once you have defined your competitors, you can start to research and analyse their strengths, weaknesses and strategies, and determine what this means in terms of threats and opportunities to your business. Pay attention to the relativities between your company and your competitors; those that are more profitable, generating better returns on capital employed, and greater total shareholder returns over a sustained period must be doing something right and this needs to be understood. Look carefully at:

- The performance of your competitors; are sales, profitability and market share rising or falling? What's behind this performance – what's working and not working?

- The direction in which your competitors say they're going. What do they say their objectives and strategies are? Does your on-the-ground experience suggest it's true or otherwise?

- The business processes and models that underpin the business and provide a competitive edge, eg product/production process, price/cost structure, distribution, etc.

All of the above will indicate a relative strength, weakness or potential threat and opportunity. In Chapter 3 Strategy Development, we discussed how to conduct a strengths and weaknesses analysis. This methodology should also be applied to competitors. **❸▶**

Success factors for improving competitiveness

While conducting competitive analyses will be beneficial, you should also consider the following to help improve the competitiveness of your business:

Institutionalise competitive analysis

Reviewing competitor activity on an ongoing rather than ad-hoc basis is more likely to alert you to changing dynamics and help you spot an issue or opportunity earlier. Establishing a formal early warning system or process can also provide potential advantage over your competitors. Consider enlisting the support of your sales force, customer services team or even the whole business to create more sensitive and forward-looking 'corporate radar'. Many retailers employ armies of competitive shoppers and sophisticated monitoring techniques to provide hard-tracking data on regional prices, stock levels, promotions and so on. Your own sales force will be in regular contact with trade buyers and is also likely to be able to provide useful information.

Mitigate the risk of proprietary information falling into the wrong hands

It may also have occurred to you that some of your competitors will be watching you watching them. To this end, consider any areas where your proprietary information could fall into the wrong hands and take steps to mitigate these risks. For example, you may wish to limit what appears in annual reports and accounts or enforce strict clear desk policies at the end of the working day.

Develop spoiler plans to counter competitive activity

If you discover that a competitor is running a test market or planning a re-launch or new launch it could be beneficial to develop plans to spoil or counter this activity and mitigate any potential threats. With more sophisticated companies relying on the results of a test market to judge whether to 'roll-out', this can be a good time to cause disruption and lessen the chance of success. This is a time, for example, when you may wish to increase promotion investment in your own brand.

Devising strategies to 'eliminate the competition' can also be effective. For example, Nike's mission in the 1980s was to 'kill Adidas'. While they failed, others have been more successful. Maws baby utensil sterilising tablets was a major pharmacy brand in the mid-1980s, until it was killed by the aggressive pricing, distribution and promotion policy of Procter & Gamble's Milton tablets.

 Key points to remember

1. Competitive analysis is most useful if done well. Ensure it is based on thorough research and that your commercial experts are involved in the process of research and analysis.

2. Ongoing competitive analysis can provide a source of competitive advantage and is powerful as part of an 'early warning radar system'. Consider how you could use the resources of your organisation to make the most of this opportunity.

3. Competitive advantage can be gained by keeping your own proprietary information secret. Conduct a risk analysis and take steps to mitigate any risks that you identify.

4. Devising spoiler strategies or strategies to 'kill your competitors' can be effective and worth considering as part of your mix.

5 Setting Objectives and Measuring Marketing Performance

Do You Know Where You're Going To? – Theme from Mahogany Diana Ross (1975)

In this chapter you will learn:

- *The purpose and benefits of setting objectives and measuring marketing performance*
- *Success factors for setting objectives*
- *How to devise useful marketing performance measures*

A recent survey of US marketing directors (1) showed that less than 20% had developed meaningful, comprehensive measures or metrics for their organisations. Those organisations that had instituted useful measures substantially outperformed their competitors in terms of revenue growth, market share and profitability. They also enjoyed greater CEO confidence in their marketing functions. So, to command a credible seat at the board table, it is imperative to define and deliver quantitative measurements that either prove that your investments are paying off, or at least provide you with the knowledge to change your plans should any activities fail to deliver adequate returns or hit plan. The purpose of this chapter is to help the majority who have not yet 'cracked the code'. It provides inspiration and advice to help you establish a complete and credible set of measures in your own organisation. First, however, let's recap as to why this is so important.

 Why bother with setting objectives and marketing performance measurement?

Goals focus attention towards goal relevant activities

The term 'Management By Objectives' (MBO) was first popularised by management guru Peter Drucker over half a century ago (2). He realised that managers who gain employee agreement to what they are trying to achieve were better able keep everyone focused and induce greater effort and persistence to fulfil those goals. By setting both organisation and individuals goals, keeping track of performance and providing feedback on performance has also been proven to enable behaviour change and ensure that goal achievement is all the more likely (3). In short, if you don't know where you're going to, how can you ever expect to reach your destination?

Increasing corporate accountability

We live in an era of increasing accountability. Shareholder scepticism and the introduction of the Sarbanes Oxley Act has rippled through the corporate world, forcing senior management – most notably the board – to demonstrate new levels of diligence and transparency in order to rebuild lost confidence. In the UK, the fact that legislation to mandate the disclosure of key marketing measures in Company Financial Reports and Accounts came very close to being instituted in 2004, only to be sidelined in a last minute volte-face, is further evidence of growing accountability demands.

Marketing is a significant expense

Marketing activities have a profound bearing on the corporate performance of many organisations. Under increasing pressure themselves, CEOs, chief financial officers (CFOs) and other board members are casting a critical eye on the marketing team and demanding more and better reporting. For a long time, marketing has been perceived as a 'fuzzy' function, and this is unsurprising when its biggest protagonists weren't too sure themselves. As Lord Leverhulme, founder of Lever Brothers famously said *"Half of what I spend is wasted. The trouble is I just don't know which half."*

Improving ability to focus investment on the most effective activities

Probably the only thing that is certain about marketing management is that activities rarely go exactly to plan. Monitoring marketing performance is vital in order to understand deviations from the plan, the size and nature of any variances and the reasons for deviations, thus enabling organisations to be better equipped to deal with them. Effective marketing performance measurement also means that marketing plans and the effectiveness of the department can be financially justified. Not only can marketing resources be most effectively deployed on activities that work but additional resources can be justified to drive profitable growth.

Success factors for setting goals or objectives

The best planning and measurements cascade down from the overall goals of the organisation and good project management technique states that goals/objectives can be best defined using the SMART acronym:

S = Specific; the objective or goal shouldn't be diffuse or nebulous but should be precisely defined

M = Measurable; it's necessary to define a method of measuring the objective/goal

A = Agreed to, achievable; all parties need to agree on the objective/goal, and it must also be achievable

R = Realistic, relevant; it must be a realistic objective and it must make sense to do it

T = Time specific; it must be completed within an agreed time scale

What should you set objectives for?

This question is easily answered in theory: what are the Key Performance Indicators (KPIs)?

KPIs are the modern equivalent of the Holy Grail, with everyone searching for the ultimate prize. Get them right to measure success; get them wrong and you can be measuring hot air. To determine what the company needs as a whole, consider and align objectives to the public statements made by the CEO/financial director. These could be as simple as the net number of contracts won to the more costly overall market share.

Where to start?

While the setting of objectives is worthy in itself, it is also the start-point for making a plan. In itself, the process is not sufficient to do this. The starting-point is to identify

Figure 5.1 *Setting objectives and targets*

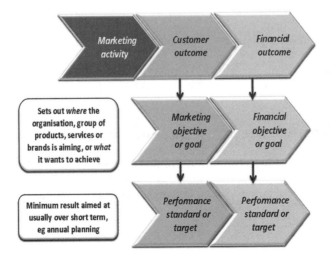

what the key activities of your function are, who the expected customer is and then in turn the primary objectives for each activity into measurable targets. Each customer outcome should also have an associated financial outcome, and each marketing objective or target should ultimately be able to be expressed as a financial objective or target.

The process of setting objectives and targets also clarifies the expected outcome of implementing the plan. Remember that it is the planning process itself that is the tool you are using to manage, not simply set objectives or targets.

 Ten minute exercise

Objective of the exercise:

- To help you start to define SMART objectives for your marketing activities

Guidelines for the exercise:

- Work through the following steps for each of the key marketing activities that you undertake:

Step	Example
1. Describe the marketing activity	Customer recruitment
2. Define the desired customer outcome	To increase the size of the customer database
3. Define the objective of the marketing activity	To acquire X new customers
4. Select the evaluation method	Number of new purchasers
5. Define the minimum performance standard or target for success	Number of net customers acquired against those lost (churn)
6. Define the financial outcome	To increase overall product sales
7. Define the financial objective	X satisfied customers with lifetime value of Y
8. Define the financial target	To increase sales by £Z in Year 1

Modern thinking emphasises the role of project management to make things happen while removing obstacles, championing causes, supporting people to achieve the best outcomes and ensuring sustained performance improvement. That is why it is important to set objectives in the context of the overall business as a whole.

Figure 5.2 *Setting objectives in context*

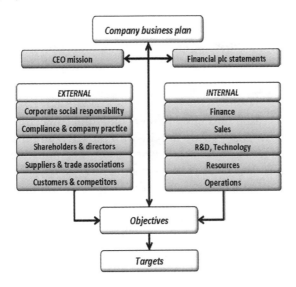

Success factors for setting marketing department or personal objectives or goals and targets

Setting objectives and targets means facing challenges head on. It also means being prepared to be measured by your ability to deal with them. This is critical for your credibility with the rest of the business.

Clarify what needs to be achieved

At the outset, agree what needs to be done, what means what and then set performance standards or targets accordingly.

Ensure regular reviews

Objectives and, in turn, targets must have numbers to ensure they are measurable. In setting objectives and targets, do as much as you can to ensure fairness by comparison and regular review.

Attainability versus challenge

If objectives or targets are set too low there may be no gain for the business. Equally, if they are set too high and you fall a long way short then both you and your team will become de-motivated. A balance is needed. What levels the company is setting overall will be your guide as to what is right.

Ensure influence and control

How well you are able to influence and control other people both within your department and beyond will affect how well you achieve your objectives.

Ensure adequate resources

Perhaps the biggest reason for failing to meet individual objectives and targets is lack of resources. Make sure that you are in sync with the CEO and the FD on this point – clarify what the budget is, who in the organisation is responsible for what and what physical resources are available. This is particularly critical for resources that are provided by other departments, especially IT.

Making decisions

Delegation is an integral part of setting objectives and everyone to whom you have delegated needs to be aware of the linkages.

Timing period

Everything must have a beginning, a middle and an end. If possible, ensure your internal departmental targets complete ahead of the company reporting requirements, just to stay a little ahead of the game. Once your personal and departmental objectives are set, now is the time to cascade your objectives and ensure all your people and activities are aligned to their achievement. It's as easy as that!

Success factors for marketing performance measurement

Knowing where you want to go or what you want to achieve is only half the battle. Equally important is being able to measure and monitor all that is going on. One could argue that the reluctance of marketing to stand up and be counted coincided with the explosion of data and the expansion of management consultants, with a mantra to measure everything. As return on investment (ROI) is the new *croix de guerre*, the marketing director must seek out measurement and embrace it as the lifeblood of the function. While it was always easy to talk away failure, it is now impossible to deny success and its source. Here are some success factors to help you create and implement a useful set of measures.

Determine a relevant, comprehensive and consistent set of measures

Determining what the measures should be is the first step to effective marketing performance measurement (MPM). The range of options is vast and sometimes contradictory. Piecemeal measures or snapshots can give limited views and are no replacement for comprehensive and ongoing perspective and insight. Some companies will prefer certain types of measures, for example, many direct marketing companies prefer recency, frequency and monetary (RFM) purchasing measures. However, there can be a danger in over-relying on a small battery of measures – it can lead to 'tunnel vision', and fail to give a true picture of the state of the business or an early warning of problems. While RFM is good for optimising sales from a customer base, it fails to provide insights on future customer lifetime value or on potential new or emerging customer segments and product opportunities, which may be vital to the long-term health of an organisation.

Marketing measurement should comprise multiple and ongoing measures. Your set of measures should provide a combination of big picture context as well as a detailed understanding of associated causes and customer effects or outcomes. Sometimes this may require new data or research to be obtained to provide a complete picture of what's going on.

Figure 5.3 describes the potential scope of a set of marketing measures. From left to right, marketing activities, associated customer outcomes and finally financial outcomes are described. These are the ultimate measures of what you are doing in marketing. They should form the 'dashboard' to show where you are at any time. The

Figure 5.3 *Translating marketing activities into measures*

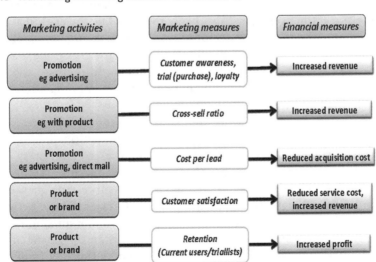

exact content and detail will be down to you. Make sure they are seen as KPIs by the rest of the business and that you always have the information to hand.

Measurement must also be consistent across activities, departments such as call centres, manufacturing and distribution depots or business units. Lack of consistency in measuring, for example, calls handled or day length, can disguise the true cost of doing business, and thus lead to erroneous comparisons. Therefore it is important to ensure that all data is clearly defined and uniformly collected and measured.

Once a set of measures has been established, it should be trialled and tested within the marketing department. Then comments and inputs from the wider organisation should be invited. Once an initial set of measures is established, it can be refined and extended over time. This is an important part of establishing a visible and credible set of measures. Then through understanding and analysis of all the measures, it should be possible to determine what's working and what's not, and diagnose and address problems when they occur.

Ensure linkage between marketing activities and customer outcomes and financial outcomes

A key challenge is likely to be the absence of clear and tested linkage between the marketing activities, performance measures used and the outcomes sought. Successful marketing measurement should link marketing activities to customer outcomes such as awareness or loyalty, and then ultimately to financial performance.

To create an effective set of measures, marketers must first identify the key business or cash flow drivers, ie what drives acquisition and retention of customers, and what drives income and influences cost. Most likely these will be the critical activities on which the marketing budget is spent, for example communications such as advertising or promotions, products and brands. Remember too that price may also be a business or cash flow driver. Consider whether you could increase the price and margin of your products and services by improving customer preference through promotion activities.

The second step is to determine the effects of these activities on customers, ie determine the possible customer outcomes such as increased awareness, usage and loyalty. Once the customer outcomes have been mapped to causal marketing activities, then the effect of each activity can be assessed. To be successful, marketers must rigorously and diligently test their assumptions. Until a clear linkage between cause and effect is established, the relevance of any preferred measures must remain a hypothesis. Once a clear linkage has been established then the financial effects of marketing activities can be assessed ie revenues, costs and ultimately, economic profit measures such as ROI, cash flow and value added. Figure 5.3 also shows how some marketing activities can translate into marketing and financial measures.

Establish a measurement-oriented culture

The path to world–class marketing excellence lies in a rigorous commitment to measurement and the performance improvements that measurement makes possible. Once these are in place, the challenge is not only to monitor and use them to improve marketing performance but to continue to challenge and improve the battery of measures. Organisations must be prepared to introduce tests and adapt improvements on a continuous basis. Responsibilities for measurement must also be allocated; training and skill development provided and rewards and promotions linked to measurable results.

 Best practice

Some companies have created a group within the marketing department responsible for performance measurement. These groups sometimes function independently of managers responsible for developing and executing plans. Some report to marketing directors or even financial directors with dotted lines to the other.

Measurement must drive improvement

Objective measurements provide a powerful call to action. They can help provide a visible and credible communications vehicle and agent for change. They can de-politicise or de-personalise the process and people involved in change. Based on effective measurement, leaders can redeploy funds into those activities that generate the best returns. This is also important to maintain credibility in the measurements themselves.

The role for marketing systems

Marketing directors who have gone furthest in implementing MPM stated that working with the IT function to create a single data repository for all marketing data was the single biggest challenge and also value added. Typically, data is often held in different systems, and bringing them together in one place is essential to establish linkages between key customer behaviour attributes, marketing activities and revenues and costs. Marketers should also be cognisant of the barriers to success but take heart that finance functions have already faced and addressed similar challenges. Potential barriers include the high cost of potential solutions and lack of funding. These can be alleviated by clearly defining needs and then using these needs as a means to evaluate the growing number of proprietary software products designed to help marketers systematically measure and communicate the results of their efforts. In selecting a system, marketers should be prepared for process change, which can accompany the introduction of such systems. Key MPM system capabilities include 'desktop' or 'dashboard' reporting, automated drill down for analysis of specific programmes and functions, and the ability to report plan versus actual. Marketing dashboards are discussed in Chapter 24 Marketing and Digital Technology. **24▶**

Types of measures

Figure 5.4 describes the journey that a typical customer takes as he/she builds a stronger relationship with a product or brand.

Figure 5.4 *Typical customer journey*

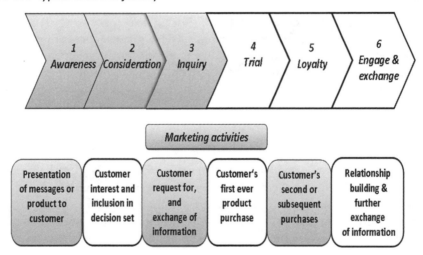

While the customer journey allows us to see the different stages of customer development and possible outcomes, each of these stages can involve a different set of measures. Analysing activities in this way can help determine where the greatest returns can be achieved, as well as determine where the most value can be added.

Marketing activities

Measuring the resources and activities devoted to achieving marketing objectives will primarily cover the nature of the activities, timing and investments.

Figure 5.5: Description of marketing activities

Description of Measure	Examples	Application
Promotion	Advertising campaign	Often one of the most expensive marketing investments. It is most useful for assessing both short- and long-term costs and benefits and includes all pre-production as well as media costs. This will also help make more meaningful judgements on 'pay-back', 'wear-out' and when to replace a campaign.
Distribution	Full revenues and cost of supply, servicing, promotion or display through to customer sale	Vital to include all costs and benefits to make meaningful assessments on relative channel effectiveness.
Product	Full revenues and production and servicing costs of new product development and range maintenance	Vital to include all costs and benefits to make meaningful assessments on where the cut-off points lie; some companies allocate a proportion of overheads to product costs to help assess true product profitability.

Marketing impact

Measuring the results of marketing activities is key. This information is useful in enabling consistent comparisons across activities and stages on the customer's journey. It enables the identification of opportunities for improving specific marketing activities, as well as redeploying funds into the most effective ones. Examples are shown in Figure 5.6.

Customer outcomes

Marketing activities can be measured and analysed in terms of their effect on customers as well as how efficiently they move them onto the next stage on their journey. Measures included are shown in Figure 5.7.

Figure 5.6 *Examples of marketing activity measurement*

Description of Measure	Examples	Application
Advertising impressions (customer coverage and frequency)	Television ratings (TVRs) or gross rating points (GRPs)	Used to assess advertising cost effectiveness but needs to be linked with purchase or usage data to provide meaningful insights on return on investment (ROI). Technology is enabling more meaningful measurement. For example, in the Netherlands (via a joint venture between Arbitron and VNU Publishing), consumers wear a pager-like device that picks up details of all the TV and radio they consume, and all purchases are scanned.
Direct marketing response	Click-throughs, enquiries, response, purchasing, payment, returns and bad debts.	Used to assess the cost-effectiveness of direct mailing, search engine or emailing campaigns. It is vital to assess the cumulative effect of all customer actions to provide a realistic assessment of campaign or customer profitability over time. It is also important to obtain comparative data across media as well as different campaigns, in order to make truecomparisons and focus investments on those that work best. Search-engine campaigns, for example, are taking an increasing share of promotional investment and can generate leads for a handful of pence with very low set-up costs.

Figure 5.7 *Measures included in marketing activities*

Description of measure	Examples	Application
Customer acquisition	Awareness, trial (first purchase) and loyalty (repeat purchase) measures; conversion (the ability to convert customers who have heard of a product to try it) can be calculated by expressing triallists over those aware as a percentage	These measures are useful in planning or assessing the effectiveness of promotion campaigns; understanding associated revenue and costs should enable the calculation of a meaningful profit or ROI.

		customers who have trialled a product) can be calculated by expressing loyalists over triallists as a percentage.	calculating revenue that can be derived from customers over time.
Customer disloyalty		Churn (percentage of customers lapsing in a fixed time period).	A credible measure that is used and widely published by many service providers and companies that sell products by subscription eg BSkyB, magazine publishers etc; we argue, however, that it is even more useful to calculate the cost of disloyalty and explore and understand the key influences on disloyalty in order that they can be addressed; possible causes include the customer acquisition method, nature of promotional offers as well as the product or service itself.
Customer satisfaction or other attitudinal measures		Satisfaction in a product or brand expressed on a scale eg 0-10; agreement with product or brand image statements expressed as a percentage of those agreeing/ disagreeing.	Some studies have proven a linkage with customer satisfaction, revenue and profitability and these should all be tested; it is also worthwhile reviewing the costs and benefits of serving differing segments, as some may prove to be less profitable than others; customer satisfaction measures can also provide an early warning of problems before they translate into lost revenue and profit.
Product or brand market share		Relative volume or monetary value of customer purchases within a category.	Some studies have proved linkages with brand awareness, share of voice (your brand's advertising expenditure as a percentage of the total category expenditure) as well as satisfaction; these should all be explored.

Best practice

Sometimes it will be necessary to commission additional quantitative research to help validate awareness, trial, usage and loyalty measures. Figure 5.8 describes a loyalty model based on customers' responses to the list of product statements. Models of this nature are most widely used in FMCG markets. Such models are useful in assessing current and predicting future consumer purchasing intentions, as well as indicating additional potential for growth.

Figure 5.8 *Customer loyalty measures*

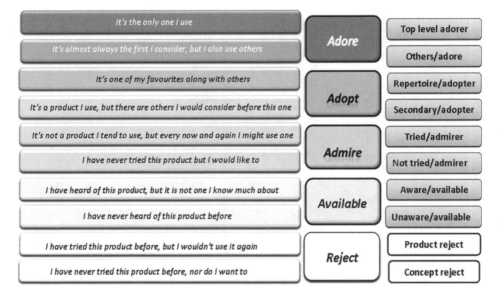

Financial impact

All measures should ultimately translate into financial outcomes as these measures are held in most esteem by financial departments and wider shareholders. They enable organisations to treat marketing decisions in the same way as any other investment. These measures are also commonly used as executive performance measures and link to remuneration. In assessing financial impact you should also assess the timescales over which profits or cash can be generated, as earlier or sooner is better than later or never.

Figure 5.9 *The financial impact of measuring marketing activities*

Description of measure	Examples	Application
Profitability	ROI eg the incremental profit derived as a result of an investment.	Probably the most widely recognised and useful financial measure; useful for assessing and comparing the relative ROIs across an entire organisation; ROI can also be benchmarked against competitors at an organisation-wide level.
Cash flow	Discounted Net Present Value (NPV) cash flow is the discounted cash an activity or event brings to the organisation over its life cycle.	Useful for assessing the cash implications of investments in new products, new plant and machinery or extra services.
Customer profit	Customer Lifetime Value (CLV) –is the cash a customer brings to the organisation over the lifetime of his/her relationship. This is sometimes discounted to take into account the cost of money,	Useful for assessing the long-term attractiveness of customer segments and marketing activities targeted at those segments; most widely used in database-driven organisations such as financial services and utilities; potential to help underpin the market value of an organisation; according to Vilfredo Pareto, some 20% of customers are responsible for 80% of profits – this assumption is worth testing to help focus your energies on the most valuable customers (4).
Brand or organisation value	A number of ways to measure brand value are discussed in Chapter 16 on Brand Management. The most visible and credible way to measure brand value is to compare the difference between the balance sheet or asset value of a company or brand and its stock-market value (derived from the share price and number of shares issued); there are also many proprietary techniques.	A number of organisations have started to include brand valuations in their annual reports and accounts; it is likely to be more useful to assess the financial or added value impact of a brand or group of brands on a regular basis using a consistent approach; most widely used in consumer goods companies.

Key points to remember

1. The process of setting objectives is critical to aligning resources throughout the organisation and ensuring that goal achievement is all the more likely.

2. Objectives should be SMART (specific, measurable, agreed/achievable, realistic and timely).

3. Effective MPM is essential to drive continuous improvement in marketing activities and financial performance. What is measured can be managed and gets done. What is not managed can't be managed and won't get done. This is essential to gain credibility at the board table.

4. Effective MPM consists of a comprehensive and consistent set of measures, will demonstrate linkage between marketing activities and customer outcomes and will express all customer outcomes as financial outcomes.

5. Customer trial and loyalty will be essential customer outcomes and therefore critical components of an effective MPM system.

6. There are few short cuts to implementing a set of effective marketing performance measures. Test the validity of measures within the marketing department and then engage and seek inputs from other senior colleagues and board members to design a practical solution.

7. Strive to embed a measurement-oriented culture within the marketing department and beyond. Tie remuneration to measures. This will help ensure continuous improvement in the set of measures as well as the effective application of the learnings from marketing measurement. In turn, this will justify the value of marketing investments, sustain competitive advantage as well as win recognition from your colleagues.

8. Focus marketing investment on the best value customers and marketing activities.

6 Customer Strategy

Knowing Me, Knowing You – Abba (1977)

In this chapter you will learn:

- *The purpose and benefits of understanding customers*
- *Different ways to segment and target customers*
- *Customer segmentation and modelling tools*
- *The 'customer journey' and relationship building tools*

In Chapter 2 The Role of Marketing in the Business, we discussed the importance of understanding and embedding customer-focused thinking throughout your entire business. Customer definition is the first critical aspect of an effective marketing strategy. **2**

The level and sophistication of customer understanding and definition required will be greater in the most competitive markets where more specific or finely tuned decisions need to be made. It's also worth noting that the understanding you need, needs only to be fit for its decision-making purpose. It is therefore often helpful to generate a working hypothesis on who customers are and what they need to make quick decisions – you can always research more specific insights at a later stage.

This chapter provides ideas on what a robust understanding of customers *could* or *should* look like in order to facilitate effective targeting and marketing decision-making. You will also find some models for segmenting, bringing to life and defining customers, as well as understanding triggers and drivers to demand and building strong customer relationships. Each model offers specific benefits and different applications to help you help your colleagues understand customers and embed customer-driven thinking in your business.

Chapter 14 Managing Market or Customer Research can be read in conjunction with this chapter, as it outlines a number of ways to unearth insights on customers and populate the models. **14**

Why bother?

- by delineating one customer segment from the next you will be able to determine exactly who to target, and who not to target

- by understanding customer needs as well as the drivers behind those needs you will be able to configure your portfolio of products to meet those needs and create new products and services

- by understanding exactly how customers consider and choose which products and services to buy, you will be able to determine how to capture their attention

- by understanding triggers and barriers to building relationships with customers you will be able to determine how to build repeat business, loyalty for, and endorsement of your products or services

Customer segmentation and targeting

Categorising customers into similar groups is vital for targeting. Needs, attitudinal or behavioural variables can be most useful to segment and delineate customers. Models based on these variables can also provide an organisation with an in-built competitive advantage and overlay on variables such as demographics, although life stage targeting may be distinctive in some markets.

Figure 6.1 *Targeting variables and their definitions*

Targeting Variable	Definition
Need (or driver)	Requirement, thing wanted (or driver that prompts the need); needs can be rational, such as convenience or emotional, such as relaxation.
Want	Requirement or thing held necessary to life or happiness; note that not all needs are wants!
Attitude	Settled mode of thinking.
Belief	Acceptance of statement, fact, thing as true, firm opinion.
Behaviour	Human action, way of conducting oneself, treatment shown towards others.

Source: Oxford English Dictionary

Maslow's Hierarchy of Needs Model

Fulfilling consumer needs is central to what marketing is all about and Abraham Maslow's Hierarchy of Needs Model is a useful start-point. His theory, proposed in his 1943 paper *A Theory of Human Motivation* suggests that as humans meet 'basic needs' they seek to satisfy successively 'higher needs'.

Figure 6.2 *Maslow's Hierarchy of Needs Model*

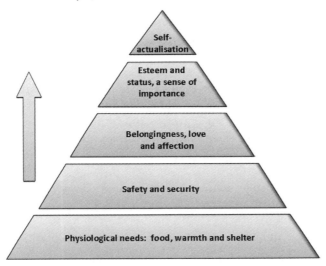

Maslow's Hierarchy of Needs (1) was originally depicted as a pyramid with five levels; higher customer needs only come into play once all the needs that are lower down in the pyramid are mainly or entirely satisfied. The five levels are described in more detail in the following sections.

Physiological needs

The first need is for the body to survive. This is obtained through the consumption of food, water and air, and by obtaining shelter. Other needs are suppressed until these needs are met. Physiological needs can control thoughts and behaviours and can cause people to feel sickness, pain and discomfort. Maslow also places sexual activity in this category, as well as bodily comfort, activity and exercise.

Safety and security

When the physiological needs are met, the need for safety and security will emerge. Maslow believes that a properly functioning society tends to provide security to its members. Sometimes the desire for safety outweighs the requirement to satisfy physiological needs completely.

Belongingness, love and affection

After physiological and safety needs are fulfilled, social needs emerge. This involves emotional or relationship needs, such as friendship, a sexual relationship and having a family. Humans want to be accepted and to belong to groups such as sporting clubs and political associations. They need to feel needed, loved or accepted by others. In the absence of these elements, people can become lonely, anxious and depressed.

Esteem and status

After belongingness, love and affection are fulfilled, there is a need for self-esteem or respect and the respect of, and recognition by, others.

Self-actualisation

Though the first four needs can be seen as 'basic', the fifth is considered a 'growth need'. Self-actualisation is the instinctual need of a human to make the most of their unique abilities and achieve personal growth and fulfilment. In describing this need, Maslow said *"A musician must make music, the artist must paint, a poet must write, if he is to be ultimately at peace with himself."* (2)

Self-actualisation can also be achieved by helping others, for example, by playing a role in the community.

In later years Maslow went on to add three other needs to his original pyramid. These are:

Cognitive needs

The need to acquire knowledge, and to understand that knowledge.

Aesthetic needs

The need to create and/or experience beauty, balance, structure, etc.

Self-transcendence

Self-transcendence sits at the top of the triangle. Maslow proposed that people who have reached self-actualisation will sometimes experience a state he referred to as "transcendence," in which they become aware of not only their own fullest potential, but the fullest potential of other human beings. It is sometimes referred to as a spiritual need or a need to discover true meaning. Some psychologists believe that the concept applies mainly to those with religious beliefs.

Maslow's theory is particularly useful to marketers who wish to position products and services, but bear in mind that hierarchies of needs will be different in different markets.

Mindsets and drivers model

The model shown in Figure 6.3 is really helpful to determine and express need-states or mindsets as well as the drivers behind those needs. The nuance implied in the word mindset is to recognise the fact that some needs may be transitory ie relevant just at a point in time. Figure 6.3 describes seven different rational and emotional gardening need-states. These are shown in the seven segments of the circle and the drivers behind those needs are shown around the circumference of the circle. Any one consumer may seek one or more of these needs. To understand how the model works, ask yourself what you get out of gardening and why. The answer is most likely covered by one of the segments of the circle. If you don't enjoy gardening, it's likely you see it as a burden (along with around 10% of others in the population). This model was originally created for, and is used by BBC Worldwide (3).

Figure 6.3 *Mindsets and Drivers Model*

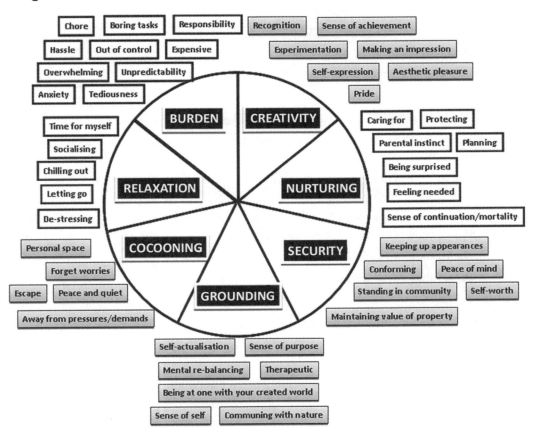

Source: BBC Gardeners' World (BBC Worldwide)

Ten minute exercise

Creating a need-states and drivers model is a useful way to help colleagues get inside the heads of customers. By helping them think from a customer's point of view they start to appreciate what customers seek, need or want in a particular market or category. This then provides a foundation that can be used to generate solutions to meet their needs – for example, better products and services.

What you need for the exercise:

- at least two people; but more is helpful in order to spark ideas off each other
- a blank flip chart

Objectives of the exercise:

- To determine customers' needs and wants and the drivers behind those needs in a particular market or category

There are two steps to the exercise:

- Step 1: to determine customer needs
- Step 2: to determine drivers behind the needs

Step 1: determine customers' needs

- Encourage the team to talk to a customer beforehand and to make notes on their needs
- The success of this exercise largely depends on the facilitators' ability and experience to distinguish needs from drivers
- A useful way to uncover needs is to ask what customers are seeking… the answers should be in the form that customers seek….'needs'
- Needs are drawn on the flip chart in 'pie' shapes
- Expect to uncover around five to ten needs in a sector

Step 2 : determine drivers behind the needs

- Drivers can be revealed by considering and asking what prompts or causes the need to exist in the first place
- Drivers are drawn around the circumference of the circle

Figure 6.4 below shows some other ways of describing, delineating and targeting consumers.

Figure 6.4 *Targeting consumers*

Targeting variable	Example
Demographics	Sex, age, social class, life stage
Geo-demographics	Location
Usage occasion	Easter, breakfast
Physical feature	Red head, oily skin, full denture wearer, shoe size
Physical condition	Overweight, asthmatic
Personal interests	Finance, golf, gardening
Media consumption	Times reader, DVD collector
Attitude	Value seeker, premium quality seeker, worrier

You will be able to list other variables that are relevant to your specific market. At a more tactical level, and of particular relevance to CRM and database marketing, you will also be able to source lists that mirror customers' needs and interests. For example, of relevance to gardening in the UK, some 350,000 gardeners are members of the Royal Horticultural Society.

Through observation and analysis it will also be possible to segment customers in your category in a meaningful way. Customer segmentation models can be based on one or more variables and vary in complexity and the number of segments. What's right for your business partly depends on where you are now and want to be in the future. It also depends on the nature of your market and how it has developed over time. As the late Professor Peter Doyle said: *'Markets don't grow, they just add segments'* (4). It is possible to identify growth opportunities by researching and thinking about your market in new ways. A good example of this is in sun-care. In the UK, original products were oil-based and positioned on creating a suntan. Today, with more overseas travel and increasing awareness of the risks of overdosing in the sun, the market has now spawned a large 'high protection' segment. In turn, this has spawned a 'children's' segment and a 'water-resistant' segment. As these segments near saturation it is very likely that others will emerge.

Segmentations have many useful applications. Figure 6.5 summarises the seven different segments in the gardening market. For ease of understanding the segments are delineated on two axes – gardening ability and the need for advice or inspiration. Applications of this segmentation include assisting in product development and focusing on and prioritising promotion investment.

Figure 6.5 *Gardening customer segments*

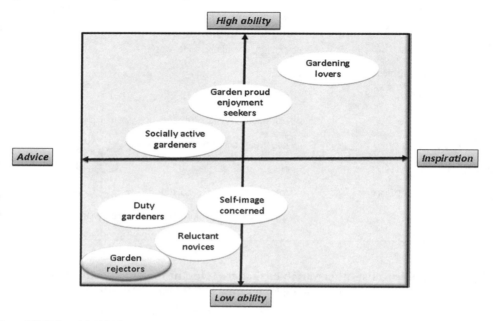

Source: BBC Gardeners' World (BBC Worldwide)

Bringing to life and personalising customer segments is a powerful way to help colleagues understand them. This can be achieved in many ways, for example, through pen portraits, vox-pops, short films and interactive CDs.

 Best practice

At BBC Worldwide, pen portraits and short films were created to help the gardening editorial team understand their potential audiences and in so doing improve the content, format, style and tone of their magazines. Bringing to life the segments also helped the BBC raise awareness of their magazines, as well as build extra credibility in the industry. It also helped the advertising team communicate with media buyers and advertisers and thus sell more advertising space. A visualisation of two of the gardening segments is shown in Figure 6.6.

Figure 6.6 *Visualisation of gardening segments*

Gardening lovers

Self-image concerned

Source: BBC Gardeners'World (BBC Worldwide)

 Team questions

When reviewing or developing your own marketing strategy, consider the relevance and usefulness of your own customer segmentation. Here are some questions you can ask your team:

- How up-to-date is our customer segmentation?
- How useful is it; could we improve on what we've got? Does it provide us with an advantage over our competitors, if not, how could we improve on it?
- What's our position in each customer segment?
- Which segment accounts for the most profit in the market?
- Where and how could we drive additional profitable growth – within segments or by creating new segments and driving overall market growth?
- How well do other colleagues in the organisation know our customers?
- Are there opportunities to improve their knowledge of customers and add extra value?

The customer journey

Understanding the customer journey and decision points along the journey provides insight on where and how you can add value to an offer, as well as how to improve trial and retention. Specifically, by understanding:

- how customers consider and choose which products and services to buy, you will be able to determine *how to capture their attention*
- triggers and barriers to building relationships with customers, you will be able to determine how to *improve or add extra value to your offer* and *build repeat business, loyalty and endorsement* of your products or services

Customers encounter products and services in many different ways and the best way of illustrating a journey is through an example.

Figure 6.7 shows a typical customer journey in the travel industry.

Figure 6.7 *The customer journey in travel*

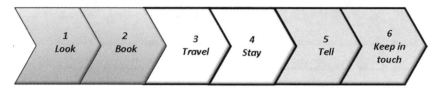

There are six steps to the traveller or holidaymaker's journey:

1. Look – before travelling or going on holiday, customers look where they'd like to go. They seek ideas and undertake research on what to do and where to go, for example, by talking to friends, looking on the Internet and speaking to travel agents.

2. Book – having decided where to go, and stay, customers then make a booking. Perhaps a flight only, perhaps hotels and car hire, perhaps a package. They can do this directly with the travel or holiday operator or via intermediaries.

3. Travel – customers then travel to their destination, by one or more modes of transport. Some may spend the entire holiday travelling and discovering new places.

4. Stay – some customers will take their own place to stay (a tent, caravan); other will choose accommodation in their chosen destination (hotel, resort, cottage, house). Some will select places that offer high service, prepared food and entertainment – others will seek out all of these things on arrival or want to self-cater.

5. Tell – during their stay, customers will talk to others and tell stories about their stay. Some will send postcards or phone home with stories. Some will take lots of photographs to show off on going home.

6. Keep in touch – on returning home some will want to keep in touch with new friends. Some may want to relive the experience, or build stronger relationships with people they have met.

This is not intended to be an exhaustive list that is relevant to all in the industry as different providers will no doubt specialise in different areas. Nevertheless the challenge for all will be broadly the same – to appeal, add value and deliver a distinctive offer to customers at one or more points on this journey. VisitBritain has a remit to attract inbound tourists to the UK at the lowest possible cost. It is also a conduit or route to market for the rest of the industry. Some ways they add value at different points on the customer's journey include:

- Look & Book – providing a technically superior flight search and booking engine

- Travel – providing a distinctive and appealing welcome at ports of entry to the UK

- Stay – making the process of travelling around the country, and especially in London, easier and less hassle by providing Oyster Cards for travel on London Transport

Tools and techniques

The relationship ladder in Figure 6.8 is a tool to look at the customer journey. It describes the steps on the journey to building strong customer relationships.

Figure 6.8 *The relationship ladder*

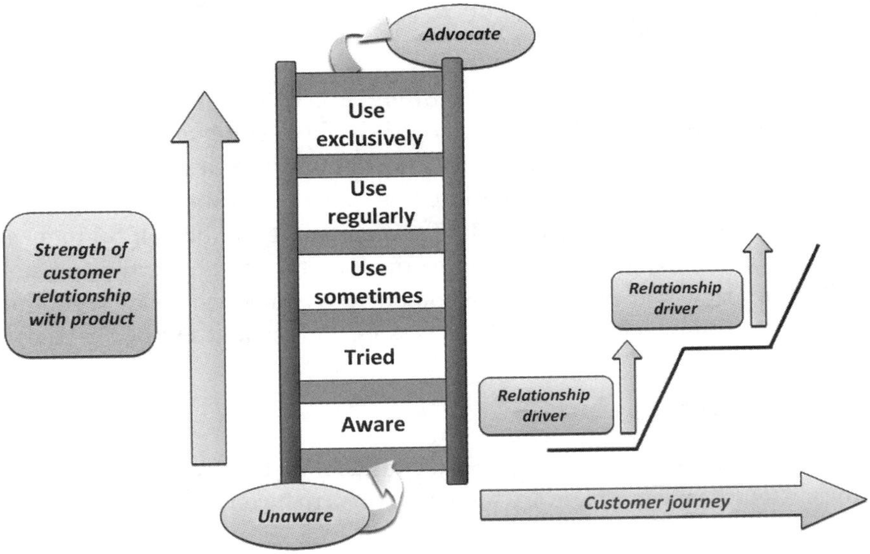

There are seven points on the journey:

1. Unaware – customers who are entirely unaware of a product or service. To build the relationship with these consumers they need to become aware of your product.

2. Aware – customers who are aware of your product but haven't yet tried it.

3. Tried – customers who have tried your product and may or may not be occasional or regular users. Can be further defined as ever tried or tried in a specific time period, for example, the last year.

4. Use sometimes – customers who use your product occasionally. Can be further defined, for example, by specifying frequency or recency of usage, for example, in last year.

5. Use regularly – customers who use your product regularly. These will be loyal users but they may also use another product at the same time. Can be further defined, for example, by specifying frequency or recency of usage, for example, in last three months.

6. Use exclusively – customers who only use your product. Most likely to be and usually defined as a subset of those who use regularly.

7. Advocates – loyal customers who recommend your product or service to their friends.

The relationship ladder is also useful in thinking through the triggers and barriers to building stronger and more profitable customer relationships. Use research to understand customers' views at each step on the journey. This can help illuminate what is driving or undermining loyalty and provide insights to help better meet customers' needs and encourage loyalty.

The number and absolute percentages of customers on each step of the ladder can also be measured and provide useful insights on the effectiveness or otherwise of your marketing activities. It can also reveal new growth opportunities. The figures can be also be tracked on an ongoing basis. It is often the case that the most loyal 20% of your customers will account for around 80% of profits, but it will be helpful to measure this precisely. It will also be helpful to define these customers as clearly as possible. It is more than probable that the 20% of customers who contribute the most profits will not be the same as those who contribute most sales. This should also be checked.

 Team questions

In developing your own marketing strategy, consider what you know and don't know about the customer journey. Here are some questions that you can ask your team:

- What do we know and not know about the customer's journey?
- What are our strengths and weaknesses at each step?
- What are the key steps and triggers and barriers at each step to using our product or service?
- What drives and inhibits customer relationships?

- Which customers contribute the most profits?
- What are the costs and benefits of moving more customers up the relationship ladder?
- What more could we find out and do to help the entire organisation better meet customers' needs and increase profitable growth?

 Key points to remember

1. Understanding customers, their needs and drivers behind their needs, is an essential foundation for building compelling and distinctive products and services, positioning and promoting products and helping your entire organisation better meet customer needs.

2. Bringing to life your customer segments is a powerful way to help your colleagues get closer to customers and understand them. It's an important early step on the journey of aligning and empowering your colleagues to better meet customer needs.

3. Understanding the customer journey will reveal rich insights on areas to add value to your offering and build stronger customer relationships.

4. The number of customers that you have at various stages on the relationship ladder and associated revenues and costs of doing business with them will have a direct impact on the profitability of your business. It is likely that 20% of your customers will account for around 80% of your profits. Make sure you're doing what's necessary to understand where the profit lies and how to increase profitable growth.

7 Product Strategy

Love Me For a Reason – The Osmonds (1974)

In this chapter you will learn:

- *What constitutes successful products and services*
- *How to influence customers to buy*
- *How to distinguish benefits and features*
- *Ways to enhance competitive advantage*

Product or service definition is the second critical aspect of marketing strategy development. In short, products or services should be designed to meet customers' needs and constitute an offering for which they will pay hard-earned cash. This chapter defines what constitutes a successful product or service and outlines some success factors for developing strong products and services.

Products versus services

The service sector accounts for an increasing proportion of gross domestic product (GDP) in most countries, and in the US and the UK the figure is now over 70%. Driven by the need to find new growth opportunities, many product manufacturers are also turning to the service sector and there is an increasing blurring of the lines between products and services. (Figure 7.1) So when devising strategies for growth, take cognisance of these dynamics as it may help you reveal more opportunities than you first thought possible.

Product or service success factors

There are several factors that help ensure successful products and services. These are outlined in the following sections.

Figure 7.1 *Products versus services*

Term	Definition	Examples of blurring
Product	n, thing or substance produced by natural process or manufacture.	Manufacturing companies providing service experiences, eg tours of whisky distilleries, home nappy delivery services.
Service	n, work provided to meet some general need.	Food retailers extending into home delivery; increasing range of products that can be accessed or downloaded online, eg research, music, TV programmes.

Source: Oxford English Dictionary

Products and services must meet needs

While this may sound extremely basic, in our experience organisations can easily lose sight of the fact that products and services must meet needs! It happens particularly often in technology markets. While some technologies are ground-breaking, more are just a collection of not-so-new features that don't meet a need or fail to find a new need. Sony Betamax and BSB digital television services are two examples that were perhaps ground-breaking but just ahead of their time. You may be able to think of many more.

 Best practice

When Akio Morita and Masara Ibuka launched the Sony Walkman in 1979, it wasn't an instant success. In fact, initial reaction was highly critical. People said that a tape player with no record button wouldn't catch on. It was only as a result of Akio Morita's confidence and vision that he persuaded his team to continue to back the idea. Through celebrity endorsement and associating the product with the up-and-coming sport of rollerblading, Sony uncovered new needs for the product – as a lifestyle extension or expression. By enabling customers to listen to their favourite music in any place, at any time and whatever they were doing, they could change or impose their own lifestyle on their surroundings, or communicate their lifestyle to others. Thus listening to, or being seen listening to a Sony Walkman became a statement of 'individuality' and 'cool' (1).

The challenge when dealing with new technologies in particular is to match the technology 'push' with the customer 'pull'. Extra effort must therefore be placed on exploring potential needs and identifying new ones.

Offer compelling and distinctive benefits

Let's also repeat another common misconception. A customer does not buy a product or service *per se*, he or she buys benefits. By definition, benefits are appealing, but they must also be distinctive. This is critical to developing, positioning and communicating a successful product. For a refresher look back to Chapter 2 The Role of Marketing in the Business. **2**

To make this more meaningful, consider the steps involved in the customer buying process. Lavidge and Steiner (2) believe that consumers do not switch from disinterested individuals to convinced consumers in one instantaneous step. Rather they approach to ultimate purchase through a series of stages in which the actual purchase is the final threshold. The steps that they believe consumers to go through are illustrated in Figure 7.2.

Figure 7.2 *Hierarchy of effects model*

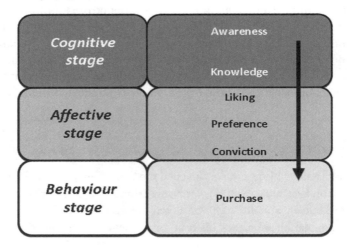

The key stages are as follows:

Cognitive Stage: In the first instance customers will be unaware of your product so it needs be on their radar and familiar to them before it can be considered. To do this your product must grab a customer's attention.

Affective Stage: Once a product is on a customer's radar he or she will either reject or consider it. To be considered a customer must decide that he or she needs it and likes it. Interest and appeal is created by *offering multiple benefits* that will enhance a customer's life.

Liking a product will only translate into preference and conviction if needs become wants or must-haves. To do this a product must stand out and offer *differential benefits* over possible alternatives.

Behaviour Stage: Last but also important, a customer must be motivated to pick your product off a shelf, or pick up a phone or click on the Internet to buy it. To do this you must ask your customer to buy and make it easy and risk-free to do so.

Behind this model is the premise that communication effects occur over time, and that consumers must fulfill each step before moving onto the next one. Typically the greater the psychological and/or economic commitment involved in the purchase of a product, for example in buying a motor vehicle or pension policy, the longer it will take to move customers along the steps. Conversely, a really inexpensive product, such as a chocolate bar, may be an impulse purchase.

Figure 7.3 describes some potential customer benefits for a motor vehicle. A useful way of uncovering benefits is to pose the question "What would buying this product mean?" and keep asking "So what?" until there are no more answers.

Figure 7.3 *What are the customer benefits?*

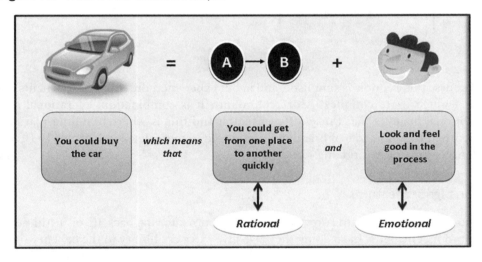

At minimum, products and services in all categories should be fit for a specific purpose – in other words they should offer certain standard or basic benefits. These benefits will be generic or the same to all products and services in a category. Sometimes they are also called table-stakes (a stake needed to enter in the game) or hygiene factors (maintenance factors that are needed to avoid dissatisfaction) (3).

For products and services to stand out and provide an advantage over competitors they must offer more than standard benefits – they must offer differential benefits. An example of a differential benefit for a motor vehicle is shown in Figure 7.4.

Figure 7.4 *Example of standard versus differential benefits*

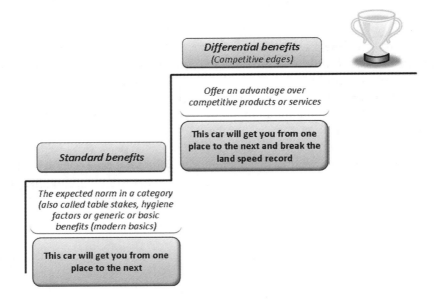

Of course this example is simplistic, and in our experience, differentiating benefits are often much more complex. More commonly, it is combinations of rational and emotional benefits that cause differentiation and this is where branding plays an important role. The role of branding is discussed in more detail in Chapter 16 Brand Management and Positioning. **16▸**

Don't ignore features

Features are important in two ways. First, they provide vital back-up or justification for product benefits. In so doing they also give extra credibility to the benefits and a 'reason why' for potential claims. Using the same motor vehicle as an example, Figure 7.5 shows how two different features support two different benefits.

Features can also play a very important role in differentiating products and services. In service markets, benefits often tend to be generic, so this is where features play a key role in helping distinguish one service from another. In addition, in some very competitive product markets, products often focus on meeting the dominant needs in a category. The consequence of this is that the products all start to offer the same highest common benefits rather than differential benefits. Again, this is where

Figure 7.5 *Examples of features/supports versus benefits*

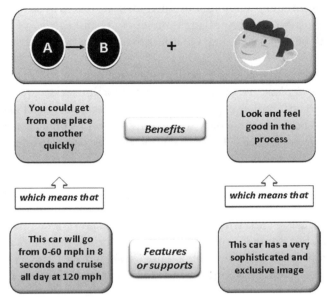

features and other factors such as branding can enhance differentiation and appeal. Again, Chapter 16 covers some of these aspects in more detail.　**16**

Beer is a category where products offer similar benefits. A predominant customer need is great taste and refreshment so the challenge for beer manufacturers is how to say this differently or justify it through different product features. Potential differentiating features include the nature of the manufacturing processes, the provenance and heritage of the beer, and the nature of the yeast.

Exceed expectations

If a product or service does not satisfy a customer need, a customer might try it once, but it's highly unlikely that he/she will do so a second time. In judging satisfaction the customer is the only arbiter of quality. It's therefore important that your product or service must do at least what it says on the tin. To generate a repeat purchase and start to create loyalty, your product must at least meet or, better still, exceed customer expectations.

US writer and management expert Tom Peters expressed this concept in a simple equation (4):

$$CP = D/E$$

Therefore, where CP = customer perceptions, D = delivery and E = expectations.

When delivery exceeds expectations, the customers will be satisfied. Conversely, when delivery does not meet expectations, customers will be less than satisfied and product improvements must be made. Applying numbers to D and E; when CP is in excess of 1, customers will be satisfied. When CP is less than 1, they will be dissatisfied.

There are many ways to measure product or service quality and many organisations will have systems in place. Tracking perceived product or service quality will provide the intelligence to ensure that products and services meet or exceed needs and enable improvements to be made if needed. It is helpful to do this on a regular and ongoing basis. Tracking performance relative to competitors is also helpful as it can reveal a performance gap that needs to be closed or maintained.

There are also advantages in establishing your own proprietary monitoring processes in order to uncover intelligence that your competitors may not have. Some organisations run regular usage and attitude surveys. Some restaurant chains hand out questionnaires with a bill, some telephone and Internet service providers assess the views of a proportion of their customers on a daily basis, and some television companies monitor audience satisfaction and ratings for every programme. There are many opportunities to invent monitoring systems that will give you an edge.

Avoid over-proliferation of products or services

For all except perhaps the very smallest organisations and those focused on very clearly defined niches, there are usually benefits in marketing more than one product or service.

However, there can also be an extreme in marketing a large a number of products and services. Too large a number can dissipate resources, use up too much management time as well as financial and other resources. In recent years, a number of organisations have taken strategic decisions to reduce the number of businesses that they

Figure 7.6 *The pros and cons of single and multiple marketing strategies*

Strategy	Pros	Cons
Single	Enables the full resources of the organisation to be deployed to support a single line and protect a 'niche'.	Growth limitations; could be vulnerable to market segmentation and new entrants in a market.
Multiple	Enables coverage of the breadth of segments in a market.	Dissipation of resources and dilution of market impact; cannibalisation risks; reduced profitability per product line.

manage or reduce the number of products (or brands) that they sell. 'Short-termism' in the investment community and the growing power of venture capital organisations means there is an increasing need to keep the big picture business situation and little picture individual product or service lines in perspective. There is also a need to ensure that proliferation of products and services is not to the detriment of the whole business as it could dilute earnings and cause share price vulnerability.

Maximise competitive advantage

Products and services need to be truly appealing and distinctive in order to succeed, and ideally they should have an in-built competitive advantage. Professor Malcolm MacDonald, Emeritus Professor at Cranfield University School of Management, identifies three broad sources of competitive advantage which are summarised in Figure 7.7 (5). When reviewing existing or devising new product or service strategies, these provide a useful checklist or palette of possibilities. Some of these possibilities may also apply at an organisation or business level, and help when reviewing corporate strategies.

Figure 7.7 *Sources of competitive advantage*

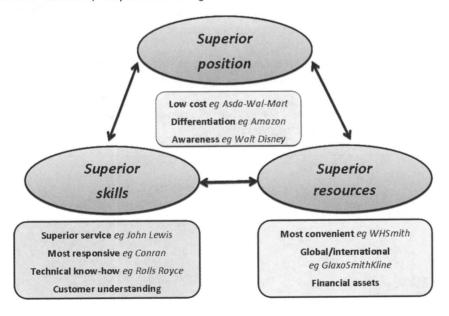

There is a fine but important line between products or services having a true competitive advantage or simply being positioned and promoted as such. It is possible to create competitive advantage through brand positioning and promotion but superior marketing skills and superior customer understanding are usually required to underpin this. Pharmaceuticals and healthcare products tend be based on superior technology whereas beers may be based on superior marketing, customer understanding or promotion. Both approaches can work in the market-place and this is where your marketing team will be able to add significant value.

Positioning products and services

Positioning products and services is a huge topic in itself and is covered in detail in Chapter 16 Brand Management and Positioning.   **16▶**

 Key points to remember

1. Products and services must meet customer needs.

2. Customers buy benefits – differential benefits rather than products *per se*.

3. Don't ignore the fact that features can help differentiate one product from another too. Features are especially helpful in differentiating services.

4. Products and services must always meet or exceed customer expectations to ensure repeat purchasing and loyalty.

5. Be careful to avoid over-proliferation of products and services to the detriment of the whole business.

8 From Strategy to Delivery

Something Better Change – The Stranglers (1977)

In this chapter you will learn:

- *Pitfalls to avoid*
- *Reasons for poor implementation*
- *Key elements of a marketing plan*
- *How to ensure successful marketing implementation*

This, of course, is what you get paid for! Strategic planning is undertaken to create a common set of goals and to allocate the resources to be able to meet them in a realistic way. In doing this, your aim should be to build a desirable and sustainable competitive advantage and, at the same time, be sufficiently flexible to meet changing circumstances.

Having devised a strategy, however, the key challenge, and what you are measured by and accountable for, is to ensure successful implementation of the strategy and successful achievement of the objectives that you have helped set and agree.

The husbanding of the strategic planning process into marketing plans and then onto successful implementation is where the business needs you most. Over and above your own job description, this is the area of activity on which you can make your mark and provide real impetus through your management skills, understanding of communications and creativity.

Pitfalls to avoid

Let's start by looking at some of the pitfalls to avoid. Strategic planning is both ambitious and concerned with the long term. Typically, it looks at periods of three years and longer, which means that some things will inevitably change unpredictably. This in turn means that there is more chance of failure or, frequently, unexpected diversion. It also means that tactics will often end up being of strategic importance.

As an example, the change dynamic comes from the actual implementation of the strategy itself, as well as emergent opportunities and threats. The importance of understanding opportunities and threats is familiar stuff to all, especially those who have already read Chapter 3 Strategy Development.   ❸

Here is a shortlist of the key things to review and monitor on an ongoing basis.

Figure 8.1 *What to look out for at the implementation stage*

Getting the strategy wrong	Reasons for poor implementation
Poorly defined objectives	Over-estimation of resources and abilities at the planning stage; lack of resources and abilities at the implementation stage.
Incomplete SWOT – Strengths & weaknesses/Opportunities & threats analysis	Underestimation of time and money required at the planning stage; new threats emerge at the implementation stage.
Insufficient attention to alternatives	Lack of co-ordination at the planning stage.
Strategies not robust enough to fulfil the objectives	Low levels of co-operation at the planning stage; insufficient know-how.
Poor interface between business and marketplace	Lack of or loss of focus; change of personnel; poor alignment of resources; poor management; poor internal communication; inadequate competence; cultural impediments; poor marketing implementation.
Not adapting to changes in the marketplace	Poor monitoring systems, feedback processes and means to learn; other internal distractions or preoccupations.

Key elements of a marketing or brand plan

There is no substitute for a marketing plan, month by month, by activity and budgeted by brand, customer category or by whatever way you have structured and are managing the marketing function.

In order to turn strategy into delivery, start by breaking down the strategic plan into a series of action plans. Allocate resources and funding and, most importantly, obtain commitment from the whole board. This is best done with an away–day and moderated workshop, where teams can develop a series of major or broad action plans or priority projects.

Once the board has handed these over, break them down into a series of specific action plans, all with responsibilities allocated and timelines detailed. Make sure that you get the right people from the appropriate departments on the case in order to enable the plan to come to fruition as a whole.

Figure 8.2 summarises the hierarchy of marketing strategies that flow from the agreed business strategy and marketing objectives. These are the key elements to cover in your marketing plan. While all marketers will be familiar with the 'four Ps' of marketing – product (or services), pricing, promotion and place (distribution/ delivery) – there are three additional Ps (physical environment, people and processes) that are relevant to service businesses ('seven Ps').

Figure 8.2 *Hierarchy of marketing (brand) strategies*

Proforma 8A takes a business issue as a starting point and illustrates the broad and specific action plans to address that issue. This format is useful at both a company-wide and individual product, service or brand level.

Proforma 8B takes a specific marketing objective as a starting point, in this instance a promotion objective for a particular brand, and illustrates the flow from strategy to broad and specific action plans. This format is useful at an individual product, service or brand level.

Proforma 8A From issues to plans

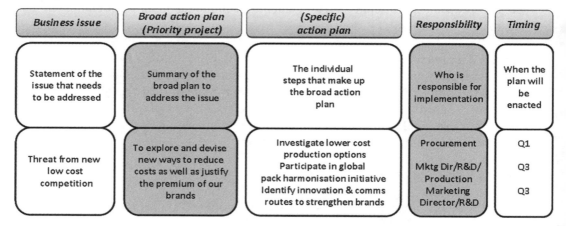

Business issue	Broad action plan (Priority project)	(Specific) action plan	Responsibility	Timing
Statement of the issue that needs to be addressed	Summary of the broad plan to address the issue	The individual steps that make up the broad action plan	Who is responsible for implementation	When the plan will be enacted
Threat from new low cost competition	To explore and devise new ways to reduce costs as well as justify the premium of our brands	Investigate lower cost production options Participate in global pack harmonisation initiative Identify innovation & comms routes to strengthen brands	Procurement Mktg Dir/R&D/ Production Marketing Director/R&D	Q1 Q3 Q3

Proforma 8B From brand marketing objectives to marketing plans

Promotion objective	Promotion strategy	Broad action plan (Priority project)	(Specific) action plan	Responsibility	Timing
The goal or purpose to be achieved. Should be SMART	Statement of how to reach the objective. Should be unambiguous and part of the brand's marketing strategy	The overall method for achieving the goal	The individual steps that make up the broad action plan	Who is responsible for implementation	When the plan will be enacted
To increase Brand X ever tried-levels among target customers (men >30) from 20 to 25%	Deliver stronger trial incentives to consumers	To devise a 3 event campaign of targeted trial events	Coupons in men's magazines Targeted mailed coupons Deep cut small size price pack	Brand Manager /Agency Brand Manager /Agency Brand Manager /Production	Feb April June

You could have a more sophisticated version which shows committed spend and budget available. Individual campaigns should also be individually planned and documented with appropriate sign–offs. These are vitally important but have been covered many times elsewhere and by now you will be well versed in using them. That is why there are simple examples here. You will be able to create more elaborate plans using software such as Excel. Only when you have such plans and tools in place will the rest of this chapter and book yield its full reward.

Success factors for ensuring effective delivery

Prioritise activities and resources

On a general business level, there is the need to rank the issues or objectives across the business and across the various functions. A simple way to do this is asking 'why?' The easier it is to answer this question the more important the issue or objective.

Establishing a clear understanding of the nature and potential impact of key business issues will make the prioritisation and allocation of resources a simpler task. From the perspective of the marketing director, this is also where market testing or evidence of research is vital in order to justify the return on investment (ROI).

Ensure staff understanding and buy-in

What do the staff think? Have they been consulted? Will it change the culture of the business? Or will the culture have to be changed for success to be achieved?

A lack of understanding of the internal cultural issues within a business is often cited as the reason for poor implementation. It is therefore vital that the marketing director, perhaps in conjunction with human resources (HR), should be the most involved.

Nevertheless a key concern should be the culture of the business and its propensity to influence change. Daft (1) defines culture as "*A series of values, standard interpretations, insights and ways of thinking that is shared by members of an organisation and passed on to new members.*" Coming to an understanding of the culture and assessing whether it should be and if so how it might be changed, may need significant consideration. This is discussed in more detail in Chapter 27 Culture Change and Brand Delivery. **27**

As marketing director, you are best placed to articulate the business objectives and create a communication concept that both reflects the corporate culture and will empower and motivate your colleagues. Read up on the subject in question, in order to gain a usable framework – marketing communications books by Paul Smith and Chris Fill are good starting points. (See Appendix 1)

Ensure staff alignment, empowerment and motivation

However, more than understanding and buy-in is needed to help you achieve your objectives. Ensuring that the whole organisation is marching united, as well as empowered and motivated, to achieve your goals, is critical. Some would argue that united movement is more important than the destination itself or mode of transport used. Bear this in mind when wrestling with finer points of strategy.

This is where a business plan, agreed by the board, can help serve as a contract to secure commitment and motivation. Beyond this, the role of HR is invaluable, ensuring that all key objectives and dependencies are reflected in the relevant individual's personal objectives. This provides a basis on which performance will be judged and rewarded. See Chapter 12 Team Motivation and Development for more ideas.   **⑫**

Moreover, accepting that there will be those inevitable and unforeseen events that will throw you off course during the year, staff should be empowered to identify, highlight and, where possible, address them. It is common for staff at a junior level in an organisation to be restricted by the objectives they have been set, and to feel that some issues are outside their area of responsibility. Empowering everyone at all levels in an organisation to be proactive in identifying and solving problems, or at least recommending solutions to management if they are unable to fully address them themselves, will lift a load off your shoulders. This concept usually results in employees being more satisfied and motivated in general.

Ensure effective management

More still is needed. It is important to monitor, measure and manage 'progress versus plan' and remain alert to address any variances.

Understanding how success will be measured is an essential part of effective management. At this level, the metrics will be the barometer of the business and will include share price, profit, capital employed, earnings and volumes. Benchmarking is important and, increasingly, environmental and social audits are being employed. Chapter 5 Setting Objectives and Measuring Marketing Performance provides a wealth of insight and information that you may find useful at this point.   **⑤**

You will find it helps to have established powerful corporate antennae so you don't just have to rely on one pair of eyes and ears. Make a point of monitoring and managing:

- Upwards in the business (ie the board) – to make sure that you have or obtain the necessary resources, as well as manage expectations. Take a look at Chapter 13 Managing the Board and Business as a Whole.   **⑬**

- Across the business – to keep an ear out for any resource issues, signs of discontent or lack of capabilities that can affect your ability to deliver. Raise the issue with the relevant director if it does not look under control. Have some constructive solutions in mind to make sure your intervention is seen in the best light.

- Downwards in the business (ie your team) – to make sure that your team delivers. Remember that some of your people will always be less capable than others. Remember also that different folks require different strokes. Take a look at Chapter

11 Day-to-Day Management for more specific advice on how to manage the various individuals in your team. **⑪▶**

- Outside the business – the importance of staying abreast of changes in the market-place cannot be overstated. This can and should be a key part of your role. External market changes can have a huge bearing on your ability to deliver. Take a look at Chapter 4 Competitive Analysis and Chapter 14 Managing Market or Customer Research to help ensure your corporate antennae are properly tuned. **④▶ ⑭▶**

Excellence in execution

Marketing initiatives that touch customers can fail if either the strategy or execution is not quite right. Ensuring excellence in marketing execution of all of the initiatives that you undertake is vital to achieve cut-through, stand-out and appeal. This is where your creativity, customer-driven skills and rigour will be needed most.

Year ahead tests

The nature of investment and risk-taking means that not all your marketing plans will achieve the results you desire. Another way of managing this is to make sure that you have a continual testing programme to probe for new growth opportunities. This should be designed to explore and test different aspects of the marketing mix, as well as different investment levels. Here are a couple of examples of relevance to either retail product and service or direct marketing businesses:

- regional tests – useful for test-marketing new products and services, as well as different levels of media investment

- mailing tests – useful for assessing product response from selected demo-graphics, as well exploring promotion variables

Whether or not to change the marketing mix after a successful test market is of continual debate. Some consumer goods companies have a strict policy of not changing the mix (on the grounds that any change is untested and unproven). Some direct marketing companies do change some elements of the promotion mix (in the knowledge that some elements of the mix may have worked better in other tests). What is right for you will depend on the culture and processes of your organisation as well as the confidence and facts at your disposal.

Key points to remember

1. Market failure can result from poor strategy or poor execution. Pay attention to both.

2. There will be many internal reasons that may inhibit effective delivery. Good people management and processes will be critical.

3. Changes will happen in the marketplace that will affect the delivery of your plans. You just don't know when, where or how. Be sure to establish proper monitoring processes or corporate antennae to stay on top of, and react to, any issues as and when they arise.

4. Develop an ongoing series of year-ahead tests to probe for extra growth. This will help you reduce the risk to the company from a potential market failure as well as ensure a series of new initiatives to drive growth.

9 Financial Management and Pricing

Money Money Money – Abba (1976)

In this chapter you will learn:

- *The success factors for financial management*
  - *Planning & budgeting*
  - *Financial controls*
- *Pricing strategies and how to price for 'profit'*
- *Forecasting methods*

Maximise profitability, and stay on and within budget, and you stay in a job. It is as simple and as important as that. Every organisation will have a set of systems and protocols that you should follow to the last detail, even if you have to re-work information from your own analyses and reports.

Beyond that, your ability to demonstrate financial competence will be an essential asset in the boardroom. Your relationship with your CEO and Financial Director (FD) will also depend on it. The aim of the chapter is not to lay out the systems or protocols that you should follow but to provide you with insights and ideas to help you maximise your financial credibility and ensure effective financial management of the business.

There are four key areas to consider:

- planning and budgeting
- ongoing financial management and control
- pricing
- forecasting

Success factors for financial planning and management

Here are few factors to help ensure success:

Planning and budgeting

Plan early

You will find the FD is always budgeting and forecasting, so you should always be in a position to respond. Normally it will be the last quarter before year-end when the financial planning process begins, but you should always have a notion of what budgets and costs will be 'next year' at any time of the year. The larger groups tend to start as early as six months into the financial year (based on board level expectations of profit before tax [PBT]) so that they can create an early consolidation and then gain board approval once the FD has had a go at imposing ceilings on cost increases.

Ensure continual learning

Make sure you continually commit to learning what works and what doesn't, so you can plan for the future with more confidence. Set up tests to assess the costs and outcomes of any new marketing activities that you have devised. These will be valuable for the planning process. Use what you have learnt to assess the impact of full implementation and create an even more robust forecast and budget.

Take your time

Consolidating the budgets and bringing all headings and codes together is something best done outside the pressures of completing them. So take a quieter period and give this as a task to one of your developing managers. Equally, work with your colleagues in finance to create the necessary software to easily roll up the budget.

Plan for unforeseen circumstances

The unforeseen will happen so do plan for it. When presenting a budget, add a bullet point narrative highlighting those elements that are critical to achievement of the overall business targets as well as the implications of any cancellations. Pre-agree what can be cut if and when there is a need, or added in should the opportunity arise.

Ensure consistent reporting

Make sure all the departments and units with budget responsibility use the same codes and work to an agreed and understood definition of what is covered by each code. This is fundamental and will help avoid confusion or misunderstanding at the planning stage as well as throughout implementation. Work with your colleagues in finance to help define the headings within the chart of accounts, if necessary.

Retain control of any contingencies

There is always the temptation to allocate a contingency plan on which everyone then relies. This is best avoided. When allocating the overall budget to your individual reports, do not allow them any contingency – keep that to yourself to help manage the overall organisation budget. This also means that when there is a problem, and consequently a need for a back-up plan, you will have to be alerted to it.

Watch your headings

Another danger lies in the heading 'other costs'. Always ensure that what goes into a heading is universally prescribed and understood. Remember, everything can go into both 'other costs' and 'contingency'. 'New product development', 'competitor research' or 'personnel development' are all projects that are undeniably in your remit and give you the opportunity to have some flexibility in spend.

Ensure many happy returns

By developing the practice of setting a return on investment (ROI) for all projects, you will become ever more cost-effective in your spend. Set a constant metric or two – for example, the value of sales expected for each £1 of marketing spend or the individual cost of customer acquisition. You may also be able to identify comparative figures from other companies as an additional benchmark.

Ongoing financial management and control

Measure, manage and realign

This is the maxim for financial responsibility. Chapter 5 Setting Objectives and Measuring Marketing Performance lays out the key principles for turning marketing measures into financial measures. With a clear understanding on where the best returns are being generated, you will be able to manage the process and work with your fellow directors to revise strategies and activities and realign resources where necessary.   **5**

Match investment sign-offs and controls to responsibility

Every major item of marketing expenditure should be associated with an internal document, which becomes both the planning document and an official purchase order. Set up or confirm a marketing activity approval or sign-off system with values appropriate to status or responsibility. Make the level too low and you will forever be signing (a director's professional blight). Make it too high and you will put yourself at unnecessary risk.

Match investment reporting to tasks

Also match investment reports to your key marketing activities or tasks. Avoid excessive detail and too-frequent reports. Ensure that all invoices are aligned with the correct project, product and code. Remember you are the marketing director, not the FD. If necessary, set up a separate project code to account for costs against new or test-marketing activities.

Take all costs quickly

Whenever you start a campaign that has a variable element or is likely to last a long time, always take the full costs from the budget immediately – at the outset of the promotion, for example. Prudence is a key financial management principle that you should follow.

Don't take cost savings too early

As a new director you have a unique opportunity to re-negotiate costs and look for savings in a way that is more difficult the longer you are in place.
However, keep these savings away from the budget. They will be a useful counter-balance for the inevitable over-spends during the year.

Ensure timely and ongoing activity measurement

Ensure some means of measuring promotions and offers during the period they are running (a sequential curve is a good start). This will provide an early warning of over- or under-performance. Consider setting up a one-page Excel analysis with a built-in graphical comparison of performance versus budget.

Monitor rolling expenditure

Keep a rolling total of what you have spent versus budget and what you are yet to spend. That way you will always know exactly where you stand when the FD unexpectedly calls, which he or she will.

Practice good supplier management

It is good practice to set up supplier agreements and create an approved list that you can review from time to time. This will put some order into managing the constant flow of new business approaches but more importantly will enable you to lay down a working relationship with every supplier. One of the key elements will be *'the budget is the budget is the budget'*.

Mix the mix

The growth of new ways in which to market products and to communicate means you need to pay attention to the mix. New channels tend to be more accurate, cost less (when set up) and give better response data.

Give some back

If you under-spend you know where the funds will go… straight to profit!

If you have a budget in the millions and follow the tips you have just been reading, you should be able to achieve this without a problem.

Regular reviews

As a marketing director, you will be called upon regularly to review progress versus budget and plan with the CEO and FD – most often on a monthly or quarterly basis. When preparing your report, align your activities to the budget headings so the status can be seen easily.

Share the results

Sharing the successes (and failures) of your marketing activities also presents an opportunity to be, as well as be seen to be, on top of your job. Consider using your company Intranet or other distribution methods to ensure that those who need to be aware of the contributions of your team, are so. Success can also provide an opportunity to celebrate and boost morale. On the other hand, failure can bring extra attention to an issue, and in turn help you fix it.

Pricing

Price is one of the original four Ps, a fundamental element of marketing. It can have a significant and rapid effect on profitability. It is therefore a tool that the marketing director should embrace and utilise to its fullest potential.

From the outset, be aware of the characteristics of the demand curve and the nature of the underlying relationship between product, price and demand. What sort of purchase is it? Frequent, luxury or distress purchase? What is the relationship between demand and price? In economic terms, what is the elasticity of demand (1)? Is demand highly elastic to price (highly responsive, for example, as with non-essentials such as chocolate) or inelastic (weakly responsive, for example, as with necessities such as water)?

Managing price is the key to that profitability, yet price management is more often than not reactive. Cost pressure or customer demands are usually the drivers. As marketing director, you should consider actively developing 'price management' as part of the marketing function. You should seek to 'manage a market' so that pricing plays a strategic role and every movement helps fulfil a specific objective such as market communications and channel management. You should also manage the response to competitors and market factors like supply and taxation, while also reinforcing relative value for the customer.

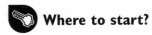 **Where to start?**

Conducting a detailed pricing analysis is a good starting point. Prepare a report that assesses your current position. The following headings provide a guide to help structure your report:

- Price structure – what are the prices of your product lines and what are relativities both within the range and versus competition? Why is this the case, how do these relate to demand and what opportunities does this present?
- Capacity, stock and pipeline – what is your capability in terms of responding to changes in demand and the relative cost of holding stock?
- Services pricing and establishing value – (if relevant) how do services add to your value proposition?
- Managing discount – what are the qualifying criteria for discounts? How do you manage the trade-offs – for example, for volume sales or early payment?
- Customer segmentation and product applications – what are the needs of different groups and how do you manage them?

From this chapter you will be able to assess relative opportunities and threats, and gauge how effectively you will be able to implement a more positive approach to pricing. As with all marketing, your aim will be to maximise customer value and profitability in the marketplace.

Principal pricing strategies

At its most simple, 'pricing for profit' means moving from 'cost plus pricing' to 'value-based pricing'. It may sound simple, but how is this executed?

The move to value-based pricing should be based on what a customer is prepared to pay for your brand rather than a competitor's. The starting point is to determine what the customer values in your product and how, as well as the way in which it is offered. Then you can add the additional value that the brand itself endows.

In order to achieve this, there are four principal pricing strategies that can be employed. These are illustrated in Figure 9.1. From the outset, it is important to understand where your brand sits and where you want it to be. Much will also depend on the market and where your brand is on its product life cycle.

The four principal pricing strategies are as follows:

Skimming

Skimming is often used by products at an early stage in the life cycle, or by those with

Figure 9.1 *Principal pricing strategies*

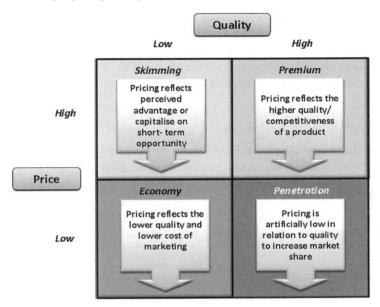

a short–term opportunity or competitive advantage, such as new technology products, new film or music releases and limited edition products.

An early high price enables the product to achieve maximum profitability from early adopters. After they have been satiated, a lower price will be needed to broaden the market. This strategy also serves to reinforce premium values, for example, for products competing in niche markets.

Premium

This strategy is most often used by products with a clear competitive advantage or large market share, thereby enabling the product to maximise profitability while also justifying the premium. The pitfall to avoid is that of setting prices too high and creating a gap in the market for lower-priced entrants. For example, the high increases of many branded goods in numerous UK markets have enabled many retail own-label entrants to establish a strong foothold.

Economy

This is most often used on no–frills products such as retailer 'basic' lines, where the apparent cost of marketing and promotion is also kept to a minimum. Profitability is contingent on the low cost of goods and other costs.

Penetration – loss leader

This strategy involves deliberately setting low prices and is most often used to gain market share or to drive retail traffic by creating the customer perception of overall low prices. An extension of this is known as everyday low pricing.

Long-term profitability is contingent on high retention or repeat purchases of the same product or on sales of other product lines.

Other pricing strategies

In addition to the above, there are a number of other pricing strategies that can be employed in specific marketing circumstances, listed as follows:

Known Value Item (KVI) pricing

Setting a low price for the most Known Value Item (KVI) within a range will help give the perception of overall low prices for the whole range. This strategy is common in retail.

Geographical/channel/segment pricing

This involves setting a different price for different regions, channels or customer segment, which can be discretely managed in order to avoid questions regarding the discrepancies.

Charm pricing

Charm pricing is setting the price so it looks lower than it is in reality ... see any petrol station.

Line pricing

Line pricing reflects the benefits of parts of the range when purchased together.

Extras pricing

This is setting the original price so that optional but desired 'extras' increase the overall price of the product or service. It is most common in restaurants.

Captive pricing

Captive pricing sets a low price for the original equipment but a high price for the refills. Ask any razor or printer buyer!

Bundle pricing

This combines several products within the same package.

Promotional pricing

This involves simple or delayed price cuts, expressed as 'money off', as a percentage off the current purchase or in coupon voucher form. 'Extra fill', 'buy one get one free' (BOGOF) or '3 for 2' are all variations of this strategy.

Value pricing

Value pricing involves responding to competitive forces in order to provide extra value – the best example, of course, being the 'sale'.

Managing price increases

Managing a price rise is an inevitable part of business. Here are a few pointers to help manage the process to your best advantage:

- Always give reasonable notice, reinforce service and brand values when communicating price rises and aim to give acceptable reasons for the rise.
- Give key customers early warning and the opportunity to buy at least once before the rise.
- Use the rise to coincide with a sales drive or offer other benefits such as just-in-time delivery.
- In consumer markets, consider using a loyalty or stocking incentive that spans the price rise, such as a collector promotional scheme or a 'money off next purchase' coupon.

Alternative strategies to improve value or profitability

Beyond manipulating the headline price to influence demand or improve profitability, here are some alternative strategies to consider:

Product improvement

Perhaps the most lasting method of improving profitability is by improving the product or reducing the costs. Make a start by looking at the overall inventory and identify any rationalisation opportunities. You could even plan to produce less of the lower margin lines, encouraging customers to trade up with a parity or matched price offer to the next line in the range.

Packaging improvement

New, easier to use packaging and better sizing can deliver more benefits. These will provide the opportunity to change prices and generate sales impetus through a re-launch or promotion, for example, from 'new and improved' to 'best ever'. In the luxury market, limited editions are a constant source of profitable promotion at prices that bring new customers to a brand.

Outer packaging improvement

Most discount structures have grown up organically, or perhaps due to limitations imposed by outer packaging availability. By taking a close look at quantities purchased in relation to your competitors and shelf displays, you may be able to move discount structures to a more positive pricing outcome with a change in quantity or display unit.

Change the minimum order size

Does the minimum order size reflect the needs of the purchaser and the types of purchase? For example, replacement – single; new – multiple, gift – single with added value packaging.

Add-on or related opportunities

By analysing which associated products and services are required, and working out what is included in the price and what is not, new add-on profit opportunities may be revealed. Here are some considerations:

- delivery and special services, for example, gift packaging
- insurance
- repairs on serviced equipment
- engineering, installation and training
- information, for example, access to a website or helpline

Proactive price management

In the retail market, retailers amend their position simply by maintaining relative positions to other retailers. As an example changing a 'we are the lowest' to the parity positioning of 'no one sells cheaper' moves up the lowest price and could encourage the whole market to move upwards.

Forecasting

Forecasting is often done by rule of thumb, for example, a percentage up or down from last year. However, there is some established managerial practice that you may find useful. First, it helps to understand the factors that go into planning decisions:

- *Expert opinion* – that's you and what you've drawn from your business marketing diaspora.
- *Intentions* – why not ask a sample of customers what their intentions are?

Bringing the two together leads to 'co-joint analysis' and the more developed 'judgemental bootstrapping', which means using the process to create a set of 'rules' to then bring about the forecast. This process is said to improve accuracy – it will certainly make the forecast more robust in the business.

Another variant of this type of analysis is called 'trade-off analysis'. It can be used to assess customer demand potential at a range of different price points. It is also particularly useful in gauging at what level to set prices in order to maximise profitability.

Accurate data provides a robust basis for extrapolation and there are a number of statistical models such as 'Box Jenkins' (2). We enter more sophisticate realms here because this applies autoregressive moving average models to find the best fit of a time series to past values of a time series, in order to make forecasts. Of course it is not essential that you understand how these sophisticated approaches work, it is more important that you understand that they exist and can find out more if needed. However always remember that a forecast is always just that– a forecast.

You can also apply your own rules to this form of forecasting, but it is important that you agree and publish the rules with the forecast itself. You may use an analogous circumstance or previous precedent to create a model for your forecast, based, for example, on what has happened in a test or similar market or brand situation. Finally, at its most sophisticated, you can bring all the elements together to create an overall econometric model. Be sure to take into account the status of relationships, pricing and communication spend levels, added to demographic changes and other factors that will all be important, such as 'fashion and fad' and competitor activity.

 Key points to remember

1. Robust financial management is not only key to maximising company profitability, it is also vital for your credibility around the boardroom table. Your aim should be to measure, monitor, manage then replan or realign.

2. Price is also the key to profit, yet we sometimes become over-preoccupied with the drive to increase market share. By paying careful attention and actively managing price, you can make a substantial improvement – specialist pricing consultants say 2% is readily achievable (3).

Structuring the Function

Build Me Up Buttercup – The Foundations (1968)

In this chapter you will learn:

- *How to structure the function*
- *Key marketing roles and relationships*
- *The functions of marketing*
- *Marketing recruitment ideas*
- *Marketing organisation options*

In the good old days, the structure of a marketing department was simple. Marketing managers managed brand managers who interfaced with everyone in respect of their brands. They were supported by a couple of specialist positions like market research and sales promotion, an assistant or two, some secretaries and it was all systems go. Not any longer. In many instances, 'what is actually covered by the marketing function?' is a question with a different answer every time.

However, the rise of information technology and changes in overall company function has meant that, in many organisations, marketers do not influence a critical customer interaction like customer service, and many do not even own the original 'four Ps' of marketing (1). The role played by marketing defines what a business is, what its ambitions are and how it wants to engage with its customers. As marketing director, ensuring the right resources are in the right places is one of the first and most important tasks you will need to undertake. This chapter is to help you.

 ## Where to start?

To understand the best way to structure a marketing department, both the organisational and business context must be considered. There are four steps to defining a successful marketing organisation:

- Step 1: Clarify what must be achieved and the interfaces with other functions
- Step 2: Define the tasks and then the best way to carry them out

- Step 3: Obtain the necessary resource either internally, through recruitment, outsourcing or sub-contracting
- Step 4: Organise the team with equipment, facilities and space

Step 1: clarify the brief

Today, marketing directors have many other names – 'customer director', 'director of brands' or 'customer experience director', to cite three. Although partly defined by name, rarely do marketing departments have their purpose and objectives clearly stated. Consequently, it is important to clarify your brief. What is it that you are being asked to achieve? What is it that you are being asked to both direct and manage?

Is the requirement to be a marketing service provider, a manager of the customer-facing functions or simply the customer data? As these functions themselves will have grown up outside marketing, it could be time to bring them back into the fold. On a fundamental level, it is your relationship with your CEO and the rest of the board that should dictate what you do, as so much of marketing at the highest level is seen as overall business strategy. From the outset, you should aim to agree a job specification with your CEO that sets out the role of your department as well as the expectations for success. It is critical that your goals are aligned with those of the organisation, as viewed by the CEO and other boardroom colleagues.

Yet most CEOs are accountants (as are many management consultants). Their upbringing brings a reductive and finite decision-making process, unused to either the complexities of multi-level communication or the subtlety and values of the creative process. The spreadsheet alone is not enough for marketing. So the closer you are to contributing to strategy creation and being able to build and navigate the brand (and the company through its communications), the more impact you will have. Summarised in Figure 10.1 are a number of many potential roles that you could undertake:

Business leader or provider of services?

As marketers, we know that the most customer-driven organisations are the most successful. So aim to be a business leader and not a manager of functions and processes or a provider of marketing services. At the heart of your role will be your contribution to strategy. You can do this by marrying the views of a visionary CEO to marketing, or by helping build the vision if it doesn't already exist. Then you need to implement this with vigour and passion, both internally and externally. You can do this by using your understanding of the customer, your knowledge of the market and your ability to create the right message and then communicate it. Customer understanding is the bedrock of marketing and the more knowledge you acquire the greater will be your contribution to the company – especially at a time of change.

Figure 10.1 *Key marketing roles and relationships*

Type	Key role	Responsibility	Relationship
Growth champion	Highly valued – used to first deliver change and then build revenue.	Sets and drives the priorities, including new product development.	Seen on a par with finance and sales; works directly with and for the CEO.
Marketing leader	Contributes to the business agenda and helps set priorities.	Develops major marketing drives; has the resources/budget to implement all activity throughout the company.	Co-ordinates with other functions, especially sales and product development.
Strategic leader	Contributes to strategy from marketing standpoint.	Drives major campaigns through operating companies.	Works closely with the CEO and heads of individual businesses.
Brand builder	Sustains the brand values and corporate identity.	Manages agency relationships and implements campaigns.	Seen as an important support to other company functions.
Standard setter and monitor	Aims to raise standards and encourage best practice.	Delivers processes and protocols; incorporates best practice into all marketing activities.	Works with individual businesses.
Marketing services provider	Provides the marketing services.	Manages agency relationships and implements campaigns.	Fulfils requested tasks to given deadlines on request from brands, product teams and sales.
Customer experience manager	Sets customer experience and service levels.	Manages the customer experience through all encounters eg call centres, online.	May be a sub-function of marketing or included in it.
Customer information manager	Understands and profiles customer and sets targets.	Manages all the data on customers and sales; enables the company to understand and meet customer needs.	May be a sub-function of marketing or included in it.
Early warning radar	Alerts the company to new opportunities and threats.	Monitors the external environment, ensures these are understood within the company.	May be a sub-function of marketing or included in it; support to the strategy development and operations.

Step 2: define the tasks

So what is the job in hand? To enable effective marketing, the function itself must be structured and organised around the ideal achievements of the organisation and the stage of the business cycle at which it finds itself. Start by determining what you are being asked to do, and with what resource and budget. The structure of your function will inevitably follow.

Figure 10.2 shows the many functions that are now considered a legitimate part of marketing. No doubt this range will have grown and changed by the time you are reading this…

Figure 10.2 *The functions of marketing*

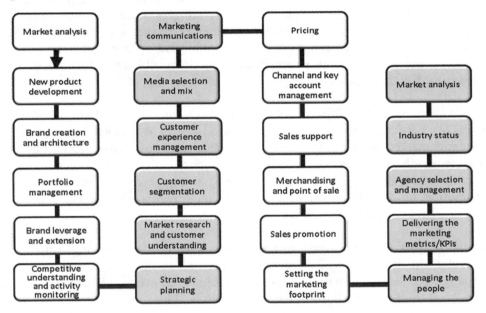

As a newly appointed marketing director, you will probably know what sort of department you are taking on, and what sort you would like, but in this changing world of marketing, let us examine the options in more detail.

Then and now

In the 1970s, the marketing function started out with in-house practitioners, able to carry out a range of activities, often as a service department to the other functions under the title of 'Publicity'.

In the 1980s, marketing departments 'outsourced' most, if not all of their activity to agencies for advertising, research, design and sales promotion. Once the management team had set the strategy, they became 'implementation project managers'. Yet the understanding of project management was to grow elsewhere in the organisation.

Brand management also developed in the 1980s. 'Category management' followed, driven by increasing customer pressure in retail and the ability to gain access to more detailed customer information. This resulted in greater involvement and effect on the business as a whole.

The more stable the industry sector or category the more likely a marketing function will not exist or be as it was originally established. In organisations where the product has high value, a long technical production process combined with an entrenched sales channel – from aircraft manufacturers and estate agencies to TV production – the sales (with some times the added 'marketing') director holds sway over decisions that affect front-line sales. Where marketing roles do exist they will often have evolved from sales and the initial remit confined to promotion – for example, producing brochures and managing trade shows. Product development is a core function beyond marketing. But this is now changing.

While every marketing department will have been formed to address the specific needs of a particular market, its current shape is likely to have evolved in response to changing market dynamics. For example, the domination of a particular retailer in a market may have inspired a trade role or the domination of a small number of suppliers may have inspired a supply role. The importance of merchandising, promotion, product development and advertising or media management in the mix may also have inspired specific roles.

Today, organisations are larger and more complex. The number of channels has widened, the importance of the brand is more universally recognised, and many organisations have international operations. However, every customer contact is important to, and has an implication for, marketing. This is most relevant now with the dawn of the Internet and other digital and technological media, and has significant ramifications for Customer Relationship Management (CRM – this is dealt with more fully in Chapter 18). **18▶**

The availability of data and more sophisticated analysis has changed the way we look at customers. Customers are not simply consumers in the marketplace. Targeting by broad demographics, simplistically interpreted and sold by the mass media, no longer holds sway. CRM has changed the way that marketing is planned and operated. Yet the IT department, with its certainty of purpose and finite rigid strictures driven by software limitations, is not the fountainhead of customer behaviour or attitudes. This is why so many CRM implementations have failed and why so many customers have been let down, as the inanimate voice in a call centre has replaced the face. This has been an area where no outside agencies existed except to understand the technology and sell it. As marketing was not involved, customer understanding and the ability to design and brand the customer encounters was non-existent. This is changing rapidly, and with it the way marketing functions and the organisation is structured.

Increasing complexity and rapid change has led to the evolution of more dynamic and flexible matrix structures in which several directors and managers interact and have multiple overlapping reports. The fundamentals remain the same. There is still a need to build the brand and deliver communications targeted at customers in order to drive sales and achieve the required profits. One requires creative cognisance, the others general management skills of co-ordination and negotiation. As so many functions can overlap or be embedded in other company functions, a high degree of people management and interpersonal skills are also needed.

The increasing availability of new channels and customer data is inspiring new marketing functions and responsibilities. Some organisations have separated the customer and customer experience from branding and from sales. In others, marketing functions have expanded to encompass the business needs. Now marketing not only creates and delivers the communication but contributes to the overall strategy, and has become the main catalyst for change and growth.

To deal with change, you must look into the future and anticipate change. In so doing, you must create a plan for change and then accumulate the necessary knowledge on which to base organisational decisions. Aim for an organisation where you can be a business leader and not a director of operating functions. Will you be given the resources, budget and facilities to implement the strategy or will you be working through other departments, for example, in other countries and autonomous businesses? Make sure that you can make decisions and clarify at what level you have to refer and by what process – at the board meeting or in a bi-lateral meeting with fellow directors? The greater the leadership role you can play, the more you will be able to make an impact on the profitability and shape of the organisation.

Step 3: obtain the resource

Deciding on resources is always a key function. History suggests that outsourcing has usually been the preferred option. However, the greater dependence on technology and the interdependence of new channels today means that some tasks must be brought in-house. What is technical should be left to the technology officer. Decide and make clear where his or her technical remit begins and ends, as well as the communication and customer experience remit. This dependency requires special attention. If you are asked to work with, or through, another function in a matrix, then your relationship with the other directors will be vital.

Whether to recruit from within or outside the organisation will be another key challenge that you may face. Bringing in new skills can often bring fresh eyes and fresh solutions. It also signals a fresh intent in tackling the challenges to the business as a whole. Equally, using existing skills enables you to retain the benefit of their experience. Usually a balance of the two is best. Whether recruiting from within or from outside the company, it is useful to have a rigorous selection procedure in order to help you make the right decisions. Proforma 10A contains some start-point principles and questions to help you prepare to conduct a job interview.

 Proforma 10A: Some job interview principles and questions

1. Purpose of an interview

To enable you to assess the candidate's:

- comprehension of, and ability to do the job
- willingness to do the job
- ability to fit in

To 'sell' the benefits of your company, and working with you, to the candidate!

2. Preparing for an interview

Make a list of the key skills and competencies that you require. For each skill, devise a question to probe and uncover evidence that they exist.

Make notes on some of the key benefits of working for your company, and you. Consider the following: at most levels in marketing, career opportunities will be important, as will be the variety and challenges of work. Maintaining a healthy work/life balance is also increasingly important.

3. Some example questions

Ability to do the job

Tell me about yourself. Talk me through your CV in 2–3 minutes, explaining your achievements and reasons for the changes at each stage. (Helps gauge ability to see the big picture, to communicate clearly and succinctly and as a consistency check on career direction and aims.)

- For each skill or area of expertise that you seek, ask for an example of an activity or event that the candidate was particularly proud of. Probe what was achieved, the steps involved, who precisely did what, and why they are proud of it.
- Tell me about your particular strengths (…and then weaknesses). Probe evidence as to why something is a strength (or weakness).
- What do you know about our company? What do you think this job entails? What problems do you foresee? How would you overcome those problems?
- What do you think you could do for us?

- Devise some 'fast-ball' questions to get the candidate to think on his/her feet, for example:
  - Why are manhole covers round?
  - What would you do to grow brand X?

Willingness to do the job

- Why are you interested in this position?
- What are the most important factors you require in a job? How should it be structured to provide you with satisfaction?
- Most people have some long-range goals. What are yours? Where do you want to be in 3–5 years' time?

Ability to fit in

- Tell me about your previous and current bosses? What kind of people are they? How would they describe you?
- Who do you find it difficult to work with?
- How would you describe your working (management) style? Tell me about your subordinates. If I phoned up XYZ and asked them about you, what would they say?
- What are your interests outside of work?

Step 4: organise the team

To maximise the effectiveness of the marketing team, you may also require new ways of working and additional resources. Communicating your intentions to the company at large can also help you start to shift perceptions and attitudes and assist you on the journey:

- a more collegiate approach means more open-plan
- interfacing with many departments means more meetings but not necessarily large meeting rooms or areas
- working with external suppliers may have implications for travel (time out of the office and travel budgets), car parking space and reception
- image storage and production may place extra demands on computer capacity and speed (as well as the Apple/PC debate)

Organisation options

Let's look as some simple organisational structures to provide a more concrete understanding of the options open to you:

Figure 10.3 *Marketing and sales interface*

Changing retail dynamics have caused an increasing blurring of the lines between sales and marketing. The enormous strength of retailer marketing, key accounts and more sophisticated abilities to measure sales both over time and to customers have given rise to specific category management and trade marketing roles – for example, sales analysis, trade promotion and merchandising. These can sit in either sales or marketing, or uncomfortably in the middle.

There is a need to recognise and manage the inevitable friction. While sales sees mainly numbers, marketing sees mainly customers. Sales also asks how many, how much and then to whom – and marketing asks the same questions but in the reverse order.

The numbers game is played every day by every outbound call centre – via speed dialling and tight scripting. Yet many potential customers are disaffected by the practice. Marketing must intrude and analyse the characteristics and behaviour of a potential customer so that the type of person can be identified and the call enabled to be more likely to result in a sale. Initiatives could also be devised to improve the likelihood of a sale –for example by prior- and post-call communication in many forms from TV to email.

When marketing deals directly with the customer as an end-user, these demarcation anomalies are more easily solved. In the end marketing needs sales and sales can increasingly benefit from marketing.

Focusing on brand management (Figure 10.4) enables effective management across all customer encounters, and focusing on category management enables accumulation of knowledge and prioritisation of resources within a category. These practices are common in consumer goods organisations.

An advantage of activity management (Figure 10.5) is the focus on key customer promotion activities, which drives growth. The main disadvantage is that this can also lead to lack of joined-up thinking in managing the number and nature of interactions with customers. This type of structure is common in financial services and other data-driven industries.

Figure 10.4 *Brand and category management*

Figure 10.5 *Activity management*

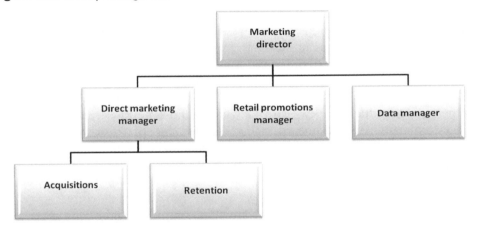

Centralised vs decentralised management

As organisations grow or acquire other companies, management practices generally increase in sophistication, for example, by combining parts of several roles into one or adding new dedicated functions. You will inevitably encounter the debate about whether and how much to centralise control or devolve responsibility to local managers. There are a number of models, with many variations. The starting point must be to understand your current business situation and needs at a specific point in time and to weigh the pros and cons of the various options.

Advantages for centralisation are more central control, economies of scale, cost control and an avoidance of duplication of effort. It is common for larger organisations competing in more stable, competitive and developed markets and where innovation costs are high, and also for masterbrand-driven organisations, and start-ups where knowledge can be shared quickly.

Advantages for decentralisation are more local control and flexibility.
It is common for companies competing in different and rapidly changing markets.

Four key areas that are often centralised are:

- research and market analysis
- budget control
- brand and digital asset management (including intellectual properties in media markets)
- product development

Equally, 'central resources' can be located in the same or different places around the group.

Project management
Another alternative to 'centralisation' is to assign 'project management' responsibility to lead a particular activity as an add-on to an existing role.

The benefit in doing this is to encourage interaction and co-operation, and help deal with ad-hoc or unusual challenges. Management by means of regular status reports and periodic roundtable reviews with all manager and key agencies, underpinned by an accessible and used dashboard, will make sure the structure works as well as possible. Chapter 20 Leading Projects provides more insights on mechanisms to run projects.   **20▶**

Matrix management
Matrix management is particularly suited to more complex organisations where there is both a vertical and horizontal flow of authority and responsibility, for example, for marketing directors overseeing the marketing operations in other countries or categories that span different countries. While conflicts of interest can sometimes arise, the benefit in this structure is also to encourage interaction and co-operation.

What's best in practice is usually likely to be a combination of elements. Deploying staff in central co-ordination or project leadership roles can be useful as stepping stones to other roles. It also helps to hone project, people management and strategic skills.

Managing in the digital age
Many businesses today are almost solely based on the web and have a purely digital relationship with their customers. As technology has evolved, companies have established functions and delivery mechanisms to manage the web site and optimise traffic and usage as well as customer contact through email with the requisite databases. Customer relationship management is covered in more detail in Chapter 18.   **18▶**

Originally, these technical departments were often set up under the management of IT but with the increasing growth and almost dominance of these new channels the function is now being brought under the wing of marketing. This has prompted recognition of the need for digital asset management (DAM).

There are two important considerations for marketing management in the digital age. Firstly that the delivery mechanism, be it print or online, should always be separate to the creation of content. Secondly that content should be the domain of the brand and/or customer manager. Best practice demands that technical development and programming should be the role of the functional or technical channel specialist, be it web site or catalogue and print, built or run internally or externally. As there is inevitably a conflict between the technical and brand demands this is best managed by having the functions separate. The inevitable comprise must balance functionality with brand impact. The eCommerce team or digital print department should be as a separate 'delivery team' whose internal customers are the brand team. Managing them will need understanding of the technology, especially as you aim to make them work better by recognising your brand and by maximising the impact of the message.

 Key points to remember

1. The way you structure and resource your department will depend on the demands of, and your relationship with, the rest of the organisation. The more you align the marketing function to the strategy of the business, the better you will be able to structure and resource positively to meet them. Moreover, you will instil confidence in the CEO and the rest of the board.

2. Marketing as a function has gone through immense changes and that will continue as long as it exists. It is exemplified by the fact that some IT pundits were predicting the end of marketing just a few years ago! There is one irrefutable bedrock on which marketers should build – the world's most successful businesses are customer-driven and marketing represents the demands from the consumer to the business and back again. As we enter a period when even those in IT are recognising the need for the whole organisation to be customer-centric, there has never been a better time to optimise the function and translate customer-centricity into marketing action and company profit.

PART 3

Operational Leadership

Day-to-Day Management

I Can See Clearly Now – Johnny Nash (1972)

In this chapter you will learn:

- *Best practices to get yourself organised*
- *How to adapt your management style to get the most from your team*
- *Best practice processes and protocols*
- *How to manage meetings!*

We all worry about strategy and long-term direction but real success can only come from your ability to get things done – consistently well, always on time and within budget. No amount of planning, certainty of direction and sense of purpose will be worth anything if your department does not function properly. Of course, the needs and skill set of becoming a senior manager have been well documented but the following chapter looks at these criteria within the specifics of marketing.

First, it covers some behaviour and time management pointers for you. Second, it covers some principles and tools that can help improve general managerial performance. The focus is on 'getting things done'.

 Best practices to get yourself organised

To have come this far in your career, you must have employed some effective time management techniques. Here is a checklist of the best:

1. Have a set of simple plans – things you have to do and by when.
2. Prioritise accordingly: make a list of things to do today, this week, this month – split it into three further sections:

   - must do
   - can wait
   - would like to do

Update this every day.

3 Keep a day book – hardback and ring-bound, as it is easier to open and write on and then remove pages when necessary. This could even be a large format day-per-page diary – write everything down, use it for lists, and set things to do.

4. Use mind maps to generate ideas and prepare documents and presentations – 30 second mind map course: use a landscape format, put the subject in the middle and write the key headings or ideas around it – you'll be surprised how much you can generate and record. (This is covered in more detail in Chapter 21 Creativity and Problem Solving). **㉑**

5. Set out your long-term aims and break them down into a series of projects, thereby knowing which will be easy (and therefore quick wins) and those that will be a hard slog (take more time and energy). (This concept was introduced in Chapter 1 Starting Out). **❶**

6. Add a delegation log in your day book or working diary.

7 Re-do and re-allocate regularly.

8. Institute processes to automate or automatically delegate some of the things you don't need to do yourself eg creating first draft replies to letters

9. Have an open door policy – if the door is open you can come in – if not…

10. Don't let people steal your time unless you want them too – say 'can we fix a meeting?'

11. Buy time – always allow an hour for any meeting or try meetings standing up – remarkably it makes them so much quicker.

12. Work faster – get up to speed through speed-reading and memory improvement.

Management style

The starting point has to be what kind of manager are you – autocratic/ directive, or empowering/permissive? In practice, you will have to be all of these styles. Do, however, be aware of the consequences of each. The more autocratic you are, the less you leave space for people to do their own thing or, as important, recognise the inappropriateness or the incompleteness of your instructions when the task has been commenced! Conversely the more empowering and permissive you are, the more holistically an issue might be considered and the more ideas may be generated. Equally, the more likely the results are to be further from your desired outcome.

When you do vary your style, it is important to be precise when something is a 'must do', for instance, when you have made a commitment to another director. However, in practice, it is best to spell out the desired outcome rather that the details of the process.

Start by asking what they would do and what they think the options are. Try not to give instant solutions to problems – help people to solve their own problems and encourage them to come to you with solutions. However, there are several pitfalls to avoid:

 Pitfalls to avoid

- The key problem in day-to-day management is *procrastination*.

- This means that with any project or task it is vital that you set a fixed completion time. The easiest way is to ask 'when can you get this done by?'

- You will need to *judge the ability* and experience of the employee, sometimes suggesting a colleague as a mentor. Act as both a coach and a cajoler, with the constant aim of getting the job done well and raising the performance of your teams.

- *Mistakes* will happen. So just put them right as best you can and analyse the reasons in order to limit future mistakes. Avoid blame and recrimination – these are negative and create resentment.

- In marketing, it is essential to manage with a *creative outcome* in mind. In practice, this will mean putting in place the right balance of formal organisation and supervision, with plenty of freedom and team encouragement thrown in.

- *Support* during the activity – a corridor water cooler moment is always helpful.

- At the end, *praise* and *recognise success*, making sure it is bestowed publicly on whoever actually did the work.

- Finally, *review* the activity and perhaps write up the methodology as a starting point for the next task. This is even more important when campaigns need to be evaluated and used as the basis for future planning.

 Management success factors

Treat everyone differently

Because every individual is different, as is every situation, the only way to manage your team is to adjust your leadership style to both the individual and the situation.

Figure 11.1 describes four styles of leadership that are appropriate, from the less experienced through to the more experienced colleagues:

1. *New joiners* are most likely to be performing below par. Typically they will lack confidence, be eager and a little hit and miss in what they do. A directing/structuring style will be most effective. View yourself as a benevolent autocrat and help them initiate, organise and undertake key tasks.

Figure 11.1 *Leadership styles*

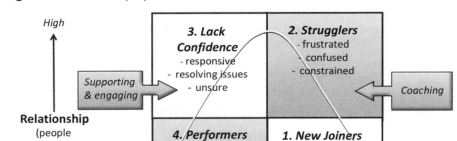
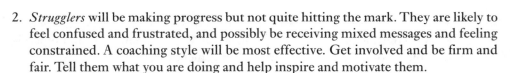

2. *Strugglers* will be making progress but not quite hitting the mark. They are likely to feel confused and frustrated, and possibly be receiving mixed messages and feeling constrained. A coaching style will be most effective. Get involved and be firm and fair. Tell them what you are doing and help inspire and motivate them.

3. *Lack confidence*; having acquired the necessary task skills, this group require *a boost to their confidence*. A supporting and engaging style will be needed so listen, understand and appreciate what is being done. Advise on issues as you see them and continue to encourage them.

4. *Performers* will be meeting, if not exceeding, your expectations for the role. The most effective style will be one that delegates (Style 4). View yourself as a futurist, and help by predicting and reflecting on what is being done. Avoid leaving them to their own devices lest they feel undervalued. Examine and measure achievements and identify ways to provide challenging learning opportunities. Remember, they also need recognition and praise for their achievements.

Management by walking about a bit

There is no substitute for a walk-around and casual interaction with your staff every now and then. Whether you are housed together or not, make time to do this. A friendly exchange, a word of encouragement or simply a smile are fantastic tools for motivation and success.

The One Minute Manager

Kenneth Blanchard (1) has espoused the benefits taking one minute out of the day to look into the faces of the people we manage. While no one ever does it in 60 seconds but it is useful reminder that people are our most important resource and that much can be achieved in a short time.

Establish protocols

While not wishing to be too dogmatic, it is important to set standards of the way people work with you and in the way they relate to others – both internally and (important in marketing) externally. We have to work with many external agencies and suppliers and their positive performance will lift our own. So, take time to make sure that your staff understand this and deal with them in a manner that you regard as appropriate. The easiest way to do this consistently is to set up a series of protocols. Ask your team to contribute and periodically update and review it. (You could start with limiting CCs on emails). Another solution is to institute end of project reviews and identify any lessons that could be applied to the rest of the team.

Establish a best practice manual

Every business has set ways of doing things and you will need to adhere to these and ensure your department also does so. It is surprising how often these processes are not formalised or have not been cohesively published. Familiarise yourself with the protocols and ensure adherence to company processes by setting up a best practice guide for the standard operating procedures. These procedures range from purchasing through to HR requirements and many other routine things. When they are followed, they can be carried out simply and quickly. When done incorrectly they can create unnecessary angst and bureaucratic nightmares.

There is one area where you will need to be insistent on others following your procedures and rules. This is in the management of the company's brands and corporate identity, which are the cornerstones of all marketing.

Another key area is the nature and format of KPIs and reports that are needed in order to properly monitor progress of your plans. The absolute basic should be a monthly status report that you receive during say, the last week of the month, to be discussed at a monthly review meeting. This meeting can be a semi-formal one-to-one or as a team, at the beginning of the following month.

 **Best practice manual**

This can be useful as an induction tool for new staff as well as a ready reference source to enable the continuing professional development of your team. Figure 11.2 provides a suggested contents list.

Figure 11.2 *The contents of a best practice manual*

Subject

Why this manual; ownership details

Organisation structure and responsibilities

Marketing function

Corporate identity

Brands and values

Best practice examples

Standard documents

Supplier relationships

Approved suppliers

Standard proformas

Visuals library

Standard slides and key presentations

Useful tools and techniques

Job specifications

Job specifications are valuable for directing and helping to prioritise the activities of your team over the medium term. This is a good place to start when meeting staff for the first time and in managing them day to day. Your organisation will most likely have an HR department that keeps copies of job specifications and, if there is a performance-related pay scheme, the key activities related to bonus achievement. The job specification will also cover the purpose of the role, key functions, direct reports, details of service and training record. If job specifications do not exist, creating and agreeing them will be a quick win.

The management structure that you inherit will have the framework for delegation and will help the department function on a day-to-day basis without you. Then you will always be able to see your intervention as a positive way to improve performance. For more details on structuring the marketing function read Chapter 10 Structuring the Function. **10**

Meeting management

Meetings are the scourge of modern-day management and will take up a vast amount of your time. As a result, many companies have evolved protocols for meetings, such as ensuring everyone stands (Asda) or that presentations are limited in time (Camelot). Applying a few simple principles with a degree of flexibility and common sense will usually be sufficient to help you work more productively. Here are a few essential tips:

Only hold a meeting if it matters

If you want to give your team an update or status report, an email will usually suffice. Equally, if one of your objectives is to build consensus or seek feedback, this is easier to do face to face.

Define the outcomes and provide a structure

Meetings are much more productive when attendees understand how it will work and what the objectives are. At the outset of any meeting, make a clear statement on what the purpose of the meeting is, as well as what the agenda will be. If this is a formal meeting, or requires the participants to prepare, then send a briefing note beforehand. If participants are required to make formal contributions to a meeting, for example, presentations, then agree a timed agenda, provide the speaker with clear guidelines on the purpose of his or her contribution, and allot a speaking time. In longer meetings, such as workshops, there is a greater risk of the purpose and desired outcomes being lost from time to time so it becomes incumbent on the moderator/chairman to be more active in managing the meeting yet still encourage participation.

Manage meeting logistics

To ensure meetings start promptly and run smoothly every time lay down a meeting mantra and delegate logistics responsibility to a member of your team. We've all been to meetings where the electronic equipment doesn't work, so make sure someone checks everything is working at least five minutes before the meeting starts. If you have external speakers, always provide them with time to set up in advance of the meeting starting. Make sure everyone arrives on time. Set out who does what regarding teas and coffees. Always have a flip-chart or whiteboard available. Always appoint a note-taker.

Appoint a chairman

Good meetings result from strong leadership. So, either take charge yourself or appoint a chairman to manage the time and get through the agenda. If you have followed the pointers so far then you will be well on the way. Another common problem in meetings is deviation from the subject matter at hand – a useful way to keep discussion on track is to get into the habit of logging issues that are tangential to the matter at hand. You can then either deal with them at the end of the meeting or on a separate occasion.

Be inclusive and constructive

The point of most meetings is two-way communication, so it is crucial to get honest input from everyone. The chairman's responsibility is to ensure even-handed and equal contributions from all and set the rules for the meeting. At the start of the meeting you may wish to remind participants that you want to hear from everyone equally and that you only want to hear constructive ideas. (We all know how easy it is to judge and shoot down ideas, and how hard it is to create them in the first place). Chapter 21 Creativity and Problem Solving provides inspiration on how to create, build and judge ideas in a meeting forum.   **21**▶

Close with a plan of action

At the end of a meeting everyone should leave knowing what's expected of them and by when. Sum up with a review of the decisions reached, and what the next plan of action will be. In turn, this will provide the start for your next agenda. In itself, this is a useful management tool for you.

How's it going?

Just like you will be asking your team members this question, expect it to be asked of you by fellow directors and the CEO. Have the latest results of the new campaign to hand and anticipate the questions so that you have answers ready – brand shares, customer penetration and number of accounts in a given category. Make up your own dashboard and, if you are fortunate to have one already set up, make sure you always have the day's update to hand.

Role of technology

New technology is a boon to the forward thinking marketing director as it can help you save time, provide timely information and alerts and manage people and processes. Many of the things discussed in this chapter can be readily achieved electronically.

Intranet-based portals are a potential repository of best practice knowledge and brand management tools. A PC with Microsoft Outlook provides a wide range of time management tools and a PDA, Blackberry, iphone or equivalent can provide similar functionality on the move. If you are not yet fully aware of the features and benefits of this technology make a note to check them out.

Key points to remember

While this chapter has been primarily concerned with the management of your resources and people, it is important to remember that marketing is about customers, products and making the most of the media. Make sure that your day-to-day planning allows time to keep in touch with customers, get feedback on your products, observe the sales force in action, go to conferences and read. In summary:

1. Plan and organise both yourself and your department.

2. Create frameworks to plan and prioritise what you need get done.

3. Monitor both formally and informally.

4. Anticipate mistakes and encourage staff.

5. Capture and document best practices to help embed working principles and protocols with your team.

6. Make sure any meetings you run are focused on achieving a specific outcome.

Team Motivation and Development

Free As a Bird – The Beatles (1995)

In this chapter you will learn:

- *How to motivate your team*
- *How to align rewards with achievement*
- *Options for developing your team*

An important quality in any candidate for a new job is 'enthusiasm'. How to build enthusiasm is considered in this chapter. There are a number of key elements that have specific relevance to marketing, over and above motivating your colleagues or developing sales promotion programmes to incentivise purchase and actions. If you are not familiar with Maslow, read or re-read Chapter 6 Customer Strategy. **6**

Behind all motivation is the desire for success, yet it also provides the process that encourages and guides behaviour. Your desire to succeed is clear, as you have achieved the status of marketing director. You must now learn to share your desire for success with those you are working with, in order to both encourage and guide them.

 ## Success factors for team motivation

Let's look at the key factors for success in team building.

The importance of culture and vision

The list of convenient Cs in Figure 12.1 should be your framework for setting goals and communicating with your team. The list you make must be relevant to your current circumstances. There are two fundamental ingredients to remember – 'culture' and 'vision'. These need to be superimposed onto the organisation itself and the environment in which you work.

In general, people need to know where an organisation is going so they understand,

Figure 12.1 *Success factors for team motivation*

Challenge	Define what you want to achieve.
Consensus	Make sure everyone understands and agrees not only what has to be done but why.
Conscientiousness	Be aware that you will need people to do what they said they were going to do.
Commitment	Seek commitment to the goals in question, both verbal and written.
Contribution	Spell out what contributions are expected and from whom.
Communication	Keep everyone informed in the most appropriate mix of ways.
Collaboration	Make sure people work well and co-operate with each other.

feel comfortable and are able to their jobs. To do this, first understand where you are and where you want to be. Then share the vision of where you want your business and brands to be in the future, and your strategy or ethos for getting there. By communicating and behaving with integrity and conviction you are more likely to instil confidence and have people wanting to be led by you.

One of the key themes of this book is how to align marketing to the vision and plans of the CEO. Embracing and influencing this core vision and translating this into the way your marketing works is vital for ultimate success. Furthermore, when the values and desires of the company are aligned with personal values, then a more productive environment is created.

We all like to think that the marketing function is full of talented people and talented people are motivated by more than money – this is at the heart of Herzberg's Theory of Motivation (1). Working for a well-managed company with a strong and positive culture is very important. Working for a great boss also counts for a great deal. Start with yourself by developing in your own mind a clear picture of who you are, what values are important to you and what you really are passionate about. Do this and it will soon rub off on those around you.

The best jobs also offer freedom and autonomy with exciting challenges and prospects for career progression. Tie these factors into the culture and vision that you espouse.

Align rewards with achievement

While money is rarely a primary motivator at senior levels, involvement in the overall success of the business and the inclusion of some form of financial motivation helps increase an individual's sense of participation and self-esteem. An individual's targets, activities and rewards should be aligned with business targets, activities and rewards. A mixture of both financial and self-esteem benefits should be reflected in any reward scheme.

While this may be possible in an overall organisation-wide scheme, you may feel the need and have the opportunity to develop your own specific programme related to the performance of the marketing function. There may also be a place for discretionary reward ie a payment or benefit for a specific reason, often non-quantifiable but nonetheless evident. In developing such a scheme, there are a number of factors that are important:

Figure 12.2 *Success factors for performance-related pay reward schemes*

Fast	Make sure that the rewards are paid promptly and the scheme starts right away.
Significant	Make sure the rewards are worthwhile.
Known	Ensure everyone is aware of and engaged with the scheme; consider using a creative overlay to do this.
Understandable	Keep it simple and easy-to-understand.
Measurable	Link rewards to task or time-related.
Attainable	Be stretching but above all be realistic in the targets.
Recognisable	Provide status; recognition is an important part of motivation.
Irrevocable	Once awarded it stays awarded!
Compatible	Should stand alone and not contradict the aims of other schemes.
Tangible	A certificate, a gift or a gong all add to the effect.

Team development

Investing in developing your team will not only be motivating to them but it is a critical part of lifting the load off your shoulders and of succession planning. Here are a number of tools that you should consider:

Feedback

Feedback is the food of champions and it is very powerful to embed this ethos into your culture and working practices. If something works well then give praise and

explain specifically what worked well and why. If it didn't work well, explain specifically what didn't work well and ask for suggestions for improvement. Then share your
own perspectives and ideas for improvement.

Training

Most staff will be motivated by learning new skills that expand their abilities and
responsibilities. Consider empowering all of your team to contribute to the continuing
professional development of others by embedding this into your cultural values and
by establishing processes to make this visible. Encourage, for example, weekly
knowledge sharing sessions (this is common-place in a consultancy environment). It
also provides a presentation platform and learning experience for the contributors
themselves.

External trainers can also inject fresh ideas. You will be aware of the increasing range
of formal business and marketing qualifications; from business studies degree courses
to the range of courses offered by the major trade associations, including the
Chartered Institute of Marketing (CIM), the Institute of Direct Marketing (IDM),
the Marketing Society and the Institute of Sales Promotion (ISP) among others.
While many of your team may have these qualifications, here are some other options to
consider:

- **On the job experience**
  Send them to the warehouse, onto the factory floor, out with the sales force and to
  sit in the call centre.

- **Time management skills**
  With so many elements to manage, time management is low cost and high payback.

- **Public-speaking skills**
  Success in marketing comes from being able to present well, so public speaking
  coaching is vital.

- **Decision-making skills**
  Education and experience is pointless if it is not used well. Today, we seem better
  informed as a society but find it ever more difficult to make decisions. Give people a
  helping hand to do so.

Mentoring

Assigning mentors or buddies to each of your team can provide an objective eye and
an independent check and balance to guide their development. Usually, mentors will
be senior team members or someone outside your department. Buddies just need to
be more experienced and can help new recruits acclimatise to a new company or new

role. You may also wish to find a mentor for yourself, for example, to hone your soft management skills – quite simply how to get the best out of people. Life coaches, if you get the right one, can be very helpful.

Support networks

We all tend to gravitate and work better in a community to which we feel we belong. You can see examples of this in everyday life – from family to classroom, from sports team to company department. These traits can be recognised by encouraging your team to build support networks. This may be via professional bodies or within your own organisation. Nowadays, software packages encouraging co-operation and knowledge-sharing are readily available, and there are many special interest groups on social networking websites. These can be developed into a knowledge management portal and a full dashboard for the whole function and activity. Again these are commonplace in professional services organisations.

Dealing with different people

This section takes a sideways look at the types of personality, how they behave when confronted with cultural and organisational change and how to deal with them. It has no scientific or quantifiable basis but comes solely from our personal experience. However, it may help you spot a problem early on and nip it in the bud. It may also save you those lengthy involvements with HR. We call them the 'changeling characters':

Commander

One who takes control and expects the commands issued to be carried out without question. Needs to be reminded of the need for clarification and explanation to maintain commitment and may resent new management and edicts that may appear to undermine status.

Controller

One who seeks to control every detail and won't let go of a single thing.
Needs to be coached to let go of old ways and be encouraged to help plan new processes that can then be better controlled.

Contender

One who thinks they should have got your job or that they are next. Decide whether they are worthy of the thought. If they are, encourage and share some responsibility. If not, make sure they are fully aware of their role and responsibilities and the limits thereto.

Constructor

One who starts to build new castles before the old ones have been knocked down. Can have new and good ideas but equally needs to be reminded of the existing job to be completed before a new one is started.

Crafty and cunning

You will need to be observant and ever watchful to spot this character because outward signs of co-operation may mask a superficial lack of acceptance and an almost malevolent execution. The Crafty is often using skills to avoid changes while the Cunning may well have their own agenda.

You will need to 'keep a straight bat' and persistently and patiently seek to reassure by restating the need for change and the subsequent beneficial outcomes. Trying to understand the hidden agenda that motivates them will be helpful. However, if the practice continues, these are rightful candidates for the HR approach to the door.

Compliant

One who simply gets on with anything they have been asked to do (usually at one pace – either frantically fast or excruciatingly slow). They tend to keep their head down. This person needs stimulation – perhaps ask them to do a task in two completely different ways and ask for a comparison and evaluation to seek the best way.

Connected

One who's usually been around a long time. Knows everyone and everything; most of which is not written down and effectively circumnavigates any process or management system. Probably wary of the change because it will 'make work' and require a lot of effort to get the connections back in place. The change may even expose them.

This is a very important person at a time of change but it can be difficult to engage them in it. Involving them as an agent of change can be risky – it will either provide great steps forward or block it altogether. However, engaging this person may be well worth the risks involved as you may at least learn some unwritten methods.

Contented

One who accepts the need for change and is prepared to work for it.
If only everyone was like this! Don't take them for granted – reinforcement, promise and a 'thank you' will go a long way.

Co-operative

One who accepts change and wholeheartedly joins in the process. Hopefully this is what all your team will become as you work to bring the change about.

Motivation at a time of change

During times of change or disruption, everything written here applies but more so. People do not mind being in a rocky boat if they know where it is going and that it is where they want to go. Your personal confidence and re-assurance are the keys to getting the best out of people in times of change.

If that time of change means you need to rationalise your team, you should now read Chapter 26 Rationalisation or Downsizing and talk to your fellow director of HR.

Dealing with HR

Today more than ever before, we are beset by regulations surrounding employment and staff. As a result, HR as a function seems to have become more concerned with compliance, seems constantly non-confrontational and will take its allotted time to achieve whatever outcomes have been agreed. Of course, your starting point for all things staff-orientated must be your fellow director of HR. Work together to plan where you want to be and what team you will need. Chapter 10 Structuring the Function should help. However, the marketing world is still peopled by people, and marketing people have to plan and create change, and help frame and drive the culture of both brand and business.

 Key points to remember

1. Team motivation and development starts with your leadership.
2. If you do not set a goal you cannot achieve it.
3. Unless you measure progress against objectives you will not know how well you are performing. This measurement gives the facility to reward performance, which will further increase the level of success.
4. The more you aim to work as a team the better the results will be.
5. Your team will always be motivated by more than money. Invest in their development, set exciting challenges and reward by enhancing their self esteem.
6. If you have problems with your team, your colleagues in HR should be an early port of call.

13 Managing the Board and Business as a Whole

Friendly Persuasion – Pat Boone (1956)

In this chapter you will learn:

- *The art of persuasion*
- *Responsibilities of the board*
- *How to work with the CEO and fellow directors*

Business groups and cultures as well as social groups can be highly complex. Each individual within a group will have a different upbringing, set of skills, needs, motivations and objectives. The larger the group, the more complex the range and nature of sub-groups and interactions will be and the more complex the management challenge.

As marketing director, you have a clear management and leadership role. In addition to managing those under your direct command, you need to manage and influence individuals such as the chief executive or managing director, as well as the board and the organisation at large. According to Robert Dorn, now Honorary Senior Fellow at the Center for Creative Leadership in Greensboro, North Carolina (1),

"The task of the creative leader is to envision and achieve organisational goals which have beneficial long-term consequences for his part of the organisation, the organisation as a whole and customers or society at large. An inseparable part of the task is to help other individuals reach their full potential, not just as contributors to the organisation but as human beings."

Few are taught how to manage at college or business school. Even fewer are taught to deal with a managing director or board. Motivating individuals and groups is a skill that is acquired over time. To encourage colleagues to help you, they need to trust you, buy into your vision and be convinced of the benefits in helping you. But not necessarily in that order!

Success factors – the art of persuasion

While the motivators for each individual and group will be very different, there are a few general factors that can help ensure success:

Marshall your arguments

Research suggests that colleagues will be inspired by a credible and motivating message. At more senior levels pure financial arguments may hold sway, but at other levels the prospect of an exciting challenge or the opportunity for personal growth, respect and advancement will be more important. You will need to marshal a combination of rational and emotional arguments to justify your strategies or directives. In addition to the business analysis that you have undertaken, you may find Figure 13.1 useful in crystallising rational benefits. A quick look at Maslow's *Hierarchy of Needs* (covered in detail in Chapter 6 Customer Strategy) may also inspire some credible emotional benefits.   **6**

Figure 13.1 *Virtuous circle of benefits*

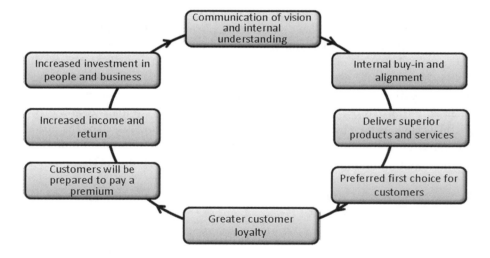

Keep telling and selling your message

Never assume that everyone in the organisation is aware of or understands your message, let alone agrees with it. In complex, multi-layered organisations, it is virtually certain that colleagues on lower rungs of the corporate ladder will be less in the know than those on higher rungs. You should therefore take every opportunity to tell and sell your message. This is an occasion when force of personality or enthusiasm can be infectious.

Best practice

Jack Welch, previously chief executive at General Electric, was a charismatic leader, and used to repeat a number of key messages in meetings that he attended. Some of his messages have become his trademarks:

- business is simple
- don't make it overly complicated
- fight bureaucracy
- face reality
- don't be afraid of change
- use the brains of your workers
- discover who has the best ideas, and put those ideas into practice

Simon Gulliford, previously marketing director at Barclays, was also known for his simple marketing mantra. When devising marketing strategies and plans, he instilled his team to ask four questions:

- Why is your product different?
- Why is it better?
- What do you want consumers to think?
- What do you want them to feel?

 Ten minute exercise

Objective of the exercise:
- To develop your own mantra to help ensure business success.

Guidelines for the exercise:
Work through the following:
- For each of the key strategies that you want to implement or behaviours you want to change (a) within your own team, and (b) across the organisation at large, generate a long list of possible messages or ideas that could motivate your colleagues.
- Distill or cluster the messages or ideas into a handful of themes.
- Make a list of potential benefits that would motivate your colleagues to do what needs to be done.
- Speak to human resources, senior colleagues or even your agency creatives to help turn your themes into a clear and motivating message.
- Start spreading the word but make sure you set an example and do as you say.

Be human

Leaders who are seen to be inclusive, empowering and friendly are far more effective than those who are seen to be autocratic, competitive and aloof (2). Experience also suggests that if a colleague feels disrespected or undervalued in any way you can be sure that he/she won't be around in the business for very long. Go out of your way to make connections and build relationships in the workplace.

- Remember names. *Hi Bill!*
- Remember names of husbands, wives or girlfriends. *How's Catherine?*
- Find and remember common interests. They are great ice breakers. *Hull City anyone?*
- Be open with feelings. Others will feel more inclined to be open too.
- Don't be Mr Angry or Mr Moody. Be Mr Calm and Collected.
- Humour goes a long way – particularly in stressful situations.
- Little touches go a long way. Send thank you notes when appropriate.
- Give praise where praise is due but only when you mean it. Say what was good and why was it good.
- Be apolitical; don't insult anyone behind their back – it will get back to them and do nothing to build your reputation!

Involve others early

Whatever project you are undertaking and whatever problem you are trying to address, there will be skills and resources outside the marketing department that can help you. Seek out diverse skills and expertise and co-opt others to help you when in need. Research also suggests that the earlier others are involved in a project, the better the outcome and smoother the process. If you are devising a work programme to address a particular problem, make a point of asking potential stakeholders and contributors for their views at an early stage. Not only can it help you anticipate potential problems and save you a lot of heartache later on, the whole process of involving others can be an invaluable part of the process of getting buy-in too.

Rise above and manage conflict

As a leader managing upwards, downwards and across the business you will inevitably encounter conflict – conflicting opinions over what to do, conflicts of responsibility as well as interpersonal conflict. This is where all your very best interpersonal and persuasion skills come into play! To deal with conflict you need to take the high ground:

- Learn the difference between aggression and assertiveness; the former is destructive and the latter constructive.

- Empathise – ask questions to find out what's important to the other person. Find out about their feelings too, say you're willing to consider alternatives and want to find the best win-win.

- Invite/suggest alternatives – clarify advantages and disadvantages. Depending on the nature of the issue, this may be better achieved by asking for it all to be written down.

- Make a decision – explain what you've decided and why. In doing this, be guided by the strategies that you've created.

Responsibilities of the board

The board of directors is ultimately responsible for the direction and management of the company. It is an entity separate from the sum of its individual directors, which makes single collective decisions. The control of the company is separated by law from the ownership of its shares, and while shareholders have powerful rights, for example, to dismiss directors or wind up a company, the directors have fiduciary and contractual relationships to the company, not the shareholders. Case law and the company's 'Articles of Association' inform the responsibilities of the board of directors; however, at present there is no single document on which to rely. Responsibility is vested in the board in the belief that groups produce better solutions to problems than individuals.

The key areas of responsibility are continually evolving, and can be summarised as follows:

- The preservation of the business and protection of the shareholders' interest is the fundamental principle

- Approve the strategy and business plan of the company. This should have been submitted by the executives & management teams (of which you will have been one)

- Ensure good governance of all that you do

- Select or remove individual directors including the chairman of the board; in practice this means supporting the chairman (particularly on a PLC board) until the chairman has to go.

- As an executive director support the chief executive/managing director at the board on the principle of 'United we stand united we fall', until he/she has to go

- Define the limits of authority for the chief executive/managing director and other directors

- Approve the appointment or removal of top managers immediately below the board

- Compile and communicate policies covering fundamental beliefs, external and internal relations, market sectors and businesses, required financial performance and planning and budgeting policies

- Review business options open to the company on an ongoing basis and ensure that meaningful plans are produced

- Allocate appropriate processes to deliver the plans

- Advise management in the compilation of plans and to assist in their implementation

- Structure and organise the company, and ensure appropriate inter-relationships

- Describe how and what it will communicate both internally and externally

- Develop and implement suitable mechanisms to ensure employee participation

- Safeguard the assets of the company and take reasonable steps to prevent and detect fraud and other irregularities

- Define how to monitor and then monitor the performance of the company

- Monitor the performance of the board (at least on an annual basis)

- Keep accounting records and prepare statutory accounts that disclose a true and fair view

- File these accounts, an annual return and other relevant documents on the public record at Companies House

- Hold the correct board and general meetings, to transact the company's business, and keep minutes thereof

There are also differences in responsibility depending on what type of board you are a member of:

- Public or private companies – the roles and responsibilities of public and private company boards differ in secondary detail. The main difference between them is the existence of external shareholders in public companies and that the shares and trading records will be generally more visible and potentially subject to scrutiny by the press. There are also strict rules on disclosure of information that can affect movement of the share price and insider trading. This usually puts extra pressure on directors to perform.

- The holding, main or 'group' board is to its subsidiaries as the independent company is to its individual businesses. They both decide what resources they will allocate to the activities for which they are responsible. The holding board's first decision is to decide whether the subsidiaries are to operate as real companies. If so, the subsidiaries will need real boards of their own, operating freely within predetermined limits of authority. If not, the holding board's management responsibilities become very great, and those of the managers of the subsidiaries become much less. The holding 'board' cannot have it both ways, and what is right is usually a question of strategy. Increasing diversification from the core business and decentralisation usually pushes decision making or 'control' down the line.

- Divisional boards operate with authority from the holding board. As a result, divisions and the authority of divisional boards can be real or apparent. Sometimes divisions exist for presentation reasons and divisional boards can often be little more than an extra level of management committee, producing less active contribution than its own subsidiaries.

- Subsidiary boards are usually where the business is done and cash is generated and where the decisions of the group board are put to the test. However, these can also be places where executive directors say the least and are most commonly frustrated. If, however, these boards operated as 'real' boards, there would be an awakening and quickening of the many directors who comprise them. Experience in dealing with conflict would be enhanced and this would make subsidiary boards more effective places for group boards to grow future talent.

Boards work best when they are:

- heterogeneous rather than homogeneous – comprised of individuals from different backgrounds and with different skills

- task focused

- performance driven

- small, usually less than ten people

- comprised of contributors not wallflowers

- democratic

Boards can fail when poorly led or when they become complacent. They can fail when they look inward rather than critically outward. They can also fail if they don't select or remove poor managers, and when decisions are driven by dominant individuals not corporate objectives. They can also fail when the board is blinkered or blind.

Success factors for working with the chief executive and board

On joining a board, be aware of the strengths of good boards and the failings of poor boards. Champion the good over the bad.

Stand up for what you believe

If you are on the board, there is generally an expectation that you subscribe to so-called 'cabinet' rules – what is discussed in the boardroom doesn't go beyond it. You must take collective responsibility for the decisions taken in the boardroom. There is also a legal responsibility that what's recorded in the board minutes is agreed by all unless anyone asks that his/her disagreement be noted to the contrary. You should also be aware, however, that pressure for conformity can rob the group of original contribution. The implication here is that you should speak up, otherwise you risk creating an illusion of unanimity when none exists. Present the facts first, and then add a degree of emotion if it helps you sell your recommendation. The chairman also has a role to play and a strong leader will ensure that everyone's view is heard. He/she should rein back dominators, including him/herself.

Celebrate your difference

As marketing director, you should also recognise and make the most of the fact that you are different from your colleagues in other functions – human resources, information technology, legal, finance etc. While it will be tedious to bang on about customers every week, you can and should bring your unique viewpoint to the boardroom.

Talk the same language

Remember too that your colleagues will not understand marketing as well as you do and that the language that you use can help or hinder clarity. It may be helpful to cover off a few basics to check you are on the same wavelength before getting into a lengthy diatribe. In the introduction to this book, we discussed the misconceptions that some people have about marketing and marketers. The subject of branding can also be misunderstood, especially in organisations that are new to branding initiatives. Brands can be seen as trivial and raise hackles unduly. Your job should be to discuss issues and opportunities at a level that your colleagues will understand and pre-empt possible misunderstandings. Some ideas to help your colleagues understand the meaning and benefits of brands are covered in Chapter 16 Brand Management and Positioning. **16**▶

Your heightened financial responsibility also means that you must be familiar with the numbers and understand and speak the language of the company report.

Find time to talk

Few CEOs, managing directors (MDs) and fellow directors are superhuman. Like you, most are ordinary human beings who are seriously time-pressed and work long days. One of the problems you will encounter is getting time to talk, so it is worth cultivating opportunities at an early stage, and try and establish a routine to do so.

Make time to get to know your boss, as well as your other colleagues – these will be invaluable to help keep you in touch with what's going on, as well as bounce ideas or take soundings and prepare the way for any recommendations you may wish to make.

Cultivate a mutual support network

It can be a lonely and vulnerable place at the top of most organisations. No one knows everything, nor can any one individual do everything alone. Everyone needs help to achieve their objectives, and you will need help too. Try to understand the hopes and fears of your colleagues and build mutually supportive relationships. This will help you align the objectives of your team with other functions and win support for any marketing initiatives that you plan to recommend. The only way the marketing function can be effective is to have close relationships with your fellow directors, especially the chief executive (CEO) and finance director (FD).

There will also be times when you encounter sticky situations, and sometimes helping others through them will motivate them to support you when the boot is on the other foot.

A little research may also be helpful. There are parallels with building relationships with your biggest customer. Would you ever meet up without doing your homework on what your customer needs first? Would you ever present to them without having a clear idea about what you could offer and at what price? The answer is probably no – so ask questions and listen to what they have to say:

- *Tell me about your role and key responsibilities.*
- *What are your job objectives; what's written down and how is achievement measured?*
- *What are key dependencies or barriers to achieving your objectives?*
- *What are your hopes and fears?*
- *How could the marketing team help you?*
- *How could you help the marketing team meet its objectives?*

Beyond your board colleagues you should also establish your own external mutual support group. Your peers, your direct reports, friends and allies in other companies may all be able to play a role. Consider appointing a personal coach or a consultant that you trust.

Key points to remember

1. Don't underestimate the need to play a 'broken record'. Keep communicating clear, credible and motivating messages to your colleagues in order to generate and maintain support behind your initiatives. Consider creating your own mantra to help you get your point across.

2. While rational (commercial) arguments will motivate your fellow directors, others are likely to be equally motivated by emotional benefits. Remember that different folks need different strokes, so use both and adjust the balance to the audience.

3. The more complex the challenge or far-reaching the project, the more important it is to involve others early in the process.

4. The board alone has responsibility for corporate performance. Boards can perform more wisely than the wisest director or more foolishly than the most foolish. The quality and suitability of a board depends not only on the people but also on how the various members of the group interact, stimulate, respect and support each other.

5. Stand up and be counted in the boardroom. While it will be inappropriate to bang on about customers to the point of boring your colleagues, the marketing director should be valued for his/her unique viewpoint.

6. Take the time to get to know your board colleagues and build mutually supportive relationships with them. Don't underestimate the importance of the emotional dimension in decision making.

7. Don't get bogged down in personal conflict(s); rise above it and help facilitate the best solution.

14 Managing Market or Customer Research

The Eyes of Truth – Enigma (1994)

In this chapter you will learn:

- *What customer insight is*
- *How to create a market research brief to get the best results*
- *Selecting and managing research agencies*
- *Ideas on qualitative and quantitative methods*

Customer research is a vital weapon in the marketing director's armoury. It fits perfectly with the marketing director's role as the customer manager and is valuable to help champion and 'hard-wire' customer-driven thinking in an organisation. The size of the global market research industry, which is worth over £12 billion (1), provides testimony to its importance. However despite the large size of the industry, many don't invest sufficiently in research or don't invest wisely. Some pay lip-service to research and use it just to support decisions they have already made. Others use research for purely evaluative purposes or to investigate the here and now. This chapter is designed to help you maximise the benefits from your investment in market or customer research. It outlines a number of principles and provides inspiration on tools and techniques to help you enhance the competitiveness of your brands and business and identify ways to add value to your bottom line.

Organisations in the consumer industries tend to give most recognition to customer research. Some have even renamed what were previously called 'market research managers' as 'customer insight managers'. Some have taken this a step further by defining what constitutes an insight and have developed their own principles and processes for unearthing and applying insights to their businesses. Others are less prescriptive and recognise that continual innovation in the methods used can also reveal new insights and in turn provide competitive advantage. A minority are highly future focused and seek to understand customers' needs tomorrow and not just today; not only does this help unearth new insights but it also helps fuel more creative and forward-looking business strategies and solutions.

What is customer insight?

Customer research at its most useful should deliver actionable insights; but without trying to be trapped by semantics, let's start with a definition.

According to the Oxford English Dictionary, insight is *'profound understanding into character or circumstances'*. To ensure that it is something that genuinely matters to customers as well as the business this is best expressed as a customer need, want or belief. To provide benefits to the marketer, the insight should point to a marketing opportunity. In other words, the insight should have a relevant and practical marketing application. So when looking for insights, consider the following:

- what is the new or unmet customer need, want or belief articulated by the insight?
- how and why is the insight important and relevant to the customer and his/her life?
- how could the insight be successfully acted upon or applied to benefit the customer and brand or business?

Once articulated, customer insights sometimes evince a widespread sense of recognition – an 'ah-ha' moment. Often they are wake-up call to something that is already known but so far not been given sufficient attention or acted upon.

 Success factors for briefing research

To maximise the benefits from your investment in research, an important first step is to prepare a research brief. Creating this is a useful mechanism to solicit input and buy-in from colleagues to your proposed research objectives and plan. Most agencies will also usually prefer to receive a written brief, as this provides greater assurance that both your objectives and needs have been thought through and agreed by your stakeholders. An additional benefit of producing a brief is that it can also be used as a checklist against which to assess agencies' responses.

The brief should set out clear objectives and expectations. A checklist of points to include in a research brief is shown in Proforma 14A.

 Proforma 14A Market research brief

Background
- What has happened to make this brief necessary?
- How does this piece of work fit with other potential initiatives within the organisation?

- What work has already been done in this area? What do you know/not know?

Business objectives

- Describe your business objectives, for example, in terms of sales and profitability, market share, growth in customer base.

Project objectives

- What is the purpose of/expected outcome from conducting this piece of work (eg to focus new product ideation)?
- What decisions will be made on the basis of the work undertaken?
- Who are the key stakeholders; what interest do they have in this project?

Guidelines

- Provide guidance on the nature of work that should or should not be undertaken.
- What are the priorities?
- What countries, markets, customer groups should be covered/receive most attention?
- Who should be involved?
- What specific information should be provided or knowledge gaps addressed?
- What are specific issues that should be considered?

Timing

- What time constraints for the project?
- What is driving any time constraints eg board meeting presentation?

Deliverables

- What should this project deliver?
- What will success feel like?
- Define any terms used (eg what constitutes a successful proposition?)
- In what form should the project be delivered (eg full debrief and report)?

Budget

- What is an appropriate investment in this project?

Bearing in mind the following can also contribute to the success of your research:

Seek input from your colleagues

In almost every situation, your colleagues will have views – usually different – on what is known and unknown about the customers and the challenge at hand, as well as future opportunities. There is huge value in canvassing their opinions on what is known, unknown and important to know at the outset of a research project. There is also huge value in hypothesising potential issues and solutions to problems, as all can be explored and developed with customers. Some consultancies will recommend facilitating working sessions to cover this ground as part of their approach. Many will not.

Include business objectives

The vast majority of briefs tend to contain clear research objectives. However, few include clear business objectives, as well as project objectives or outcomes. Given that the end-result of any research commissioned should ultimately help facilitate the achievement of your business and project objectives, both of these should always be included. Furthermore, your desired business or project outcomes may have a signifi-cant bearing on the optimum research approach.

Ensure scope is not limiting

Making unwarranted assumptions can result in an overly narrow research focus and limit the benefits of any work undertaken. In other words, if you ask the wrong questions, or inadvertently exclude exploration of a particular area from research, you are likely to get the wrong answers! As well as ensuring that all key issues are explored, research should be briefed to ensure that the proper contextual understanding will be gained. For example, this could have a bearing on the range and nature of competitors considered and customers' decision making processes – all could skew the potential findings and conclusions.

Don't be too prescriptive

While it can be helpful to fully describe the nature of your customers to ensure that the right demographics and other variables are included in a research sample, don't be too prescriptive about the approach that should be used. This could limit the creativity of the response and, in turn, limit the insights that are revealed.

For example, including influencers or opinion leaders such as industry experts in a research sample can help address some promotion and product development chal-lenges. Typically, these people have more knowledge than customers and their views either influence or lead mainstream customer opinion. Customers from other countries, or expatriates, can also help reveal insights on 'best practices' and ways to accelerate development of particular markets. The opinions of US or Japanese consumers, for example, can be useful in some service markets as the US and Japan can be more 'sophisticated' than in Europe. Non-customers or recently lapsed customers can also be as useful as customers themselves when exploring business or brand issues. Those who have never consumed or tried a brand may provide insights on why they have never tried it and reveal inherent promotion weaknesses. Lapsed customers may provide insights on why they have lapsed and reveal inherent product weaknesses.

Investing some of your budget in researching the world about us is particularly useful when investigating trends. While trends may have customer or social outcomes, they are sometimes politically, economically and technologically driven. There are many ways to explore the world about us, including web-surfing and talking to experts and journalists. The Internet is an increasingly powerful source of information and insight. There is a huge variety of sites that contain information and opinions on trends, product reviews and competitor performance and strategies. Some contain discussion boards and blogs and, as we all know, advances in technology are fuelling increasingly rich multi-media content.

Don't ask for the kitchen sink

Trying to do too much can blur the focus for a piece of work and risk dissipating effort. Sometimes it is better to conduct two or three sequential studies, or more frequent studies.

Do enter into dialogue

Some organisations refuse to discuss their briefs with agencies or will only do so in writing. Most agencies view this as unhelpful – it also sends a warning signal as to the kind of relationship an agency might expect from working with you. If you want someone to help you, help them understand your needs and make time to talk to them.

Be clear what you know and don't know

Most organisations tend to overstate what is known. If part of the research challenge is to build on previous work, be sure to provide an indication of what you know at the briefing stage so there are no surprises on either side.

Managing research

There are three main options for managing research within your organisation and the pros and cons of these options are outlined in Figure 14.1. What's right for you will depend on the size and nature of your research workload and budget. The majority of organisations tend to maintain a small in-house research management resource and sub-contract the planning, fieldwork and analysis to consultancies. The large and diverse range of research expertise available means you can buy in considerable skills at a modest cost.

Figure 14.1 *Managing research options*

In-house research management option	Pros and cons	Application
Marketing managers responsible for commissioning their own research	Helps forge close customer understanding; helps enable skill development; helps ensure research delivers commercial benefits; cost saving in not having a part or full-time in-house research specialist.	Most useful for smaller organisations and where there is a need to train specific individuals to acquire research skills.
Research manager/ team as managers, or internal experts	Helps create in-house centre of expertise; extra cost; marketing managers risk being one step removed from customers and external agencies; some risk in research not delivering maximum commercial benefits.	Most useful for organisations with ongoing research needs and where there is a need to accumulate, share or disseminate knowledge across the organisation and establish 'best practice'.
Research team as doers	Enables accumulation of customer knowledge, potentially leading to greater leverage and competitive advantage; potential cost savings; in-house culture and team perceptions may influence the value and credibility ie perceived independence of work undertaken.	Most useful when a high volume of specific skills are needed.

Sourcing and selecting agencies

Asking around tends to be the most commonly used means of sourcing or shortlisting agencies. Other useful sources include the Internet as well as professional associations and their handbooks (2). When creating a shortlist of agencies to respond to a brief, include a range of different types of agency as each is likely to have different specialist areas, respond to a brief differently and offer varying benefits. Different types of agency include; pure market research, marketing and new product development consultancies, communications agencies and management consultancies.

While many agencies will provide proposals free of charge, there is increasing antipathy to long shortlists. Three is likely to provide a good spectrum of ideas, a fair indication of costs and also be fair and motivating to the agencies concerned.

Pitch meetings, sometimes called 'beauty parades', are useful to compare approaches and gauge the quality of personnel within an agency. In inviting an agency to pitch, be clear what is expected of them and who will attend. Also be sure to check and meet the people who will do the work. Be equally clear to your own team what is expected of them. Circulate a hard copy of a proposal document to your team beforehand to save time and ask everyone to prepare questions to ask. Also consider creating a list or scorecard of criteria against which the agencies can be assessed.

As regards pricing, it is more often than not the case that you get what you pay for. While the approach to costing proposals across countries and agencies may differ, the underlying elements of a quotation remain similar. These are listed in Proforma 14B. The key challenge in comparing research proposals is to compare like with like and ask questions so you can make sure you know what the similarities and differences are:

- Generally the staff costs will be the dominant element and this will depend on time involved, as well as the seniority and experience of staff.

- The type of deliverable will also have a bearing on the costs and should be discussed and agreed at the outset. Deliverables typically reflect the effort and skill that go into their preparation and can range enormously in detail and quality. If you haven't worked with an agency before, ask to see an example of a typical deliverable.

- The number and nature of respondents to be recruited will also have a bearing on costs. Make sure this is not dissimilar. Also be aware of differences across countries. In the UK and mainland Europe, groups usually comprise 6-8 respondents, whereas in the US, 8-10 is the norm.

- The nature of research viewing facilities also has a bearing on costs. Using research facilities is very much the norm in the US, where this has spawned an industry within the industry. However, in the UK and mainland Europe, group locations vary. Groups held in homes or pubs rather than viewing facilities are much cheaper.

 Proforma 14B – Costing considerations

Consultant's time
- Attend and prepare for meetings.
- Development of recruitment screener.
- Development of questionnaires/discussion guide.
- Create research stimulus.
- Conduct fieldwork.
- Analyse and prepare report on findings.
- Present findings.

- Project management.
- Travel.

Field services
- Viewing facility rental and catering.
- Recruitment of respondents.
- Incentives for respondents.
- Meals and refreshments for respondents and observers.
- Audio, video or other form of recording or transmission.
- Hire of equipment eg laptops with Internet access.

Expenses
- Consultant's travel, parking, accommodation, subsistence.
- Research transcription.
- Creative services, for preparing and producing research stimulus and presentation materials.
- Photography.

Managing agencies

The most important thing to remember when managing research agencies, as with other agencies, is that they are people. The more you motivate and get on with them, the more they will go out of their way to help you. After all, for everyone, not just you, this is a job that pays the bills, and this is always more motivating when learning new things and working with interesting people on interesting challenges. Having agreed a budget that provides a reasonable return for effort, the people within the agency should want to do everything in their power to help you, both as a business and an individual. The motivation will also be to win applause and subsequently more work. Conversely, if they feel they've been backed into a corner they will be less motivated. Bear in mind that motivation works at many levels – there is likely to be a Finance Director (FD) lurking in the background to make sure that the consultant doesn't spend more than the budgeted amount of time on a job!

There are few other factors to bear in mind to help ensure a successful research outcome and ensure a successful agency working relationship:

- Recruitment – the quality of research and nature of insights partly depends on the quality of respondents and the quality of recruitment. In the UK and Europe, recruitment of respondents tends to be a 'cottage industry' and driven by 'snowballing' (whereby one subject recommends connecting with another), whereas in the US, recruitment tends to be driven by databases. In the UK, there is also an unfortunate rise in the number of professional interviewees and it is vital to allow sufficient time and/or money to ensure quality recruitment. It is also useful to ensure diversity within the constraints of the sample and mandate the number of people in a research sample who have participated in research before.

- Database recruitment – recruiting respondents from in-house databases can be problematic too. First, because data protection legislation means individuals may not be approached for research unless they have previously given their consent. Second, because there may be inadequate numbers of individuals in proximity to research locations. Make sure you have the necessary 'permissions' and discuss what you've got and not got at the briefing stage so any issues can be anticipated and dealt with in the response to your brief.

- Attend qualitative research – it is usually invaluable to see and hear the customers first hand and you should encourage your colleagues to do so too. However, do bear in mind that watching just one group or interview is likely to provide a misread. Watching just one interaction is even forbidden by some agencies.

- Work hand in hand – most consultants will understand and respect your political and business challenges. Some will enjoy helping you address both and view it as part of their job. To this end, be open about all facets of your problems and share new news as it emerges. The more the agency knows, the more it should be able to help you. Introduce your senior management to your agency at an early stage, as they may have different interpretations on your requirements. This may also have a bearing on a recommended approach and if you do this too late, it won't be possible to take their views into account.

- Presentations and debriefs – there are many ways of presenting and debriefing findings and conclusions, and budget is usually the main limiting factor. Make any desired outcomes and guidelines clear at the briefing stage so your needs can be met. Make a point of reviewing and discussing the researcher's report in as final a form as possible before the final debrief. This is most important when senior management will attend the debrief. This should help both parties manage expectations and ensure no nasty surprises.

- Meeting time – the key challenge is to enable your agency to present the key messages and achieve your desired outcomes. Some organisations enforce time limits but you should use your judgement and bend the rules if needed. One hour is often too short to present, discuss and agree the key findings and next steps. Three hours is sometimes too long.

- Chapter 15 Managing Agencies also provides more insights and ideas on this subject.   **15**

Qualitative vs. quantitative research methodologies

There are two main types of research – qualitative and quantitative. Historically, the two disciplines have operated independently, largely because of the different skills and infrastructure required with little crossover between them. Figure 14.2 shows the pros and cons of each.

Figure 14.2 *Qualitative versus quantitative research*

Research method	Pros	Cons
Qualitative research is used to describe the approach taken when opinions are sought from a relatively small number of respondents, usually by means of individual interviews or group discussions. This form of investigation makes use of relatively flexible 'discussion guides' rather than pre-structured questionnaires.	Enables exploration and explanation of issues and opportunities eg causes behind types of behaviour. Answers questions such as 'why?', 'what if?' and 'how to'?	Decision-making substance is sometimes limited by the number of respondents.
Quantitative research seeks to make numerical or probabilistic measurements. In most cases, this involves the statistical analysis of the answers given to a structured set of questions (as in a survey questionnaire).	Enables measurable comparisons between sets of data (between groups of people and points in time). Answers questions such as 'how much?' or 'how many?'	Larger sample sizes required to obtain decision-making information. Usually higher cost. Usually takes longer to set up Usually less good at providing understanding ie answering the 'why?' questions

Today, however, there is an increasing overlap and blurring of the division between the two types of research and this is providing new benefits for users. For example, using simple proformas or voting methods in qualitative research can help researchers obtain more robust insights or comparatives across a sample. This is particularly useful in assessing the relative appeal of ideas, for example, for new products or services. While quantitative studies have usually allowed the inclusion of open–ended questions (at an extra cost), this is now being taken further by some online techniques, whereby the respondents can generate their own 'why' answers as part of the methodology.

Given the usually much higher cost of quantitative versus qualitative research and the longer elapsed timescales involved, it is usually advisable to conduct qualitative research before quantitative and use the former to inform and shape the latter. Conversely, there may be times when it is more expedient and cost effective to first conduct 'dipstick' or a short piece of quantitative research to determine where, for example, the country, market or customer group focus for qualitative research should be.

Qualitative research

The research industry has historically and sometimes disparagingly associated with focus groups but today the range of methodologies and applications is much wider. Focus groups or group discussions remain the default research method for many and are certainly cost effective in researching large numbers of people. Depending on the challenge you face, however, you should question long and hard whether it should be the sole method used. Group discussions are useful for generating and building ideas by co-opting the inherent creativity of the group, whereas they are less useful in understanding each individual's attitudes and motivations. At the other end of the spectrum, in-depth one-on-one interviews are most useful in understanding an individual's personal attitudes and motivations, but less useful in generating ideas. Figure 14.3 summarises the spectrum of options.

Figure 14.3 *Relative benefits of qualitative research methods*

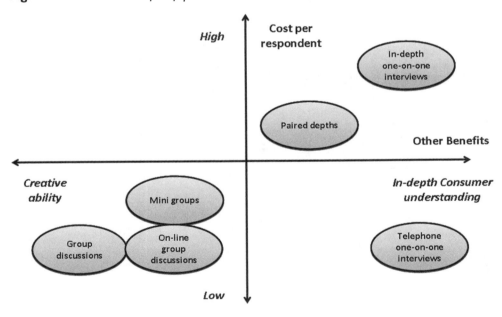

Figure 14.4 looks at the advantages and disadvantages of these methods in more detail.

Figure 14.4 *Advantages and disadvantages of qualitative research methods*

Method	Pros and cons	Application
Group discussions (focus groups or creative workshops)	Economic use of moderator and facility time; enables sharing, building and challenging of ideas; limited opportunity to understand individual attitudes and beliefs; peer groups can be more open and honest.	The most common research technique; has universal application; useful for idea generation and building (especially when using stimulus or exercises designed to stimulate unconventional responses).
Mini-group discussions	Combination of group and in-depth benefits.	Suitable when respondents are hard to find and when more detailed discussion is required.
Paired depths	Combination of group and in-depth benefits.	Useful to explore decision-making in family groups eg couples.
In-depth one-on-one interviews (idis) (conducted face-to-face)	Enables in-depth understanding of individual attitudes, beliefs and motivations; easier to schedule; conducting idis in homes also allows contextual observation; greater use of moderator time, means it is more expensive per respondent.	Most useful for understanding customers and how they live their lives; suitable for more confidential and sensitive topics eg healthcare, personal finance, and hard to recruit respondents eg high net worth, business people.
Online verbal discussions (with respondents linked via the Internet)	Contingent on technology; puts some limits on the spontaneity and detailed nature of interactions; costs are similar to face-to-face group discussions but lower for text interactions.	Useful for exploring Internet sites and computer applications; also useful for hard-to-reach respondents. Text conversations can be useful for idea sharing and building.
Telephone discussions	More spontaneous than online discussions; some limitations in distributing and discussing visual stimuli (although these issues can be overcome by using the Internet); cheaper than face-to-face idis.	Useful to research respondents in remote locations as well as respondents who have limited time eg business to business (b2b respondents).

In highly researched consumer markets it is harder and harder to unearth new insights. Thus, using a bricolage or variety of methods and techniques, is more likely to reveal new insights. To help you go beyond the obvious and reveal genuinely new insights and ideas to drive business growth, Figure 14.5 outlines three strategies and a range of techniques to consider when planning a qualitative research study.

Context

Much research presumes that customers can tell you everything that you want to know – this is only partially true. For example, what customers don't say or show in their expressions can sometimes be more revealing. Furthermore, as conducting research in a research facility is an artificial situation, it can be difficult to obtain a proper contextual understanding on customers, their lives, what's important to them and what influences the choices that they make. Research methods should, therefore, not only involve questioning but observation and listening. Visiting a customer's home or working environment to see what influences their lives, as well as watch them consume or use products and services, can reveal new insights on drivers and barriers to usage which can point to a myriad of new communication and product development opportunities.

Challenge

As what customers think and feel is based on their own frame of reference, ie historical experiences and memory, they often need to be provoked to reveal what may be unconsidered, hidden or forgotten. To do this they need to be taken out of their comfort zones and given new experiences to challenge their existing views and prejudices. For example, by being asked to try a product for the first time, it will be possible to unearth new insights on competitive relativities as well as drivers and barriers to increased consumption.

Collaboration

Today we live in an increasingly connected society with a greater free-flow of information and collaboration. In the software world this has enabled 'open-source' development and it is now truer than ever that insight and ideas can come from anywhere. The notion and principles of 'open-source' development can justifiably be applied by researchers and marketers that want to help their businesses innovate and stay one step ahead. The principles can be applied to both who, how to and where to research. In this increasingly digital age, the mechanisms to bring respondents together and co-opt their help to devise new solutions to problems can only increase in both scope and scale, with our imagination being the only limiting factor. Even in non-digital technology markets, some companies actively solicit ideas from external sources, for example, Procter & Gamble, through their 'Connect and Develop' programme.

Figure 14.5 *Qualitative research strategies and methods*

Strategy	Method	Application
Context: understand the context in which people make choices, and what drives choice	Ethnography – observing customers in places where they buy or use products; enables observation of behaviour and behavioural influences.	Useful to explore opportunities for new forms of marketing communications and product development; suitable for sensitive topics and to serve as a memory jogger.
	Diaries and scrapbook pre-tasks (in either hard copy or audio- video form) – asking customers to record what they do over a period of time, as well as record ideas and influences.	Useful and value-for-money means of recording detailed insights over an extended time period; easy-to-create in digital form and incorporate into debriefs.
	Timelines – asking customers to describe and/or visualise their experiences with a category or brand over time.	Useful to explore a customer's relationship with a category or brand, and identify and visualise emotional drivers and barriers to usage.
	Semiotics – observation and interpretation of symbols and signs.	Useful to unearth cultural insights and influences and add new shades of connotation to all aspects of life.
Challenge: give customers new experiences to challenge their existing way of doing things.	Conflict groups – groups involving customers with opposing or divergent opinions eg product loyalists and rejectors.	Useful to explore drivers and barriers to purchasing and usage, as well as provoke insights on the strength of opinions and what might prompt switching.
	Trial or inflation – asking customers to try a product or increase the usage of a product over a period of time.	Useful to explore drivers and barriers to trial as well as potential to increase usage.
Collaboration: use customers and experts as part of the creative process or as an 'open-source' to develop marketing ideas and solutions.	Creativity groups or workshops – involving customers in the creative process ie a form of brainstorming (with or without stimulus).	Useful to create solutions for a wide range of marketing problems eg communications campaigns and new products; works best when customers are asked to spontaneously create ideas (and then use stimulus to explore and build ideas in more detail). A number of examples of potential stimulus are discussed in Chapte 23. New Product Development.
	Expert groups – presenting or pitching ideas to experts or customers who have specific skills or knowledge.	Useful to 'pressure-test' and engineer more future oriented product ideas, communication, promotion and sales strategies and tactics.

23

Quantitative research

The high cost of quantitative research means that it is usually more cost-effective to invest in qualitative research prior to quantitative research so the former can shape the latter. Costs tend to depend on sample size and time length of the interview or the number of questions asked as both impact on the time needed to conduct fieldwork and analyse the responses. The role that computers play in the data collection and analysis process, as well as the type of software used, will also have a bearing on costs and form of deliverable. The advent of the Internet means that quantitative research conducted by this means is also lower cost. There are four broad types of quantitative research. These are explained in Figure 14.6 .

Figure 14.6 *Advantages and disadvantages of quantitative research methods*

Method	Pros and cons	Application
Face-to-face surveys	Can be totally tailored to needs; useful when visual stimulus needs to be assessed; longer time to set up, conduct fieldwork and analyse findings; usually recruited by door-to-door or street interviewing.	Useful for larger scale assessments eg product and communication tests, usage and attitude surveys.
Omnibus surveys	Many proprietary surveys targeted at different individuals; can be tailored to address as few as one question; short turnaround time.	Useful for smaller scale usage and attitude surveys ie when budgets are limited.
Telephone surveys	Fieldwork is less time-consuming than for face-to-face surveys; requires a database of respondents and phone numbers.	Suitable for easier rather than harder to answer questions; less suitable when visual stimulus is involved.
Internet or mobile phone surveys	Growing number of providers and range of techniques; short turnaround time; some combine basic qualitative and quantitative.	Particularly useful for researching customers in Internet or related markets and for conducting large-scale research in a short amount of time.

An increasing range of proprietary quantitative methods are available to meet some specific needs. These include methods that measure and predict advertising effectiveness and product sales; some have established global databases with 'norms' that enable comparative assessment. Some methods also include both qualitative and quantitative research elements and offer some of the benefits of both.

Statistical significance

When interpreting qualitative research findings it is important to understand what differences are meaningful or significant. Statistical significance is said to exist when a difference between samples/responses is large enough to be attributed to something other than expected sampling error. When a statistic is significant, it simply means that the statistic is reliable. It doesn't necessarily mean the finding is important or that it has any decision-making relevance. To say that a significant difference or relationship exists only tells half the story. When a relationship exists, it is important to evaluate its strength. Significant relationships can be strong, moderate, or weak. The differences can be large or small – it just depends on the sample size.

Larger sample sizes are needed to provide greater reliability or decision-making confidence. The level of confidence needed should be considered at the quantitative research design stage and reflected in the sample size. While there are different ways to calculate statistically significant variances, there is much debate over the validity of the different methods. Figure 14.7 provides an indication of the relationship between sample sizes and levels at which variances start to become significant. The calculations assume a 95% confidence level (which means that they will be reliable in 95 out of 100 instances). A number of proprietary statistical significance calculators can be found on the Internet and two are mentioned in the references (3).

Figure 14.7 *The relationship between sample size and statistical significance*

Sample size	Variance in response that is 'significant'	Variance in response (as a % of the sample size)
100	8-14	8-14
200	8-10	4-5
300	7-9	3
400	6-7	2
500	6-7	1.5
1,000	4-5	1

Source: prconline.com

Key points to remember

1. Research at its most useful should deliver actionable insights ie insights on needs or wants that point to a new business or brand opportunity.

2. Preparing a clear and comprehensive research brief is an important first step towards a successful research project. Describe your needs or requirements, uses of the research as well as business and project objectives, and desired deliverables or outcomes.

3. Build an open, close and supportive working relationship with your agency to help you get more for your money, improve the quality of research deliverable and ensure it helps you make more progress to meeting your objectives.

4. To unearth new and meaningful insights, avoid reliance on a single research methodology. While groups are cost-effective, consider the increasingly large range of alternatives to help provide more insightful findings.

5. Quantitative research can be expensive – conduct qualitative research before quantitative as a matter of course and make sure the quantitative design is fit for the decision-making purpose that it is intended.

15 Managing Agencies

It Takes Two – Marvin Gaye and Kim Weston (1967)

In this chapter you will learn:

- *The agency landscape; different agency types and how they work*
- *The role that the marketing director should play*
- *How brief, select and manage agencies to get the best results*

Agencies will be both the bane and boon of your life. They can be a pain, with their constant new business approaches and annoyingly difficult to be realistic about budgets. Yet they can transform the performance of your brand, your business and yourself. The benefits by far outweigh the negatives, and with careful and thoughtful management, even the negatives can all be virtually eliminated. This chapter is designed to help you obtain the most from agencies.

The agency landscape

Let's start by helping you understand the agency landscape. Originally, the landscape was dominated by advertising agencies. They were the main appointment and assumed intellectual partnership with the client – in effect being 'Agency of Record'. Not only did they produce the 'big ad', they also influenced many of the other marketing decisions. As this practice grew the advertising agencies often gathered affiliates across various functions and around the world. Sometimes they became part of an international group. Above all, the client and agency alike saw its prime responsibility as providing the creative lead and strategic direction.

Historically, there were three types of agency within advertising:

- The full service agency (FSA). Here, the agency creates the advertisement and plans and buys the media space to carry it.

- The creative shop, also called the 'hot shop'. The agency only creates the advertisement and has nothing to do with media planning or buying.

- The media independent. This agency is only concerned with planning and buying media space and has no involvement with creating the advertisement. Some specialise by media type.

In reality, the creative shops grew out of the FSAs as their key creative personnel moved to set up their own agencies. Similarly, the media independents grew out of the FSAs as they became stand-alone profit centres or the media specialists set up their own agencies.

The choice was either an FSA as a one-stop shop, or going 'à la carte' and picking different agencies to do different bits of the campaign. In reality, the FSA often used specialist independent agencies and was effectively going à la carte on your behalf. In this case, the FSA was evolving into a marketing communications consultancy.

Figure 15.1 *Traditional agency landscape*

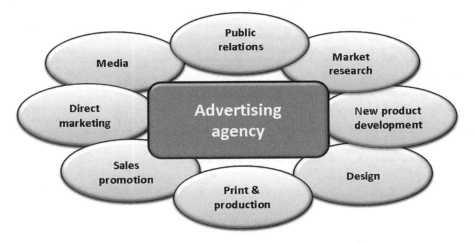

Today the landscape is much more diverse, with a broad range of specialist marketing agencies. Faced with eroding margins from advertising, the larger groups, most notably WPP and Omnicom, as well as most of the others, have sought to increase revenues and profitability through diversification (the acquisition of specialist agencies, which have hitherto had higher margins). The fragmentation of media, demand for marketing specialisms, more robust strategic advice as well as pressure to deliver sustained growth (and sometimes internal straight-jacketing by the quoted multinational groups) has prompted many break-aways and start-ups to enter the market. The result is that there are now many multinational conglomerates (largely consisting of separately managed and run companies) as well as many small independently owned organisations operating in the marketing services arena.

Figure 15.2 provides an overview of the services available in the market and which remuneration method is the most prevalent.

Figure 15.2 *The current agency landscape*

Consulting	Data	Campaigns	Implementation
Market research	Database system development	Copy writing & creative production	Call centre in-bound
Marketing strategy & product development	Database management	Media buying List buying	Web content & interactive support
Brand development & positioning	Analysis & planning	Letter shop & digital print	Handling & fulfilment
Creative direction & campaigns	Customer segment & targeting	Design & digital production	Experiential & sampling
eStrategy & development	Out-sourcing & interim management	Online campaigns	Public relations
Public relations & sponsorship	Digital asset management	eMail/sms/ mobile/web2.0	Call centre out-bound
CRM & customer channel planning	CRM implementation	Promotion & merchandising	Pay per click + affiliates

Intellectual = Fees	Value added = Cost plus	Service = Price list

Choosing the right agency is always going to be difficult especially when some claim to do everything. Figure 15.3 provides some ideas to consider as you start to look around:

How do agencies charge?

Historically, advertising agencies earned most, if not all, their income by commissions paid to them by the media owners. Typically, revenue was charged at 15 or 17.5% of the media spend plus advertising production costs. The cost of creating the advertisements was included in the invoice paid by the client for media space – hidden within the total or 'above the line' cost. Other promotional activity, such as sales promotion, direct marketing and public relations where media space was not bought, was referred to as 'below the line', also a euphemism for lower importance. However, clients

Figure 15.3 *characteristics of agencies*

Type of agency	Key selection criteria and considerations
Large	Status, process; maybe formulaic, need to get the right team.
Small	Specialists, commitment, value proposition; ask about the specialisms and overheads.
Advertising	Creativity or service; not necessarily the best strategists, tends to be the lead creative and umbrella for all messages and all media - you can manage this integration yourself or ask a full service/integrated media agency to do it for you.
PR	Relationships with the media, tenacity or ideas generation; PR has the capacity to deliver huge payback or be worse than a waste of time; keeping PR disciplined and in line with the communication strategy and marketing objectives is an amorphous task, try and set measureable outcomes.
Research	Specialist understanding of your target audience, techniques, fieldwork and analysis skills; fieldwork is often undertaken by juniors who lack commercial nous so explore who does what as well as abilities to unearth insights that point to practical opportunities and solutions.
Sales Promotion	Effectiveness, creative ability, brand relevance; sales promotions can deliver great results (and problems if not professionally handled), the best solutions comprise brand messages as well as the incentives - probe understanding of the strategic and tactical imperatives.
Internet	Technical expertise, creativity and brand understanding; an agency that is technically biased will put emphasis on the performance of the process - lots of traffic and clicks through but what about your brand? Make sure that your branding and message are understood and used.

became aware that their agencies were receiving commissions from the media and asked that this, in whole or part, be handed over to them. This passing of commissions received over to the client, or 'commissions rebating', reduced the income earned by advertising agencies, and additional revenue was sought from the client by way of fees and retainers. In some instances, where the agency only created the advertisement and did not buy media space on behalf of their client, fees – either a percentage of media costs or an amalgam of salaries, time, and overheads – were the norm.

The origins of the creative work being paid for by commission for the media are long gone and have been replaced by more transparent charging. Fundamentally, salaries, time, overheads and expenses tend to dictate charging mechanisms, although a minority operate 'value-based charging' and 'reward-based' fees.

Looking to the future

The agency landscape continues to evolve, in that many of the new channels and new media are technology-based, and agencies operating within these areas may have less understanding of the communications values.

The agency landscape is also changing at an increasing speed and becoming more complex – with extensive behind-the-scenes networking on behalf of clients. Agency networks also operate increasingly across borders as media and brands go transnational.

Traditional media planning relied heavily on very blunt socio-economic groupings and with hindsight is proving to have been relied upon too much. The growth of emarketing has generated vast amounts of data. It is the effective use of this data that will define promotional activity in the future.

If the UK and European market is to follow that of the US, it is likely that there will be a continued polarisation in the market, with a consolidation at the larger end and more new entrants at the smaller end.

All of this brings into sharp focus the need for positive and active management of a basket of agencies by management that knows clearly what they need and have to achieve. Highly experienced people will be found in an increasing variety of places and value propositions will differ markedly.

The new role for the marketing director

With the growth in new digital channels and delivery methods, there is a growing plethora of agency types and functions, for example, insight, search engine optimisation, advertising, creative and new technology delivery. It is your job to manage delivery and you must weigh up and balance effectiveness in reaching your customer target with getting your brand message across. Seek out those who fully recognise this. It is not always as easy as it seems. Those agencies that specialise in the web and all things 'e' tend to rely on the measurements that they create, site visits, clicks etc. As effective as 'opportunities to see' as a measurement are, they represent only the media and not the strength of the message.

Custody of the brand is also vital. The marketing director must have a clear brand vision and strategy, translated into a clear plan, which multiple agencies can understand and work to. This should be evidenced in a robust brand definition to provide the strategic glue to brief agencies and bind their activities together.

Creativity is important, not only to achieve cut-through and project a clear and distinctive brand, but to compensate for the technical limitations of many of the new media whose creative platform is limited. For example, the impact generated by the hand-held device is nothing compared to that of the billboard.

Increasingly, creativity and campaign development should extend into any medium. In order to justify the increasing cost and be noticed, advertising has to work in conjunction with direct marketing, sales promotion, public relations, sponsorship and all the other elements like never before. Otherwise, the brand and its positioning can easily slip into a series of unconnected campaigns, by different agencies, aimed at varying targeted audiences, using a whole panoply of new media. The elements within the promotional mix must be increasingly integrated. This was the original intention of integrated marketing communications, which many agencies sought to provide but few actually did.

Now it is your job. It should be your aim to have the central spine of a campaign espousing the brand and its values, which will serve as the creative wellspring for all other communications. Your job will be to find the ideas that can travel and become a creative lead. However, as great ideas will come from more and more places you will need a greater awareness of the range of different agencies and should seek out the agency with the appropriate resources and intent to provide this creative umbrella. Those agencies with a technical bias will need creative management and input, while those agencies with an emphasis on creative communication and traditional media will need to be constantly reminded of the other channels and routes to market. Collaboration within and across agencies will become more important in order to implement truly integrated campaigns.

Consequently, the search for creativity and the instillation of collaborative working practices should be an intrinsic part of the briefing process to every agency, of every complexion.

Briefing agencies

The brief is one of the most important documents and processes for any marketing department. The more intellectual the agency, the more you should bare your soul and give as much detail and strategic substantiation as you are able. It is not practical to provide a detailed proforma for every type of client brief, but asking your agency how they wish to be briefed is a good option. Ask what information they use internally and supply the information under their headings. For a more communications-oriented challenge, this would typically include:

- Background the brief – what has happened in the past and with what effect?
- What has necessitated this brief?
- Brand marketing objectives/desired outcomes.
- Customer definition and the reason why he or she buys.
- Position of the brand or product compared with the competition through the perception of the target audience.
- Single-minded proposition, being the one main thing needed to be communicated.
- Substantiation, or justification, for this single-minded proposition.
- Brand personality and style, and tone of communication.
- Time of the campaign in terms of start date and duration.
- Budget.
- Sign-offs covering who is responsible to check work in progress.

If you seek a competitive pitch, you should spell out the selection process and the criteria for your selection. Moreover, now is the time to agree the performance criteria that you expect from the agency. If the pitch is going to be long and involved be prepared to pay for it. It need not be a large amount but it will show how serious, professional and fair-minded as a client you aim to be. Ensure also that all agencies in the pitch are treated the same.

Agency selection

There is one simple test to apply before all others. Do you like them and want to work with them? If you don't, then don't proceed.

Figure 15.4 shows a cost-effective and effort-saving approach to new agency selection. If you have a larger multi-site or multi-national operation then you may have to consider creating an agency roster. Individual managers are free to use any agency, as long as it is on the roster. The roster appointment would come after the credentials stage.

You need to understand what resource you have and decide where you will need agency input. Then aim to build up knowledge of what agencies are out there and create an ordered file and library of the work. Use trade listings to keep the information up to date.

If you set a formal review date, say, once a year, this gives the 'business development' agency person a framework and no false hopes. It will also enable you to manage the approaches in a professional way – a simple, appreciative yet explanatory response is all that is needed.

Rather than a long and unnecessary beauty parade of pitches, ask six for 'credentials'. See how much they have tried to learn about your issues rather than their own prowess. Then, if you decide you wish to move, select three or four for a full pitch (this is the time that procurement procedures can be carried out). Make sure the brief is as full as possible and that you see the agency in action.

Equally, bring in some colleagues to see the final pitches with you – the full selection team should see all the presentations. Make your choice but still speak openly and frankly to all the participants. Then start to work very hard to make the new relationship as productive as possible.

Figure 15.4 *Agency selection process*

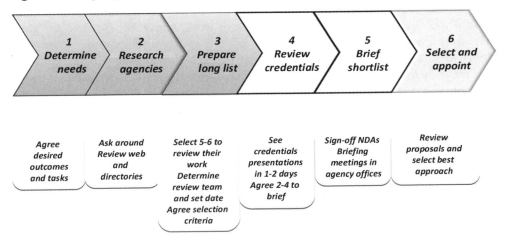

Success factors for working with an agency

Here are a few rules of thumb for working with agencies. They should be tailored depending on the type of agency:

Don't move agency quickly and often

Often in a new role you may find that the agency roster you have inherited does not have the qualities and capabilities you will need. In these circumstances, beware of moving too radically and too soon. Probably one of the biggest mistakes and wasted opportunities is moving agencies too quickly and too often. It is especially tempting when you first get the job. Remember the old adage 'if it ain't broke don't fix it'. In this situation, the incumbent agencies will have been doing the job they had been asked to do so let them carry on until you need a new job done. At that time, you can assess whether they are suitable or not. Only when there is no further benefit in continuing the relationship should you consider a move.

An agency represents one of your best sources of knowledge regarding your new company and the job you have to do. A simple thought – ask each incumbent what they would like to have done under your predecessor or what they think your priorities should be. You'll be surprised how much feedback you get and how enthusiastic this will make your agency partners. More importantly, it could give you some early quick wins that will highlight your arrival and build the corporate fecundity for your appointment.

Make yourself available to answer questions (at the pitch stage)

Should you decide to seek pitches for a piece of work, remember that like any good marketer, agencies are often only as good as their ability to truly understand your objectives and needs. Some organisations, particularly those in the public sector, will only make themselves available via email and even then the responses can be sanitised. Not only is it disheartening, and disrespectful to agencies, but you also risk depriving yourself of quality responses. If the work is truly important to you, make a senior member of your team, or yourself, available to answer questions.

Ensure no surprises

At the briefing stage, make clear any guidelines so the agency can factor this into their work programmes. This will help them meet your internal reporting requirements and service standards, as well as avoid any cost surprises. So, make a point to:

- agree and set performance criteria
- spell out the internal process by which work is approved
- set out what documentation you would like ie a proposal, call/meeting report or a status report

Be open and inclusive but manage the 'lines'

One of the greatest difficulties you may face will be to manage multiple agency relationships. Some agencies will inevitably have specialisms that others don't. Being inclusive, setting the tone and taking the lead in order to encourage collaborative working will help you crack a multitude of problems. Equally, make clear to all where their responsibilities start and end to avoid any wasting energy managing demarcation issues. This will help you focus and leverage their combined resources to maximum effect. Consider:

- having a quarterly review – a relationship health check; make it two-way
- sharing results
- using agency relationships to build the confidence of your own team – by giving then some autonomy within the agreed relationship and letting them present and manage meetings

Understand and appreciate your agency

The main motivator for the people working within most agencies, as well as the corporate entities themselves, is the stimulation of working on challenging projects and creating not only satisfied but positively delighted clients (who will give them more work).

Make a point of understanding the agency, the people within them and what makes them tick. The stronger your relationship, the more they will go out of their way to help you out. It can be a lonely life at the top, and there may be times when you need a sounding board, a sage, a mentor or a just a quick favour to help you through thick and thin.

Also make a point of understanding agency charging and payment terms and ensure the capability of your organisation to meet them. There will always be very good reasons why an agency's charging and payment terms are as they are, and there is nothing more likely to inhibit a promising relationship than for you or your procurement or finance departments to cause undue angst (and wasted time) by losing or sitting on invoices.

Work at the relationship

Finally, remember that it takes two to make a relationship and two to break it. If you feel that a new strategy or creative approach is needed, be upfront and say so. It is not necessary to change agency every time – if mistakes are made give the agency the opportunity to put it right. Not only will you end up with an improved output but also a stronger relationship.

As a human being, you may have an off-day, and your agency colleague may also have an off-day. So give a little to get a little. Underneath it all, everyone has the same basic thoughts and feelings. If you are paying an agency to help you, never be in doubt that they are on your side. Let your agency know you are also on their side. An occasional 'thank you' can go a long way. Careers can be made through good relationships.

Key points to remember

1. Agencies can make a positive and powerful input to your work, and can even be your alter ego. As the agency landscape is constantly changing, make sure you remain abreast of its changing nature. Keep a watchful eye on what is happening and check out the odd new agency or service that you feel may be relevant. Keep an eye on people moves too, especially if it is happening in one of your agencies.

2. Developing creative and truly integrated campaigns will require more proactive management of your agencies. As guardian of the brand, you will need robust tools and management skills to help keep your agencies on strategy and ensure effective implementation through multiple media. Your management skills will be essential to ensure collaborative working, manage demarcation lines and instill and set the tone.

16 Brand Management and Positioning

Brand New Friend – Lloyd Cole and the Commotions (1985)

In this chapter you will learn:

- *Common brand problems*
- *Types and benefits of brands*
- *How to position or reposition a product or corporate brand*
- *Brand architecture and options for managing a portfolio of brands*
- *Options for valuing brands*
- *Brand positioning tools*

Despite the fact that awareness of brands is high and that many books have been written on the subject, branding is a frequently misunderstood concept. This is partly due to the fact that many brands have evolved by accident rather than deliberate management. Many businesses started out by bearing the names of their founders, for example, Boots (1849), Heinz (1869), Ford (1903) and Disney (1925), but it is only in relatively recent times that many have been managed as 'brands'. In today's competitive environment there are huge risks in failing to manage such important assets in any other way.

The aim of this chapter is to provide insights and ideas to help marketers in different situations realise extra value from their assets by thinking about and better managing them as 'brands'. For marketing directors embarking on a corporate branding exercise or embracing branding in an organisation less familiar with these concepts, it is likely you will face those who don't understand and need to be reassured, rallied and sometimes cajoled into appreciating the benefits that branding can offer. For marketing directors working in organisations with an abundance of brand experience, the main challenge is likely to be maintaining stand-out and appeal. For those also responsible for a range of brands, the challenge is likely be optimising the value of the portfolio as a whole. This chapter also contains a number of tools and techniques to help you develop and define your brands.

Common brand problems

Loss of salience, stand-out and resonance with customers can occur to all brands at some point in their lives. Problems also occur when brands appeal only to the heart *or* head. Examples of brands that appeal primarily to the heart are fashion brands. In good times this can be a recipe for very high margins. However, when fashions become unfashionable, as happened to Laura Ashley's flowery look in the early 1990s, this can cause catastrophic sales and profit decline. Examples of brands that appeal primarily to the head are price-led brands. Price-led brands tend to be vulnerable as they have only one weapon to compete with other brands. This was the problem that befell Tesco in the 1970s, when its 'pile it high, sell it cheap' ethos became less relevant as consumers started to demand higher quality.

Brand planning

A vital part of the strategic planning described in Chapter 3 is to assess and maximise fitness to compete. The same processes apply to brand planning and a good place to start is to determine brand strength or fitness to compete. Ideally, you should conduct research to provide an objective and robust assessment of brand strength.   **❸**

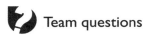 Team questions

As a short-cut, ask yourself and your colleagues the following questions:

- Is our organisation or portfolio of products or services *well known?*
- Has our organisation or portfolio of products or services got a *clear and distinctive image?*
- Are customers particularly *loyal* to our organisation or portfolio of products or services?
- Do our colleagues value and think about our organisation, or its products or services as one or more *brands?* Do our colleagues all think and *act in concert* to help our brands build the same clear, appealing and distinctive reputation in the eyes of customers?

If the answer to all of the above questions is 'yes' then it is likely that you already have a reasonably strong brand. If the answer to any single question is 'no', then it's more likely that your offering may not yet be a brand, could be strengthened, as could the management processes you employ.

Benefits of brands

Helping colleagues understand what a brand is and appreciate the benefits is a common challenge and a precursor to brand planning, especially in organisations that are new to branding.

 Ten minute exercise

Objective of the exercise:
To help colleagues start to appreciate that brands are all around us, and start to appreciate some of the benefits and characteristics of strong brands.
There are four steps to the exercise:

- Step 1: generate a list of favourite product or service brands.

- Step 2: for each brand, discuss what influences purchasing.

- Step 3: listen to the responses and probe what your colleagues think and feel about their favourite brands ie what are the rational and emotional/self image reasons for buying them.

- Step 4: in conclusion, ask your colleagues what they think sets their favourite brand apart from others.

Lessons learned
This exercise should reveal a handful of points about brands including:

- It is relatively easy to create a list of favourite products or service brands. This helps demonstrate that brands are all around us and *have high awareness*. Brands that spring to mind include: BMW, Coca Cola, Disney, John Lewis (at least in the UK), Levi's, Microsoft, Nike and Virgin.

- It is also easy to explain why brands have been chosen over other products and services. This is because strong brands have a *clear and distinctive image that sets them apart*.

- Strong brands tend to strike some kind of bond or relationship with customers. Typically they appeal at multiple levels – usually for a combination of rational and emotional reasons. This is because strong brands offer a *combination of strong rational and emotional benefits*. For example, BMW cars have an exclusive and quality image (German engineering), Coca Cola is a refreshing drink that brings people together, Disneyland offers an exciting day out, especially for kids and families, Levis is fashionable and hard wearing (rivets, stitching), Nike offers performance sportswear with a competitive attitude, Microsoft enables a host of useful and inspirational personal and business activities and Virgin offers innovative and good value products and services (and aims to be a customer champion).

- It is also likely to be evident that not all products and services are brands. Through analogy, if all products and services are people, then only brands are friends. This is because only brands forge deep and enduring relationships (with customers).

What is a brand?

Some simple definitions may also be helpful to help your colleagues grasp the concepts:

'A brand is powerful shorthand for the complex package of emotional and rational benefits, and personality traits that drive customer choice, build enduring relationships and differentiate from competition.'

Other definitions emphasise different facets of a brand. For example, David Aaker (1) describes brands as *a symbol (such as a logo, trademark or package design) that is intended to identify and differentiate goods or services.* Hugh Davidson (2) explains that brands *arouse expectations about quality, price, purpose and performance and promise specific benefits.* Interbrand (3) describes the end benefit of a brand as making it *valued and valuable.*

Our preference is a simple epithet...

PRODUCTS ARE PEOPLE

BRANDS ARE FRIENDS

What is brand positioning?

At the heart of a brand's positioning is its 'essence' or 'promise' ie the key (rational and emotional) benefits that it offers customers. Over time, a personality and image also tend to surround the brand to help the customer relate to and recognise it. Brand positioning is:

- a simple, concise description of the nature of the offer
- a statement of the most motivating and differentiating rational and/or emotional benefits to the target customer
- the compelling reason to believe the benefit

A 'positioning statement' is often created to summarise the various elements of a brand and define what the 'take-out' should be in the customers' eyes.

There are many brand positioning models and formats, such as brand pyramids or arrows, brand onions, and brand strengths or muscles, but the following distils the key elements into a very simple form. It is used by a number of advertising agencies for developing and assessing advertising:

(BRAND NAME) is the brand of (CATEGORY) that to
(TARGET) offers the benefit of (BENEFIT) because
(REASON WHY)

For example, FAIRY is the brand of WASHING UP LIQUID

that to BUSY HOUSEWIVES (WITHOUT DISHWASHERS)

offers the competitive benefit of

MORE CLEANING POWER THAT IS KIND TO HANDS *because*

**IT HAS A CONCENTRATED FORMULA WHICH IS MILD
ON THE SKIN**

 Why bother with brands?

For those embracing branding for the first time or trying to win corporate support for
a new branding or re-branding initiative, compile a list of reasons why the organisation should bother, to help secure buy-in. Here are some reasons why it can be worthwhile investing in brands or applying the concept of branding to an organisation. Use
these as a start-point to create your own list:

- Brands provide a framework to develop customer communications, brief
  agencies and initiate brand-building activities to deliver a consistent customer
  take-out.
- Brands help present an attractive and distinctive face or set of values to drive
  customer purchasing or choice.
- Brands command premium prices by appealing and driving demand more than
  competition.
- Brands drive loyalty and repeat sales by delivering ahead of expectations.
- Brands can be extended via new products or services or into new markets by
  building deep relationships with customers.
- Brands provide a vehicle to align the hearts and minds of people in an organisation, drive culture change and focus the activities of different departments and
  interests to a common goal.
- Brands can be unifying forces that bring together different functions and people
  to unlock new synergies and generate cost savings or new revenue opportunities.
- Brands can add substantial value to an organisation. The difference between

book value and shareholder or market value of an organisation can vary enormously and this difference is largely attributable to intangible assets such as brands. Potential purchasers will need to pay a significant premium to buy shares and gain control over an organisation with strong brands. A recent study in the US (4) showed that the total value of equity in the top 150 US companies was 180% over book value in 2004 and that this had grown from a 30% over book value in 1984.

Figure 16.1 summarises some of the incremental benefits accrued as brands grow in strength. Nike, Coca-Cola and Walt Disney (5) are examples of brands in the third category – they have strong personalities and built strong and enduring customer relationships – sometimes so-called 'power brands'.

Figure 16.1 *Benefits of brands*

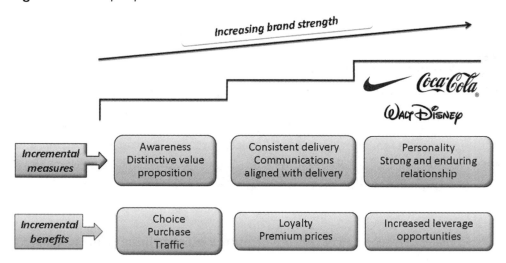

Dealing with problem brands – whether to sell, divest or revitalise

Building on Chapter 3 Strategy Development, Figure 16.2 describes four broad options to deal with problem brands. ❸

 Team questions

To help decide what to do, here are some questions consider with your colleagues:

Do you understand the reasons behind your brand's performance?

• If not, conduct customer research to find out both why, and whether there is upside potential to revitalise the brand. A common reason for brand decline is failing to

Figure 16.2 *Options for dealing with problem brands*

Option	Pros	Cons
To do nothing	No real pros.	Unplanned, loss of control, potential vulnerability to competitive threats/takeover.
To sell the brand	Ability to realise quick, short-term profit gain.	Potential profit loss if the brand has higher value in balance sheet than can be realised from a sale.
To manage the brand as a 'cash cow'	Planned decline; ability to realise long-term profit gain.	Continued decline in sales and possibly market share.
To invest in revitalising and repositioning the brand	Potential to restore growth.	Short to long-term investment required; risk attached to outcome.

stay relevant or in tune with customer needs. The questions outlined in the section on brand planning provide start–point to do this.

Where does your brand fit in your corporate portfolio?

- As every organisation will face a different and unique set of circumstances, decisions should really be made in the context of your own organisation's corporate strategy and portfolio and in light of wider shareholder, market and customer issues and opportunities.

- In recent years, a number of high-profile consumer goods organisations have sold off many 'non-core' brands in order to focus their resources on a smaller number of core brands. Brands that have been retained by these organisations appear to be larger, more distinctive and more stretchable and have lower sales maintenance costs. Brands that have been sold tend to be smaller and more focused on niches.

Is the brand performance inhibiting the value of the company?

- In recent years there seem to be a growing number of purchasers of 'ailing' brands including venture capitalists and other businesses specialising in these segments. If your share price drops too low you could be vulnerable to predators who think they could do a better job than you. You may need to move quickly to pre-empt threats from predators.

Is it possible to revitalise the brand?

Best practice

- There are many examples of brands on a seemingly downward track being revitalised through inventive repositioning or more proactive management. For example:

- Lucozade was launched in 1927, and was positioned as an 'aid to recovery'. By the early 1980s it had an old-fashioned image and poor sales. The brand was repositioned as an 'everyday energy drink' in 1986 and advertised by decathlete, Daley Thomson. A series of line extensions have since consolidated its position as a leading sports drink (6).

- Tesco's 'pile it high and sell it cheap' and 'Green Shield stamps' offer became increasingly irrelevant when consumers started to demand better quality, wider choice and a different lifestyle in the early 1970s. In the late 1970s, Ian McLaurin took the chain upmarket, and since the early 1980s, Tesco's has repositioned itself on a value and service platform, claiming that 'every little helps'. Since the repositioning, Tesco's overall image has improved and it has become both the UK's largest supermarket and a growing international force (7).

 Success factors for positioning or repositioning brands

A logical but tailored and flexible process

Approaches to positioning and repositioning brands should be tailored to individual circumstances. When dealing with organisation brands, particular attention needs to be paid to the human change management factors.

At the outset, document and agree the steps and timeframes that will be involved, both to manage costs and expectations. If this is the first time that you are undertaking a positioning or repositioning exercise it is likely that you will encounter many unexpected issues and may benefit from bringing in an agency to help. An agency should be able to foresee, plan for and adapt to the unexpected as well as provide resources and momentum to keep the process on track. This should also help you keep your eye on the big picture and free up your time to manage upwards, downwards and across the organisation as needs arise.

There are two broad approaches to positioning or repositioning a brand:

- Inside Out: involves internal collaborative working to generate and hypothesise possible solutions. In this instance, the customer has limited input to strategy creation but is useful as a sense-check and to refine implementation of the strategy. Most useful for corporate brand challenges or for brands in less competitive markets where internal strengths, dynamics and stakeholder agreement are critical to success.

- Outside In: research led to unearth customer insights on which to reposition the brand. Most useful for brands in highly competitive markets eg fast-moving consumer goods (FMCG) where positioning nuances are critical to success.

If you need help repositioning (or managing, selling and acquiring) brands get in touch with one of the many consultancies that specialise in this area.

Ensure top-team engagement and buy-in

Top-team engagement and buy-in is critical in the case of organisation branding exercises – when brand strategy can be interwoven with organisation strategy. Not only will the top team be able to contribute valuable insights and information but their endorsement and involvement in implementation of the strategy will be needed to send a signal to unite and direct the organisation as a whole.

Furthermore, fast and clear communications with the board will be needed to resolve legacy issues – for example, that impact adversely on some areas but have a positive effect on the organisation as a whole.

Build on the strengths of the past but look to the future

Successful repositionings tend be founded on true or latent brand strengths (as seen through the eyes of customers). Often these strengths must be re-expressed or contemporised to help a brand better appeal and stand out. This might involve piggy backing on a new trend, looking at the brand in a different context or adding to strength.

To do this effectively a clear view of existing, perceived or latent brand strengths and future customer circumstances, needs and wants will be required. For example, Lucozade's repositioning took the same rational brand strength (ie glucose/energy-giving qualities) and positioned it in the context of the nation's increasing interest in health, sports and sporting achievements rather than as an aid to recuperation. This enabled the brand to add an emotional lifestyle and self-image benefit to its long-standing curative benefits.

Importance of brand personality as a differentiator

How it speaks to customers or relates on a person-to-person basis can be a powerful differentiator. This is particularly the case in consumer goods and services markets where there may be little to set brands apart on purely rational grounds. For example, in mobile telephony (often a very intangible commodity), Orange is seen as optimistic, colourful and forward looking. This was originally summed up in the promise – *'The future's bright – the future's Orange'*.

Use customers to identify or check sources of competitiveness or as co-creators

As customers are the ultimate decision-makers or arbiters of choice, successful brand positionings must be rooted in their psyche. Whether you are creating an appealing and differentiating positioning from the 'inside out' or 'outside in' it makes sense to use customers at least as a 'sense-check' at some part in the process.

Ensure the brand positioning model used is fit for purpose

A common problem with positioning models is that they can be interpreted in different ways and can be unsuited to the purpose that they are intended. Problems can also arise through over simplicity or too much detail. Some models are more suitable for communications development. Others are more suitable for use in competitive and customer-driven markets. Others are more useful for aligning internal teams, empowering behaviour change and catalysing brand building activities. At the end of this chapter, we describe a handful of positioning models as inspiration for your own brand building activities. All can be mixed and matched to your specific needs.

Managing a portfolio of brands

A problem encountered by larger organisations – especially those recently involved in a merger or acquisition activity – is managing or avoiding cannibalisation between several brands in the same category. This is both a threat and an opportunity. The threat is that customers can receive mixed messages and be confused. The opportunity is to present an appealing and distinctive range of choices to discrete customer groups. The key is to manage the various brands or brand elements to the advantage of the portfolio as a whole rather than the individual brands. This means making choices on what brands or brand architectural elements drive choice as well as meeting the needs of the organisation as a whole.

Brand architecture?

Let's now look at brand architecture. Brand architecture provides a structure for the brand to support the elements and vice versa.
Brand architecture is a model that defines:

- the relationship between the brand elements ie sub–brands/variants and the parent or master brand
- the relationship between each of the sub–brands/variants

Brand architecture strategies

It is easy to overcomplicate discussions on brand architecture but for simplicity there are three 'basic' strategic options (see Figures 16.3 and 16.4) (8).

Figure 16.3 *Brand architecture options*

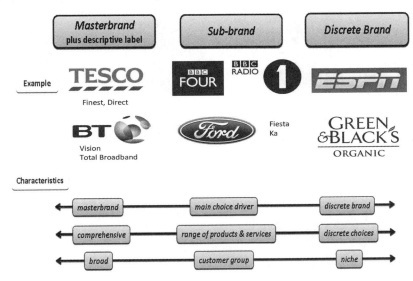

Figure 16.4 *Brand architecture options*

Option	Description	Application/benefit
Masterbrand (sometimes called an umbrella brand or parent brand)	A single brand name used as the main label on a broad range of products and services eg BT, Disney, retail brands eg Tesco, Boots and international/global brands eg Mars, Nescafé, Microsoft.	Most commonly used for corporate brands to build a distinctive identity and drive purchasing across a range of related products or services.
Sub-brand	A product or service bearing two brand names – one is usually subsidiary to the other eg Ford Fiesta and Ford Ka, BBC FOUR and BBC Radio 1.	Most commonly used for brands seeking to accrue trust and endorsement from the main brand yet build a distinctive personality or focus on a discrete customer group.
Discrete brand	A product or service bearing a separate and distinct brand name to the organisation's main brand eg ESPN (owned by The Walt Disney Company) and Green & Black's (owned by Cadbury plc).	Most commonly used by organisations who wish to compete in several segments of a market eg mass and premium, where there may be a risk of compromising or diluting the image of one or both brands.

Figure 16.5 *Alternative types of brand*

Option	Description	Application/benefit
Co-branding	The combination of two or more different brands eg on a product or promotion, to create synergies.	Useful to help piggyback a brand on another; eg to enhance image (where an older brand partners with a younger more fashionable one to influence choice); to access new customers, eg Avis car hire and Marriott hotels associate with British Airways to gain access to BA's customers.
Own or own-label brands	Products or services marketed by retailers or other service providers; take many forms eg masterbrand plus descriptive label eg Tesco Value and Tesco Finest, sub-brands eg Boots No 7, George at Asda, Sainsbury's Novon or discrete brands eg Marks and Spencer's Per Una range.	The precise benefits depend on the application; the products or services contribute to the image of the masterbrand itself, or help differentiate, add value and exclusivity to the specific products and services.
Ingredient brands	Product or service brands that are components or ingredients in another brand.	Used to improve quality perceptions, add value or extra differential to the host brand eg Intel chips in PCs, Goretex fabric in outdoor clothing, Zeiss lens in spectacles and cameras, Sweetex in drinks.
Combination brands	Refers to the combination of two or more different brands to form a new brand eg LloydsTSB, Cheltenham and Gloucester, Abbott Mead Vickers (AMV).	Used to maintain consumer awareness, reputation and goodwill; eg in financial and professional services as a result of M&A activity; can cause confusion if the consequences are not thought through and managed.
Niche brands	Refers to brands focused on serving the needs of a niche eg a customer niche eg Simple skincare (sensitive skin), geographic niche (local brewers), trade niche eg Unichem (serves pharmacies).	Often protected or protectable by their ability to service the needs better than competitors or identify with customers better.

Beyond the relatively straightforward brand architecture options outlined above, there are many other ways to classify brands. Just thinking about brands around you can provide inspiration on ways to build and manage your own brand. Figure 16.5 shows five more ideas.

Success factors for managing brands (and portfolios of brands)

Embed processes to manage and enhance all brand encounters

Creating and embedding frameworks, processes or procedures into the infrastructure of organisations is essential to ensure effective brand management. For example, positioning models can act as a lens to focus brand-building activities (Figure 16.6). This helps ensure a consistent, appealing and distinctive customer take-out through all brand encounters (eg online promotions, products etc) rather than allow mixed messages to cause confusion. Brand management guidelines or brand asset management systems hosted on an organisation's intranet also serve the same purpose for more disparate groups. Other examples of useful brand management processes include:

- checklists to assess whether activities are 'on-brand' and make financial sense and thus help make decisions

- tracking studies to monitor brand image

Figure 16.6 *Brand framework as a lens*

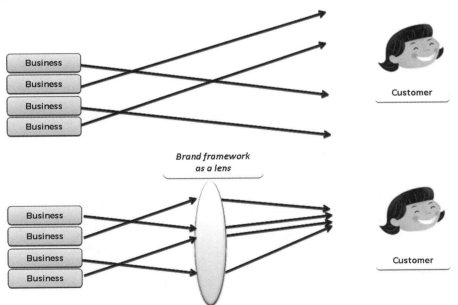

Clear and accountable portfolio brand management structure

Empowering an individual with the authority to oversee the brands in a portfolio is important to make investment decisions across brands. In matrix organisations, portfolio and brand managers are useful to plan, communicate, co-ordinate and align activities across a category and through the organisation as a whole.

Map brands to discrete customer segments

In organisations with several brands in a category, it is important to map brands to discrete or mutually exclusive customer segments in order to avoid cannibalisation risks while still providing headroom for growth. This tends to be easier if segments are primarily associated with discrete customer needs or attitudes rather than demographics, as these variables are easier to build into and clearer for customers to see in the positioning of a brand (see Chapter 7 Product Strategy). Brands positioned on the basis of needs or attitudes are also easier to stretch across category boundaries, which provides further headroom for growth. ⬤▸

 Brand positioning tools and techniques

This section describes some tools and models to position or reposition brands to prolong life and increase value. While each tool or model has its own pros and cons, the most important factor in choosing and using a brand positioning model is that it is fit for the purpose for which it is intended.

Figure 16.7 *Brand pyramid or arrow (deodorant)*

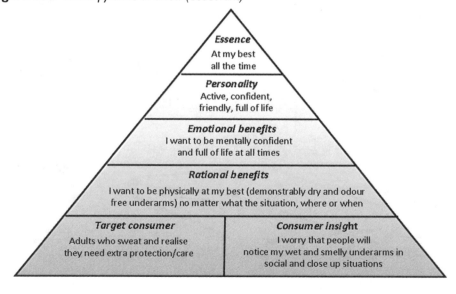

A brand pyramid or arrow is a positioning framework founded on a clear definition or description of the relevant customer insight or need.

- The top of the pyramid or arrow describes the essence of the brand ie what the brand offers or promises the customer.
- Underneath the essence is the brand personality – how the brand speaks to consumers.
- The next two layers describe the emotional and rational benefits that the brand offers consumers.
- The foundation of the pyramid outlines who the brand is targeted at (the target consumer) and the consumer insight on which the positioning is founded. Aim to describe customers in terms of their needs as well as demographics as this provides a more specific target definition.

Application/benefit

- The model is most useful for brands in more competitive ie customer-driven markets such as consumer goods, as clear and specific insights can provide much needed colour and emotion for a differentiated positioning.
- Insight-based positioning statements are also useful for managing international brands, in that the insights on which they are based can also be verified and aligned across countries.

Figure 16.8 *Brand onion (coffee)*

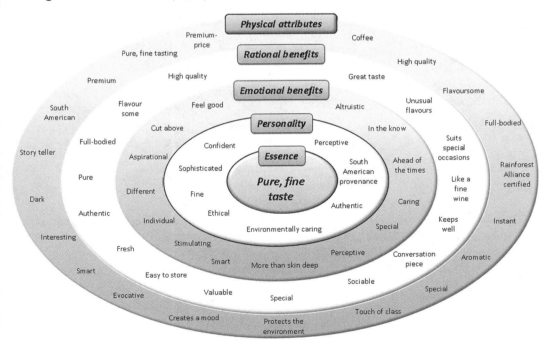

As the name suggests a Brand Onion is analogous to the vegetable of the same name. The layers of the onion can be peeled away to reveal the essence or core of the brand. Let's hope your essence doesn't make you cry!

Application/benefit

- This model is useful as a tool to think about, describe and define a brand from a customer point of view cf. peeling an onion. Moving from the outside to the inside of the model reflects the sequence of what a customer would see, think and feel and then conclude about a brand.
- The expanded and more 'loose' content is useful for presenting brand research findings and catalysing idea generation.
- Less suitable for focusing or managing brand communications.

Figure 16.9 *Brand strengths or muscles (confectionery)*

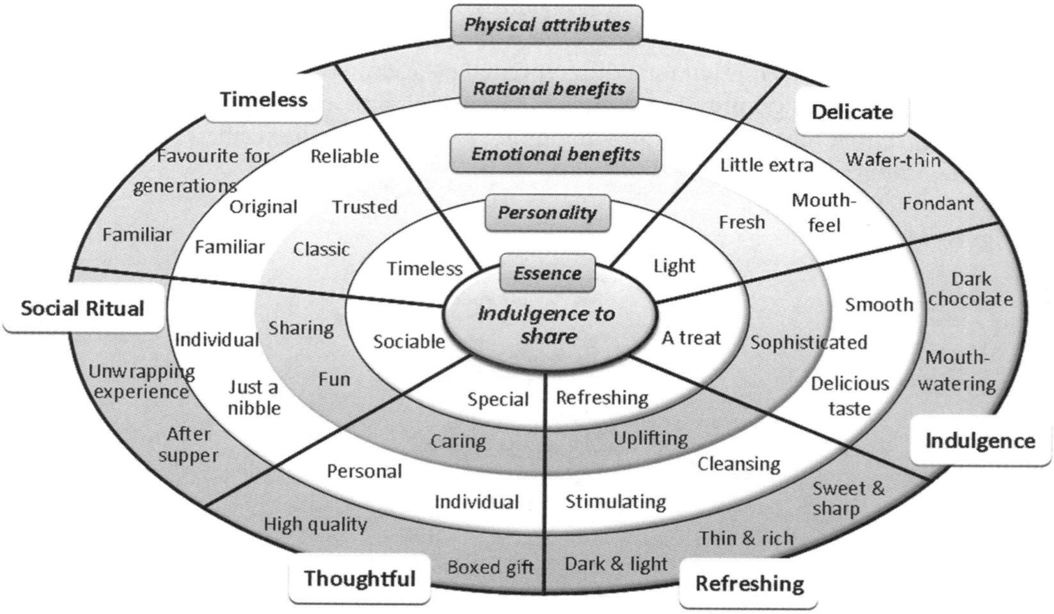

Brand strengths or 'muscles' are strengths upon which a product, service or organisation brand can draw. They can be:

- factual strengths/triggers
- known emotional strengths/triggers
- desired/necessary/latent strengths/triggers

Brand strengths or muscles can be presented in several ways:

* Figure 16.9 shows a muscle model for a confectionery brand and how it has been derived from a brand onion, whereby the different brand facets have been divided into like-minded groups.
* Figure 16.10 shows a muscle model for Nigerian energy company, Oando Energy Group (9) whereby the four muscles describe 'what the organisation wants to be seen as in the customers' eyes' ie a set of objectives together with an overarching brand vision.

Application/benefit

* Muscles are particularly useful for complex brands, especially organisation or service brands where people are critical to delivering the brand.
* Muscles also have the complexity to be recognised and allow a degree of 'stretch' to be built into the brand, which can be motivating to employees.
* Muscles can be translated into concrete objectives either individually or in combination.
* They can also be used to assess current versus desired position by activity or functional area within an organisation. By focusing on the differences between a current and desired position, they also enable the creation of new strategies and activities to help deliver the desired customer essence.

Figure 16.10 *Brand muscles (Oando Energy Group)*

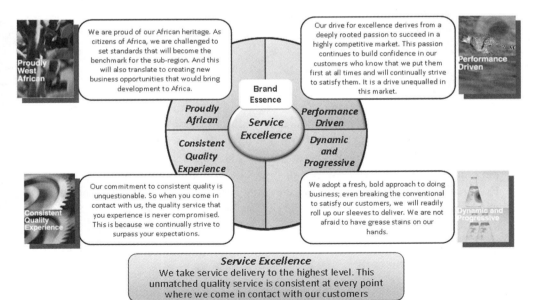

Brand personality

Figure 16.11 *Brand personality (Agatha Christie)*

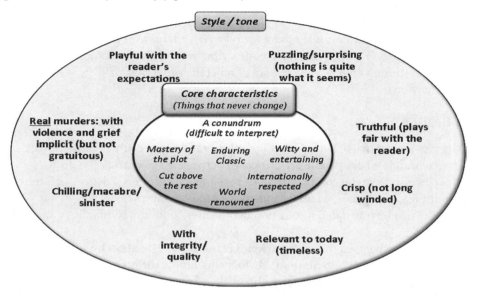

Brand personality (10) defines the core behaviours/ beliefs of the brand as well as how it should communicate ie look and speak. In reflects the idea that brands have a personality like humans.

Application/benefit

- The concept of a brand having a personality is also useful to help colleagues to understand and engage with the concept of a brand.
- It is also useful in helping define a brand. Think about the kind of personalities that you admire or have as friends – rarely are they bland and boring! Injecting colour, personality, even a few flaws into your brand helps make it stand out.
- Personality is particularly critical to ensuring brand stand-out in organisations where people are central to the delivery of the brand such as services and media organisations.

Brand style and the tone

Brand style and tone (10) is complementary to brand personality. They are most usefully expressed in pictures to bring to life dos and don'ts.

Figure 16.12 *Brand style and tone (Agatha Christie)*

Agatha Christie Ltd (A Chorion company)

Application/benefit

- Brand style and tone is particularly useful for bringing to life how to express and how not to express the brand by delineating what is and what isn't correct.

Rebranding or renaming

Globalisation, mergers and acquisitions and the drive for economies of scale has prompted many brands to change names in recent years. Successes include Cif (Jif-UK) and Veet (Immac-UK). There have also been some notable failures including Consignia (The Post Office-UK) and Choco Krispies (Coco Pops-UK). This clearly suggests that name changes need careful consideration and should not be undertaken lightly.

The first part of any brand replacement strategy should be a robust and customer driven assessment of the risks and rewards involved:

- What is the nature of the brand equity and its value to customers (as well as other stakeholders ie staff, distributors and opinion formers)?
- How do brand perceptions differ by country?
- What are the important category drivers and how does your brand compare with these?
- What attributes of your brand are distinctive and appealing?
- What is the commercial justification for change?

The second part of any replacement strategy is to choose a name. There will inevitably be some risks with particular names and these should be understood as part of the process of planning a change.

Understanding the common, appealing and distinctive elements of the brands in different countries will provide guidelines on what should be retained. Understanding the different, unappealing and indistinctive elements will provide guidelines on what should be changed. Throughout the process you need to be particularly careful to check availability of trademark registrations and that any invented names do not have unintended meanings in different countries.

Once you have chosen a new name you should also conduct a risk assessment of changing your brand to a particular new name.

- Where could you confuse customers?
- Where could you lose customers?
- Where could your reputation suffer?

In so doing, don't under-estimate the degree of difficulty that you will face. Think through all of the ways that your customers encounter, buy and consume your brand to minimise the risks of losing valuable consumers.

Valuing brands

Everyone agrees that brands are valuable but few agree how to value them. According to Jeremy Bullmore (11), *"The only time you can be sure about the value of your brand is just after you have sold it."* How best to value a brand depends on the purpose of the valuation itself:

- To measure performance and reward staff?
- To allocate an appropriate marketing investment?
- To measure the disposal or acquisition value of a company, division, or brand?
- To show intangibles in your balance sheet?

In the business of selling a business the intangible values of reputation and customer goodwill are recognised as just that – 'goodwill'. But now we in marketing can define and measure goodwill with increasing sophistication. Several UK agencies have successfully developed formulae and inspired trust which means that brand valuations are now fully accepted by the City. So much so that the brands have now become assets on the balance sheet of a number of companies and some transactions have realised brand values well in excess of the traditional value of a business.

Here are four methods for valuing brands:

Cost

- The historical or real-time cost of developing and establishing the brand to its current position – from research, design to advertising and media spend. Marketing and brand shares are easily established as are media spends in a given market. As the historical cost of developing a brand bears little relationship to its future income generating potential this method is likely to generate the 'lowest' valuation.

Lifetime value

- The lifetime value is the sum of future earnings or cash flows from your customer base. This figure should then be discounted using a rate of investment return based on the risk profile of the investment to derive a net present value (NPV) of the future income streams. This is at the heart of day-to-day decision making, particularly in direct marketing.

  - How many customers?
  - What is their average spend; what is the product profitability?
  - How frequent is the spend?
  - How much does it cost to service them?

- How long do you keep a customer?
- What is the rate of loss or churn?
- How much does it cost to acquire a new customer?

Shareholder or market value

- The value of an organisation involves understanding the contribution made by a brand or brands. Increasing value simply means making the stock price go up or increasing dividends. Dividends come from cash flow, and the stock price reflects the City's expectations for the organisation's ability to generate cash flows in the future. In basic terms, the value of the organisation is the discounted net present value (NPV) of the stream of cash flows that are expected to be generated in the future. The income and costs must then be attributed to one or more brands. This method helps derive the current economic value of the brand to its current owner in its current use.

Brand equity or incremental income

- The net present value (NPV) that a brand commands in shaping awareness, trial, preference and loyalty over and above a non-branded product. This is a conventional 'customer' view. Superior differentiation correlates with premium pricing and superior relevance correlates with market share and lower costs. Hence understanding how brands outperform their competitors on these measures provides a guide to value.

By adding brand equity to customer lifetime value you reach a fair business valuation which can be expected to positively influence the overall worth of the business.

Combining both shareholder value and brand equity approaches also provides a more robust measure. So as a marketing director, it is your job to:

- Increase cash flows in volume and number.
- Accelerate cash flows so that they start as early as possible.
- Extend cash flows so they last as long as possible.
- Minimise the risk to cash flows so that surprises are avoided.
- Maximise brand awareness, trial, preference and loyalty.

In other words you have to prolong the lifecycle of your brand(s)!

With the correct information to hand the calculations are straightforward. If you need external assistance then Harvard have kindly prepared a spreadsheet to one of the formulae and it is available to purchase via the Internet (12).

Key points to remember

1. While awareness of brands is high, the concept of branding is frequently misunderstood and you should not underestimate the need to explain the benefits of brands to colleagues. In a nutshell, brands are a simple way of expressing benefits so customers understand and relate to them.

2. Strong brands have high awareness, a clear and distinctive image and a combination of strong rational and emotional benefits and personality traits. To endure in the hearts and minds of customers, you need to ensure they stay in tune with changing customer needs and trends.

3. If you don't have a strong brand, you have four choices. Do nothing, sell it, 'milk it' or revitalise it. If your brand is declining, conduct research to understand why and help you decide what to do.

4. Brands offer many benefits; they drive customer purchasing and choice, enable premium pricing and can add significant organisational value.

5. Positioning or repositioning brands (especially at an organisation or corporate level) requires a logical but tailored and flexible process as well as commitment from the top.

6. Successful brand repositioning usually builds on the true or latent brand strengths and involves re-expressing them to enhance future relevance.

7. Don't underestimate the power of personality as a differentiator.

8. Positioning models are vital for effective brand management. Make sure yours is not just a useful document that can be understood by others, but is practically suited for the purpose for which it is intended.

9. Faced with a choice of brand assets to use and how best to architect your brand, work out what drives purchasing first and create a simple rather than complex solution so it will be clear and understandable for customers.

10. To help build an enduring brand in the eyes of customers you need to monitor the present and future and plan for the short and long term. Embed processes to manage and enhance all brand encounters, ensure clear and accountable brand management and institute monitoring systems to help track and enhance performance.

11. Change brand names with extreme caution. Make sure you do thorough assessment of the risks and the rewards. Develop plans to mitigate all risks in choosing and changing names.

12. To maximise brand value, aim to extend the lifecycle of the brand and maximise related cash flows.

Optimising Customer Communications

Light my Fire – The Doors (1967)

In this chapter you will learn:

- *How to ensure communications meet your marketing objectives*
- *How to assess a creative idea*
- *How to create a compelling message*
- *Media options*
- *Pitfalls to avoid*

We all take for granted that our agencies and creative suppliers will have mastered the basic fundamentals of good communications – the truth is, often they haven't. You may be called upon to put it right. Indeed, you may make it your business to do so.

 **Where to start?**

From the outset, you need to decide what your objectives are. Generally, it is possible to see communication objectives as supporting one or more of three marketing strategies:

- Brand switching: promotional activity is aimed at consumers switching from your competitors' brand to your brand (inter-brand switching) or from one of your brands to another of your brands (intra-brand switching). Consumers will switch to test the market, so encourage them to switch to one of your brands.

- Increasing purchase or usage: the action required is for consumers to buy or use your product more often, thereby increasing sales from the existing customer base.

- Modifying attitudes: promotional activity is aimed at changing customers' perception of your product, brand and/or company, perhaps to correct a misconception or improve stand-out. An element of this is contained within the other two objectives, but can be an objective in itself.

Consider, by way of an example, the UK promotional activity over the past few years of Kellogg's, in support of their Cornflakes brand. First, it was 'Have you forgotten how good they taste?' intended to encourage consumers away from competitors' brands (such as Shredded Wheat), other alternatives (such as toast), or other Kelloggs brands (such as Rice Krispies). This, therefore, was inter- and intra-brand switching. The next stage was 'They're not just for breakfast'. This was intended to get consumers eating Cornflakes on other occasions, as a 'guilt-free' snack.   The aim was to extend usage and increase the purchase cycle of the product.

The last stage was 'Serving the nation's health'. In this instance, Kellogg's set out to associate the brand with healthy eating and position it as an integral part of a healthy diet. This was also reflected in the increased amount of information carried on the packaging.

Kellogg's devised communications to move consumers through all three of the above marketing strategies sequentially. But what is *your* objective?

There are two key ingredients for successful communications. The first is the message and the second is the media. Let's start with the message:

Creating a compelling message

Here are six pointers to help your message hit the mark. These, together with a clear articulation of the objectives or desired outcomes of your communication, can form the essential elements of a creative brief:

1. **Creative brand positioning**
   The foundation of all communications must come from the brand itself. This means values, corporate identity and tone of voice. All this must be built upon to secure the current positioning and lay the foundation for a planned future position. For help in defining brand positioning, take another look at Chapter 16 Brand Management and Positioning.   **16**

2. **Key take-out**
   Remember that consumers don't buy products, they buy benefits – differentiated benefits (Chapter 2 The Role of Marketing in the Business). Make sure that you define a clear take-out or essence for your brand and that this reflects those key benefits. Also bear in mind that the take-out is not necessarily the same as a slogan. Many slogans are simply a distillation of features, and this is not really what consumers will be motivated to buy. The overall take-out from communications is likely to be most evident in what is seen rather than read.   **2**

3. **Relevance to target audience**
   For communication to be of interest and relevance to the target audience, it must

resonate with their hearts and minds. It must fit in with and build on the way they think; for example, their needs and beliefs. It must not fundamentally disconnect with their current brand perceptions. Make a point of defining your target with as much richness as possible. Go beyond demographics and include the psychographics too.

The message may also need to be relevant in terms of time, location or occasion. Remember the words of Don Peppers and Martha Rogers, the originators of 'One to One marketing'– "timely, specific and appropriate" (1). Can you define that time, location and occasion?

4. **Personality and style and tone of voice**
   A brand's personality is a key element of its competitive bulwark. Think about your partner, husband or wife – if they were bland, would you have ever gone near them, let alone ever started to date? It is important to define your brand's differentiating personality as this will be invested in all communications. It will affect all audiovisual elements – the vocabulary used, dialect, intonation, setting and atmosphere of a scene.

5. **Pay attention to detail**
   Brands are virtual but finite entities in themselves so sensitivity as to what is right for a brand is vital in order to sustain the brand itself. For example, beware of some tools of sales promotion, such as money-off offers on premium brands that can undermine the value of the brand and make consumers more price-sensitive. Armani never allows the retailers carrying their stock to discount the price. What guidelines do you have to make sure your communications are always on brand?

6. **Call to action**
   This is probably the one most important element of any marketing communication – *What is the intended action that you wish to communicate?* What do you expect the reader/viewer/listener to do as a result of your communication? This relates back to your objectives. If this is not clear, they are not going to work it out for you, they will just ignore it.

Evaluating your creative idea

Most peoples' reaction when a great new idea has been created is to say one of two things... 'Why didn't we think of it before?' or 'Someone must have already thought of it '.

So here's a checklist to help you decide whether it is good enough to go with, whether it needs development (and if so, how), or whether it misses the mark, therefore meaning that you need to go back to the drawing board. This list should work not just for brand communications but all communications. So think about the idea, and ask yourself if it is:

- differentiated: your promotional activity must establish you (that is your product, your brand and/or your company) as being different from and better than the competition. If it doesn't, why are you doing it?
- impactful (substantial): research indicates that people working and living in the London area can be exposed to approximately 1,200 advertisements a day. This includes logos on other people's clothing, estate agents 'for sale' boards, carrier bags and so on. With all this going on, if your promotional activity is not impactful, do you really think your target audience is going to notice it?
- clear: the message must be crystal clear so that it is understood. Your target audience has much to do and your promotional activity must be to the point. The only time when consumers work through long messages is when they have time to fill, such as waiting for a train. Remember the seven-word rule – more than seven words on a poster advertisement and most people will not have the time to read them.
- believable: the message must be credible to be believed and acted upon. This means there must be a solid reason for justifying the benefit that your brand offers consumers.
- relevant: the message must of course be relevant to the audience for which it is primarily intended. As an example an advertisement for a suntan range, which featured naked ladies succeeded in dramatically increasing awareness (and sales), but it had a greater impact on men and not just the intended female audience.
- campaignable: your message will take time to build up levels of awareness and understanding among the target audience. Each campaign must build upon the previous ones. This can only be achieved with consistency. Ask yourself:
  - where's this idea going?
  - has it got the legs to be repeatable in a different form and stand the test of time?

Final words on words

We also know that some trigger words are more effective than others. 'New', 'now' and 'free' are examples of trigger, or buzz, words that come readily to mind. However, there is one that can be the watchword to good communication (as can the thought behind it). This word is 'because'.

In using 'because', you are forced into giving a reason why you seek a particular customer reaction. Everyone responds more readily when given a reason.

And a final management point that is worth reinforcing. Never make a creative decision without taking cognisance of your competitors. Otherwise you may end up having a communication that looks identical to your competitors or those adjacent to it.

If you feel that an intended communication is wrong and don't want to run it for professional reasons then don't. Full stop. You can usually run the communication later when you are happy with it. Even if not, no communication is better than the wrong one. Many a career has been derailed by making the wrong decision.

Selecting the media mix

One of the biggest challenges of marketing today is the allocation of budget and ensuring the optimum use of the media itself. The fragmentation of media through the proliferation of channels and titles and the many forms of message filtering through the Internet are all converging on a screen near or on your desk. We also see a constant stream of new media emerging, such as TV on trains or a new 'social site' with a cunning plan to leverage its traffic. This, combined with the advent of CRM, provides the ability to talk to customers in ever smaller but targeted groups.

This volatile and increasingly diverse media landscape also means that it is essential to plot a path and keep a constant look-out for a better one. So, in deciding on your media mix, build on what has been done before, judge what has been most successful and then allocate a portion to 'new media' and 'opportunities'.

As you build response and effect data you will be able to more accurately allocate the budget for optimum effect. At the heart of the decision-making, there will always be a large element of judgement in choosing new media but they do come with the ability to accurately measure performance – albeit comparatively.

Overall, there is a growth in blurring and overlap between the different media. New ones are increasingly emerging, containing features and benefits of the others. Digital technology is inspiring more innovative posters or ambient media – moving, rapidly changing banks of posters, for example, on the London Underground and at airports. It is also enabling Internet Protocol TV (IPTV) – TV advertisements or short films can be delivered via the Internet.

One way of making sense of the media mix and the broad range of options that are available is to summarise them on a simple chart. This can be used in a number of ways: as an aid to overall planning, to provide inspiration, to check all alternatives have been considered and to help allocate budgets. For instance, budget weighting can be indicated by strength of colour.

The four broad and different types of media are:

- mass media – largely the range of broadcast, print and other options that provide high reach
- sales – largely where the customer is the physical presence of the product/service or can be influenced by a sales person
- direct – largely where consumers receive individual communication in their homes
- eCommerce – the range of electronic or digital communications media (it may be more appropriate to combine the last two).

Figure 17.1 *The media mix*

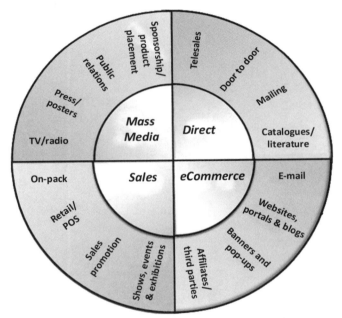

While not intended to be a comprehensive analysis, here are a few top-line observations on the applications, benefits and limitations of the different media.

As the analysis in Figure 17.2 shows, the Internet can provide a communication channel to recreate every element of marketing activity virtually. Yet still it is seen by many as ephemeral and an add-on to other communications activities. There is, however, an opportunity to see the web as 'Marketing Central' – a hub, or means of integrating all your marketing activities. Opportunities afforded by this emerging medium are detailed in the following section.

Figure 17.2 *Applications, benefits and limitations of different media*

Media	Application	Pros	Cons
TV	Brand building	Mass communication; increasing range of niche alternatives	High production costs
Radio	Good for local targeting and rapid response	Immediacy, newsy; some innovative packages eg weather-related	Audio only
Press	Suitable for interest groups or rapid communications	Relevance and immediacy	Time delay with monthly magazines
Posters	Good for frequently used/consumer brands	High impact and frequency	Less suitable for complex messages
PR	Raising brand status and broadening reach	Easier to generate for new products/ with research	Harder to measure; harder to ensure brand link
Sponsorship	Raising brand status; building customer relationships	Enables precision targeting – to both b2b and b2c audiences	Can run away with budgets as additional investment may be needed to secure benefits beyond awareness
Product placement	Raising brand status	Enables precision targeting	Can be too subliminal
On-pack	Facilitating impulse purchase	Immediacy	Many legal limitations so need to ensure compliance
Retail and point of sale	Facilitating sell-in and sell-through	Can be targeted at trade and customer sectors	Requires tailoring to accounts
Sales promotion	Encouraging trial or loyalty; bringing forward sales; alternative to cost cutting	Immediacy; more brand building potential if not price-driven	Risk of brand devaluation if too monetarily driven

Trade shows, events and exhibitions	Encouraging trial or loyalty; building brand image; meeting and building customer relationships	High impact; can be targeted at local audiences	Low reach; additional investment may be needed to secure benefits beyond awareness
Telesales	High customer impact; suitable for more complex sales and to overcome inertia	Intrusive; tailored to needs	One poor agent can undo so much good work!
Direct mail	Specific targeting	Enables precision targeting; tangibility	Need to overcome perceptions of junk mail
Catalogues and literature	Selling a product range; useful in conjunction with eCommerce	Enables precision targeting; tangibility; added brand value	Need to inject brand values/benefits to avoid commoditisation
Face-to-face (in home)	High customer impact; suitable for more complex sales and to overcome inertia	Intrusive; tailored to needs; nature of person and environment can have relationship building advantages	One poor encounter can undo so much good work!
Email	Useful for providing brand reminders	Enables precision targeting; low cost	Need to overcome spam perceptions and spam filters; important to ensure acceptance and deliver value
Banners and pop-ups	Extending the message	Enables precision targeting; need to remain aware of the options	Pop-up ads are increasingly seen as irritating and blocked
Websites portals and blogs	Brand and relationship building; reinforcing other media	Can be customer search driven; many marketing possibilities; opportunity to make 'Marketing Central' - a hub for all your marketing activities	Need to ensure ease of usage and provide added value
Affiliates/third parties	Ability to reach third-party customers; raising brand status	Broader targeting and endorsement	Requires close management/good network provider

Marketing and the Internet

While this book was being written the effect of new web usages and portals have given rise to the label Web 2.0. The digital world is well and truly upon us. This emphasises the problem that technology and its uses is changing at a rate to make any book obsolete by the time it is published. Yet there are some underlying principles that seem to have emerged.

The whole foundation of the Internet is in its universality and acceptance. This means that far-flung businesses and brands can now reach markets with greater ease and acceptance.

Having said that, some research indicates that the percentage of the world's population that either owns – or has practical access to – a computer with Internet access is only about 10%. What is certain, however, is that Internet access is high and still growing in the developed world. For example, home Internet penetration in many North European countries now exceeds 70% (2), although this does not mean that they are frequent or passionate users. The advent of broadband is also fueling convergence and the increasing availability of TV on demand and video telephony. Thus any screen, anywhere, can be both for business and entertainment, meaning that the communication opportunities are boundless.

Some see three types of businesses. The traditional businesses (bricks), Internet businesses (clicks), and businesses that use both (bricks and clicks). Let's look at some fundamentals to guide your approach.

Internet marketing – push or pull?

This book cannot keep you abreast of the ever-changing digital world so keep yourself up to date by constantly reading and seeking knowledge. There are however some fundamentals to address.

Reaching customers as a push strategy is difficult, owing to the wide dislike of spam. Consumer-directed messages are also seen as intrusive and filtering devices screen out companies' messages.

However what can be effective is the use of banners and links from high traffic sites with a common audience and a non-competitive offering. The growth of price comparison sites and affiliates is also an important development.

Online searches and shopping means that the Internet works well as a pull tool, allowing customers to demand products and buy them through the same distribution channel. The Internet can also be used within the distribution channel, such as Intranet and Extranet tools, allowing online re-stocking and communications.

What is not always recognised is that the Internet turns many of the traditional communications models upside down. For example, traditionally a company was proactive in promoting to a customer and the customer was reactive. With the Internet, however, the company is now passive or reactive and the customer is proactive in seeking out the company's website. Much promotional activity is required off-line in order to drive customers to the company's website, enabling them to regain the proactive position.

Pay-per-click advertising

In 2008 online advertising expenditure overtook that of traditional media. The biggest sector is pay-per-click (PPC) on Google. The best example of a perfect market there has ever been; the greater the demand the higher the cost. The more successful you are, the more your competitors can see how much to spend to beat you into a poorer position. Yet as a form of advertising it has the same limitation as newspaper classified ads – your message is limited to a set number of characters with constancies of typeface and colour!

The more you spend in this area the more you need to be aware of software and agencies who constantly seek out the algorithms and other criteria that Google lays down to optimise the ranking. However, from a marketing perspective, too often the message is one of simply availability or price which means many end up having the same message, consequently relying on their ranking for optimum response; this is costly and inevitably at the expense of the brand. So it is important to always try to build your brand rationale and differentials into PPC.

The performance of PPC is based solely on what the potential customer is searching for. This is inevitably a manifestation of the status quo. It is axiomatic that it is only what the customer knows about that the customer searches for! Great if you are in an established sector with an existing product, but not if you are launching a new product in a new sector with a new brand! (Try searching for 'new' and all you get is 'news').

Increasing expenditure on PPC will eventually reach a level that other media or a mix of media will be cost effective especially to help build your brand. For example when the UK property portals took hold, house builders found that their online traffic rose when supported by press and television advertising. It should therefore be no surprise that major online brands from Expedia to moneysupermarket are now significant advertisers.

Website, usability and SEO

The website can and should be 'Marketing Central'. Many organisations – for example, mail order specialists – currently see their catalogue as being separate from their website. In truth, they are one and the same thing, as both are alternatives to the traditional shop window. The digital age means all marketing assets can be stored in one content-rich 'asset' management system, which in itself can lead to even more customised messages, delivered to more accurately targeted consumers at the most appropriate time.

The more reliant your business is on a web site the more you must pay attention to site usability, ease of navigation and its effectiveness in carrying messages and taking transactions as measured by usage and volume.

The way the site is constructed and the words used are key considerations in the art of search engine optimisation – all can affect demand and the quality of demand.

Usability and search engine optimisation (SEO), as well as PPC, fall into the 'painting the Forth Bridge' category of management. It's never finished and it is a constant battle against the elements.

The nature of the pull concept also creates new marketing opportunities, for example, to attract new customers and establish new relationships that are both permissible and potentially enduring.

 Pitfalls to avoid

Vance Packard (3) said *"the medium is the message"* nearly half a century ago – this holds more truth today than ever before. The limitations of technology mean that one message may have to look very similar to others. Or does it?

Those working in Internet marketing are mostly from a technology background and the breakthrough they have developed has been a singular solution. This means they have seen a technical capability, not a communication vehicle. So far, they have only seen the Internet as its own narrow application, not as part of a strategic whole.

Websites are often crowded on the front page and while this can drive traffic this also inhibits communication effectiveness However, the rules of communication and consumer behaviour still stand. A headline to grab attention – a clear instant affirmation that this is the website the customer wants to see – has to be superimposed on a simple and easy-to-follow logic rather than a crowded index. Research indicates that if you cannot find what you want on a website within two minutes and four clicks, they are likely to move away. Loyalty, as they say, is only 'click deep'.

Success factors to make the most of your website

The marketing director of today must embrace marketing in the digital age (in our research for this book we found a significant number who did not).

Here are six success factors to help you on your way:

Marketing objectives remain the same
Consider the purpose of a printed flyer. Most likely it is to trigger a call to a call centre or visit to a shop to ask for more information or place an order. The website can address both of these objectives equally well.

Think from consumer point of view
If I use the Internet I am engaging with technology. If a child uses the Internet, they are keeping in touch with their friends. It is important to see the use of technology through the eyes of the customer. Understand the benefits the customer seeks – do not get stuck on the technology.

Ensure your branding is as strong as it can be
There is more creative potential in technology than you may think. Treat it with equal respect to other media and invest the same creative input. This must be consistent with the creative content of all other communication tools.

Strategy! Strategy! Strategy!
Internet activity has grown and has now been around long enough to be a core part of your overall strategy, not just a series of 'tacked on' activities.

Test! Test! Test!
Technology means you can change and adapt everything at any time. Testing with a small sample/budget remains the prudent way forward, but you can now speed up the cycle, from a test to full scale.

Monitor, measure and review
In an environment that is constantly changing, make sure you stay up-to-date by continuing to monitor and review how the Internet is changing, and what this means. There is also an increasing range and sophistication of measurement opportunities to help you stay ahead of the curve. While Google Analytics and other web tracking software can provide hard facts on what's working and what's not, there is a danger in putting too much reliance on these tools as they provide numbers, not understanding on why people click. Make sure you use both quantitative and qualitative research methods to get a holistic understanding to optimise your site.

Budget and activity allocation

The arrival of the digital world has led to a completely new range of marketing activities, in the main driving down the cost of reproduction and enabling more accurate individual targeting. Increasingly the Internet becomes the primary gate keeper and PPC impinges on the entire marketing budget. Some companies spend millions on PPC. The way to determine a sensible activity mix and budget allocation is to start with a simple KPI –what is the marketing cost to achieve a unit of sales? Then it is a simple calculation to compare media and the relative value of them.

 Key points to remember

Two factors emerge as being of the highest strategic importance:

1. Ensure clarity and impact of message. To be seen and heard, your message must have impact. This is increasingly important in a fragmenting, multi-media world. For your message to be understood and acted upon it must be clear and consistent. Wherever your brand is seen and heard, make sure the message reflects the benefits you want to project and ensure that the tone of voice and the look and feel are equally engaging.

2. Ensure message consistency through integrated communications. The temptation in a multi-media world is to spread investment too thinly. Media proliferation can dissipate both the brand message and brand impact, leading to mixed messages. The bigger the spend, the more you can seek to dominate a given media. Aiming to be dominant to achieve impact is always desirable. So take your brand positioning as a creative framework, find an expression that works in at least one dominant medium and then use this as a lead idea for all the others.

18 Customer Relationship Management and Database Marketing

Getting Closer – Paul McCartney (1979)

In this chapter you will learn:

- *What CRM is*
- *The role and benefits of CRM and how data can help improve the performance of your marketing*
- *How to introduce CRM to your marketing*
- *How to build stronger customer relationships using CRM*

This chapter is designed to help you recognise the benefits of CRM and database marketing. In particular, it will help you identify and utilise messaging opportunities to build customer dialogue and loyalty. Implementing CRM programmes has implications beyond marketing and you will no doubt have read about many so-called failures – from IT systems failures to poor ROI. This is an opportunity for marketing to take centre stage. 'Delivering products to our customers to make a profit' is the definition of marketing itself. So, 'carpe diem' and grasp the opportunity to lead the way.

At the heart of CRM is the customer, and reading this chapter will help you appreciate how data and digital can enhance your marketing success. The subject is covered in depth both to provide a reference source and help you work closely with the IT project teams.

Defining CRM

Every company will have its own definition. This will depend on the nature of your business, the stage of development and the degree to which there is a financial benefit from servicing and developing customers. Here is our definition; *'CRM is the understanding, acquisition, servicing, development and retention of customers for profit by an organisation with a truly customer-focused culture, using an integrated, customer-centric contact strategy, systems and processes.'*

🖰 Why bother with CRM?

"Hello Mrs Jones, would you like the same sausages you had last week and how did young Terry do in his exams?"

The local butcher is a dying breed, but in their heyday they knew all the customers by name and were able to remember their likes and dislikes, and even some of their family history. The clever butcher could use this to advantage, creating customer loyalty and helping customers to buy more of the things they liked.

Many companies yearn for this ability to target customers and offer them more of the products and services they are most likely to buy on an individual basis.

The revolution in IT has brought about a major change in the way large organisations understand their customers and the way this understanding can be used. This change has redefined the role of marketing and how we communicate with customers.

Barriers to introducing CRM

Lack of customer centricity

IT-led CRM puts the process before the customer. It confuses sales with marketing. It sells a system not a solution. Technology is not marketing. At the heart of CRM is the customer, not the process, and for this reason, marketing should take the lead. Yet this is increasingly not the case.

Customer definition and segmentation is where CRM has to be at its most accurate. A company-wide definition of a customer that is universally understood and translates from current data and knowledge is essential. Missing this point has led to the two main reasons there has been so much disenchantment with CRM.

First, not enough is done at the outset to understand the role and impact of CRM in terms of marketing. Second, marketing strategy does not sufficiently encompass the new CRM-enabled multi-channel environment.

CRM provides a history of an individual, which provides a basis for personal communication with each and every customer. It then provides the means to make targeted, appropriate and cost-effective contact.

CRM is intrinsic in its operation and meets extrinsic media in terms of response. However, beware the naivety of some CRM providers when they propose extrapolating self-completed customer response data into campaign planning models. Instead, they should be analysing this data demographically and psychographically to establish buying behaviour and the reasons for that behaviour. Marketing needs to make sure that the customer drives the introduction of CRM.

The role of the marketing director

The marketer's role lies in understanding customer behaviour, in anticipating it and shaping it to the profit of the company. That is why both marketing and brands exist. The IT world, born of logic and fuelled by ever-increasing data capacity, seeks to encroach across all areas of business. Due to the way in which it has been developed and sold, CRM technology believed it already encompassed marketing. It did not; but of course marketing must relate to technology, embrace it and use it to gather information that can be used to customise products, services and promotions to customers. The aim must be to have the best of both worlds; technology that delivers a better process and marketing that makes the most of it.

CRM flows through all channels – the Internet, CD and digital media, print and TV. The data enables both proposition, product, inducement and even payment to be personalised – and delivered at the most appropriate time and, probably most importantly of all, cost effectively. It demands integrated marketing like never before.

The marketing director must recognise and champion the effects on marketing planning and production. Contact with a specific customer at a time that is relevant to them. Consequently, it is this customer 'event', not the annual marketing plan that triggers marketing activity. So, marketing planning has to be 'customer event' driven. This should mean a great deal of pre-planning and pre-development of the communication events and elements.

The espoused *lifetime value of the customer* is not necessary in order to justify multichannel CRM-enabled customer contact. Response and sales are more robust measurements than prompted awareness and always have been. Measurement of response and your ability to make optimum use of the measures are key. Technology gives better understanding, which leads to more efficient targeting. However, the maximum benefits will be driven by creativity and communication – the right message and branding.

Costs and benefits of introducing CRM

The benefits and effects of CRM can be far-reaching. Some initiatives will be aimed at increasing revenue – retaining and selling more to customers. Others will be aimed at improving efficiencies or reducing costs in customer service. Beyond this, CRM can have a deep-rooted effect on the working practices, systems, processes and culture of an organisation. It can have a profound effect on people's skills, their development and training. As well as being a force for positive change. There are many intermediary stages in implementation, each having its own cost and benefits. To generate benefits, CRM should be recognised as an investment, and the marketing director must play a key role in assessing the costs and benefits. One or more of four types of investment are usually needed:

- research and data management to understand more about customers
- efficient systems and processes to service customers no matter which communication channel they prefer to use
- marketing or promotion expenditure
- investment in organisation-wide cultural change and people skills to improve a customer's brand experience and generate more opportunities for customer contact and relationship building.

 ## Success factors for introducing CRM

There are five key factors to ensure success:

A board-driven strategic business approach

The board must fully understand the implications and possibilities of CRM and take 'ownership' to drive change, throughout the organisation. Try to achieve 'one vision' for the project. This means you may have to work hard to understand, define, integrate and align needs and views across functions.

Ensure short-term wins

Short-term wins should be identified to deliver returns within the same financial year that activities are initiated. For example, identify key target groups and how to communicate to them. This will give confidence in the strategy and help justify future investment.

Deliver revenue gains and operational efficiency

Any CRM project should generate additional revenues and improve operational efficiency. Customer service improvements should also be expected – these could have further positive effects on the brand and revenues – but will need to be identified as part of a planning and implementation programme.

Intense implementation, strong project management

CRM is best implemented by a marketing-led, cross-company project team involving marketing, sales, customer service (call centre), HR, training and IT. This should deliver a clear vision and must be translated into a hard-nosed financial implementation plan that can be executed across departmental boundaries. This will require a combination of bridge-building and strong project management – initiatives will need ownership, leadership and drive at board level and project champions throughout the organisation.

The importance of strong project management is a key reason why many organisations employ third parties. Get good project management in place and you can devote more time to bridge the 'politics' and historic gaps between departments.

Setting up CRM projects and re-training staff is expensive and is a difficult decision to take in the absence of any concrete evidence that a good ROI is possible. That is why in some circumstances, using external suppliers to undertake controlled tests is also an opportune first step.

 **CRM implementation process**

Here is a step by step process to help you implement CRM in your business.

Figure 18.1 *CRM Implementation Process*

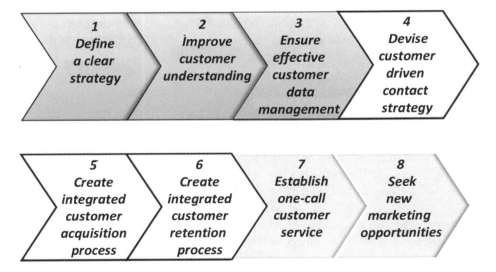

Step 1: define a clear strategy and integrate it into all aspects of the business plan

Adopting CRM will require the board to adopt a new vision of how it wishes to run the company and as marketing director for you to gain board acceptance of the complexity and impact of this vision on all aspects of the business.

A commitment to organisational and cultural change will be required to realise the full benefit of the financial investment. This vision should be translated first into a strategy and then into a hard-nosed financial implementation plan. After testing, it will need to be integrated into the organisation's overall business plan. It should give clear expectations of ROI over specified timescales.

Often CRM is seen purely as an IT investment to implement a multi-channel contact management platform across the company or in a customer service call centre. This is potentially a large investment but while benefits should be seen in improved and more efficient customer service and in centralising data management, a tangible financial return is often difficult to evaluate.

Step 2: improve customer understanding

The programme must be supported by a clear understanding of the customer. Faced with a myriad of choice, customer loyalty is only as good as your last contact... *and your customer is rarely that loyal.* Customers should be profiled and segmented not only to determine potential and marketing action, but also to measure their attitudes and transactional behaviour when dealing with your brand. We all know that customers can be fickle and their loyalty transient. How can you expect a customer to be loyal to a large multi-national when the individual they interact with is different every time? It is important to get a statistical fix on the level of customer satisfaction in order to proactively manage the experience and deal with unhappy customers. This must come from all potential contact points with the organisation.

Superimposed on this strategy is a need to recognise customers with high existing or potential lifetime values and prioritise their customer service treatment accordingly. There is a need to know what a customer has bought from you, the value, the channel, and when. It will involve collecting key pieces of information in order to target accurately and cost efficiently and maximise customer value.

Customer segmentation facilitates more targeted selling of both existing and additional products and services to customers with the highest propensity to buy. It will also identify the channel through which they are likely to be most responsive. This requires an understanding of the key triggers in the buying process and how the careful collection of profile, interest and timing data in a cost-efficient way can help the process.

Profiling customers as well as gathering purchase data enables clusters or segments of customers to be identified who are best targets for specific products and services. Further segmentation can cover channel – or combination of channels – to further refine targeting and enhance response. The complexity of the segmentation required depends on the nature of the response. In some cases basic profile data is sufficient, but occasionally this needs to be refined by attitudinal data and/or by previous response/purchase data. The better the segmentation, the more cost-efficient the marketing campaign is likely to be. It is also important to collate other key data to avoid customer service issues and complaints. For example, create and maintain a suppression file of 'gone-aways', 'died', 'do not contact', 'customer service issue' etc to be used in all initiatives. In turn this will help project the right brand values and help improve response rates.

The timing of initiatives is often more important than very refined profiling. Some products and services have a strong seasonality, some have regular renewal dates and some have a well-defined life cycle. Gathering data on expected purchase timings or making an educated guess is often important in generating additional profitable business.

Monitoring the response, orders, sales value and cost of sale from marketing initiatives to customers is also important. Learning about the profile of customers that have a greater propensity to respond and convert is obviously best done from actual results. This becomes the key factor once there is a history of campaigns to draw on. It may also influence adjustments to the profile data being collected.

Defining clear customer segments is also useful for product development. Understanding the common needs of particular clusters of customers is useful for both product improvement and new product development. Previous purchasing information and channel preferences can add to that understanding.

Step 3: ensure effective customer data management

Let's start by emphasising that data from many sources may yield new sales opportunities, for example, from service records or guarantee registrations, but also that it must be accurate or 'clean'. Data is the lifeblood of IT and CRM so tread carefully. However, as 'knowledge is power', do acquire as much knowledge as you can. Initially, ask what data is available and what the CRM system will produce.

Let's look at the data processes and what is actually collected. Essentially, CRM enables marketing to deliver a sales message to specific customers at the optimum time.

There are essentially four types of customer data that can be collected:

- profile
- attitudinal
- contact
- transactional

Collecting consistent and accurate data is hard work, so a clear strategy needs to be devised to define how data is collected and used to generate additional business. Once the customer data required to drive the CRM programme has been decided, the method of gathering it and then keeping it updated needs to be agreed. The process will often involve several sources and rely on people across the organisation to recognise the significance of the information so they do the job consistently well. Regular updating of processes and routines will be required where data is combined from several sources.

These processes should include the addition of new customers and flagging or marking of lapsed customers. An important consideration is whether data is collected 'in real time' or polled at regular intervals.

Contact data that is collected in real time tends to suppress proactive initiatives (eg where a customer has a current issue or has just enquired about the product to be promoted). However, to hold contact data alongside transactional and profile data in one all-encompassing customer platform means expensive system implementation. It sometimes may not be completely necessary. There are a number of alternatives that can be just as effective by being as customer-centric as you can be with your information.

Accurate data collection should be encouraged at all times. To 'talk' to a customer on a personal basis, make sure the name is correctly spelt and the address is properly recorded. Customer data from order processing systems may need checking and enhancing before proactive campaigns can be successfully undertaken (see improved customer understanding). Improvements to the transactional system, together with the re-training of staff, should be implemented where necessary to prevent this being a continuing problem.

A customer-centric repository is required to hold all types of data. The system needs to be carefully specified so that it is consistent with the data strategy but flexible enough to be modified/added to at reasonable cost to support a developing CRM strategy.

Query and analysis tools are also needed so that the marketing department (rather than the IT Department) can interrogate, understand and manage the data. Queries and reports should be able to produce what is required to support campaigns. Once customer campaigns have been initiated, the fact that a customer has been selected for a particular campaign and the outcome (if any) needs to be added to the customer record. The results of campaigns then need to be included in future selections as part of the overall customer contact strategy. This can be both positive and negative. Information may be used to suppress a record from future similar campaigns or to positively select for the next one.

Step 4: devise customer-driven contact strategy

A contact strategy needs to be customer-driven and decided for different segments of customers according to sales potential. Consider what is known about customers' preferences either by information gathering or from practical experience. Within this, some customers will not justify any proactive contact at all. A clear part of the strategy needs to anticipate the customer response, not be based simply on their sales potential. The customer needs to hear relevant and well-timed propositions frequently enough to keep your organisation top-of-mind – but not so often that you turn them off.

Digital technology needs to be empowered and integrated with more traditional contact techniques. Some channels of communication are less intrusive than others so can be used more frequently. For example, consider how often outbound sales calls can be made to a customer before it becomes a nuisance, compared to a mailing or email. Combinations of more than one channel, while more expensive, often offer better cost per sale.

If the customer is to receive a combination of propositions through one or several channels over a period of time then there needs to be a consistent creative approach and series of messages across all channels. This also needs to be reflected in the tone of voice and the verbal message, if using the phone.

A customer contact strategy should not just involve out-bound activities. Consideration needs to be given to what can be gained from an incoming contact in terms of immediate business or if this is not possible or infrequent, in terms of information. In these circumstances, an organisation can move from very little customer contact to too much for the customers with most potential. Therefore, a customer campaign history needs to be maintained and monitored so that good customers are not selected for too many campaigns. Too often, customer service is doing a good job but more could be achieved if its remit is extended to helping to exceed customer expectations. To achieve this, there needs to be immediate access to customer contact information and a clear strategy devised for what is said to which groups of customers in what circumstances.

If maximising the opportunity to develop customers is to be realised, managing the customer relationship has to be seen by all involved as part of an integrated process. Customer questions and service issues must be dealt with skilfully and effectively, and at the same time key pieces of information should be collected. To many organisations, this involves a cultural change. Staff who are not sales-focused may need to develop skills outside their primary remit. This is not an easy process and takes an experienced, structured approach over a period of time.

Step 5: create integrated customer acquisition process

The customer management, contact and acquisition process should be seen as one continuous spectrum to gain maximum benefit.

By understanding the profile of customers who have bought certain products through certain channels, prospect data can be sought with a similar profile to refine and fuel more cost-effective future customer acquisition activity.

By researching customers' and unconverted prospects' reactions to the sales process, lessons can be learned to improve the buying experience and hence the conversion rates. This needs to be monitored and reviewed as the combination of communication channels that the customer can potentially use increases.

Analysing the value of customer segments can also inform sales force priorities and potentially leave more time for prospecting. Most companies in the B2B sector have a field sales force. From a salesman's point of view, there is only one relationship the customer should have and that is with him. However, in many cases, the number of customers that have been built up over the years means that the sales force does not have sufficient resources to service and develop them all effectively. As a result, customers and business opportunities could be lost. Accounts should be analysed, prioritised, and supported by a cost-effective servicing and development strategy. This strategy should combine field sales, telesales and direct marketing. Due to historic organisational structures, 'politics' and personalities, companies do not always implement the best CRM/customer acquisition strategy. Your strategy should be based on a full review of the customer base using the following criteria:

- existing customer sales and profitability
- existing customer future potential
- service/direct contact needs of customers
- existing customer relationships with internal sales staff
- new sales potential within the sales force territories

Step 6: create integrated customer development and retention process

As with new business acquisition, customer development and retention activities will involve data selection, product proposition, channel, creative execution and sales process. Pilot testing activities is a cost-effective way to assess the risks and rewards. The sample must be large enough to be representative and scaleable to a national picture. The results must be accurately analysed. Look for early quick wins by anticipating the outcomes of the data.

To improve retention, first understand why and when customers stop buying or switch to other brands. The issues may, in part, be to do with the competitiveness of your product offering and/or with the quality of customer service. They may also be influenced by market volatility. Research your lost customers to find out. It may help you to win them back, but just as significantly, the findings will help you ensure that you lose less of them in the future.

Customer service must be made part of a company's culture, and flow from the CEO down to the lowest paid employee. It can be improved by empowering staff with responsibility, knowledge, access to information and authority to act without upward referral. There must be a company policy for various aspects of customer service, so that your employees are clear on what actions they can take. Within this policy, authority levels can be set so that staff know which actions are outside their personal authority. This will help ensure a consistent approach to dealing with customer issues. The increase in customer communication channels adds to the complexity of customer interaction but also provides the potential for lower-cost customer service.

Establish clear procedures to deal with customers who contact the organisation to 'cancel' an order. This must be regarded as an opportunity to rescue the situation, and not simply to accept the cancellation as an administrative exercise. Staff should be trained to 're-sell' when this situation arises. If resources allow, train specific staff in rescue skills to be allocated to customer order cancellations.

Having said this, it is not cost-efficient to try and save every customer – some churn is inevitable. Indeed, some customers consistently shop around whatever you do. As part of a retention strategy, customers need to be profiled by their potential lifetime value. So different strategies and expenditure limits can be set to save certain customer groups or make them less vulnerable. Segmenting customers for different retention strategies is equally as important as the segmentation for development strategies.

A strong proactive development programme with many positive contacts not only adds value to the worth of a customer but helps the retention. Customers increasingly expect consistently good customer service experience – so you will need to consider how to do more. Reward schemes can also improve retention as long as the customer sees it as straightforward and of real value compared to the competition. Achieving this at a worthwhile cost is often difficult. Generally, the more products a customer has bought from you, the less likely they are to leave, especially if the product has some inherent inertia associated with it eg transferring a bank account.

The argument that it is more cost-effective to sell an extra product or service to an existing customer than to acquire a new customer is generally true. The limitation is usually the customer's perception on how far the brand will 'stretch'. Clearly, the company also needs to determine which markets it wants to be in, taking into account market share and revenues against competition, margins and the ability to service the product portfolio cost-effectively. In some cases, the customer would expect a certain product to be an acceptable brand extension but the company sees only marginal value in it. Alternatively, the company may have identified gaps in their product portfolio, which the customer does not see as a logical extension. Product portfolio management, in line with customer needs, is a key element.

Step 7: establish one-call customer service

Often a new marketing director will not have had experience in call centre management. However, it is a vital ingredient in the success of a CRM initiative. Staff in a call centre can do a great deal to add value to a customer's brand experience by having an upbeat attitude and a helpful disposition. Formal training and ongoing supervision are essential. Call monitoring and coaching should be undertaken by first-line supervision and management. This will motivate staff and really drive home the CRM culture.

No matter how good a customer service agent is, if they cannot help the customer in 'one-call', the customer is unlikely to be happy. This means a level of knowledge, combined with access to all relevant customer information, with empowerment and authority to make decisions within controlled limits. A one-call solution that makes the customer happy is also more cost-efficient for the business. Bringing this together culturally and systems-wise is often requires major CRM investment – and to justify it purely on customer service and efficiency grounds is usually difficult. However, as part of a total CRM strategy that can deliver significant revenue gains, the investment has more appeal.

Equally, no matter how good the people and supporting systems, the customer is not going to be happy if calls or emails are not answered in a reasonable time. Make sure that there are sufficient staff, with working hour flexibility, to provide the level of service through the working week. There will always be a trade-off between cost and service and the business needs to decide what service levels are justified. This needs regular monitoring and adapting.

Trends in customer satisfaction and service being provided should also be tracked. It is not okay to assume that if service levels are there, or thereabouts, then everything is okay. Often, it is the 'top to tail' contact experience that causes dissatisfaction. The technology may improve the customer service experience but poor utilisation could be symptomatic of other problems – poor and too infrequently changed messages, poor routing and inadequate management.

Most customer service call centres confront the issue of how to provide the best service at the lowest cost. The common approach is to make the call centre generate revenue streams in its own right. Four ways of doing this are:

- premium customer service or technical support paid for by the customer as part of a top-of-the-range product
- premium rate lines offering additional support or specialised information
- collection of information that feeds a subsequent sales process
- sales created at the back end of a service/support call

Again, this requires a carefully structured execution over a period of time with significant changes to culture and skill sets, but it can be done. Equally, be aware of the growing customer backlash against premium rate telephone numbers. Investing in providing free phone numbers or investing in new technologies such as voice over Internet protocol (VOIP) may provide better returns in the long run. Integrating telephone systems with computers will also generate immediate benefits such as caller recognition.

Step 8: seek new marketing opportunities

CRM brings in a host of opportunities to target customers, build customer value and create new revenue streams. The proliferation of potential channels leads to three fundamental changes in marketing thinking:

- the need to recognise the brand across every channel means a tightening of corporate identity
- the need to create an over-spanning creative communication umbrella, which transcends all media
- the need to consider the most effective integrated combination of channels

Make sure you understand the potential role of all the channels and their associated costs and benefits. For example, the advancement of digital content and functionality provides the ability to deliver customised messages cheaply and quickly in new ways.

While a full-year campaign plan will be a necessity, you will also need to be more customer-event driven. Pre-planning response to known events has potential to deliver quick wins. For example, contract renewals can be planned with sufficient marketing impact to overcome churn and raise renewal levels.

Finally, there will be restructuring opportunities. Customer segment managers may be better able to align and deliver the internal capabilities of the organisation to the needs of these segments.

Introducing CRM to your marketing

This section is designed to help you recognise the benefits of CRM and help ensure successful marketing implementation.

Think from a customer point of view

Turning the much-vaunted strategy into action means helping your organisation see things from a customer standpoint. This means:

- developing customer communications in the context of the data and the platforms
- re-planning the marketing strategy in the new process and contact environment
- re-structuring the organisation to maximise the benefits
- engaging the sales teams and highlighting selling opportunities
- asking suppliers to contribute more
- when necessary, re-briefing IT

Encourage new creative approaches

Marketing is the creative lead in your organisation so use this to devise new creative methods to capture customer information that can help you target and better meet the needs of your customer – consider for example, competitions, incentives and research. Marketing has always managed creativity in business communications and it is creativity that will produce the most effective brand communication and customer satisfaction. Evaluate the role of all aspects of customer contact in a new relational matrix to optimise data collection and management and channel communication.

Champion better customer understanding

CRM will provide more opportunities to understand your customers and assess and improve the effectiveness and profitability of your marketing activities.

By comparing records and researching customers you can profile your customer more accurately and also monitor behaviour and attitudinal change. This can be added to the more traditional measures:

- purchase data – including recency/frequency/monetary purchasing or new/moderate/heavy/declining/lapsed purchaser 'condition'
- demographics
- lifestyle
- geo–demographics – while postcode information from the PAF (Postcode Address File) is useful, this is even more so with overlays from Acorn, Mosaic and Cameo

By creating a target group and then attaching a profile, marketing becomes so much more specific and accurate. You can also go on to develop a lifetime value for each customer. This is the type of analysis that retailers such as Tesco are already doing via Clubcard schemes. It is a key reason for Tesco's success.

Use of customer records will enable feedback to be used to focus future activity on those customers which yield the most profit and through the channels which cost least. Or to focus activities on those areas that need most attention.

Building stronger customer relationships

There are five steps to building stronger relationships and creating competitive advantage for your business or brand:

Figure 18.2 *Building stronger customer relationships*

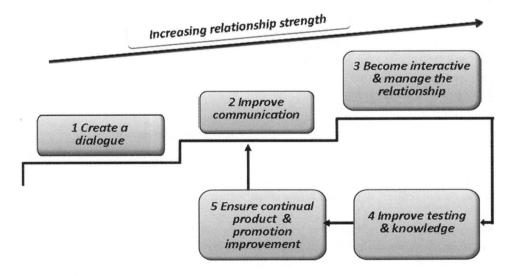

Step 1: create a dialogue

• commence and build a relationship

Step 2: improve communication

• appropriate message, related offer, optimum timing
• re-defined roles for the communication mix
• re-defined channels
• the optimum communication and appropriate cost for each customer activity

Step 3: become interactive and manage the relationship

• explain and help the customer to help themselves and the organisation
• involve the customer, the usage of the product, the brand imagery, the retailer and supplier where deemed appropriate
• add response to all communication

Step 4: improve testing and knowledge

• constantly monitor activity
• become driven by customer events and actions
• evaluate on an ongoing evaluation basis – modify current campaign
• ask 'what ifs' and follow this train of thought constantly

Use an external implementation facility if necessary, to model/test implementation, or as an overspill or a full facility. This should combine:

• response fulfilment and contact management
• fast and capacious database management
• call centre and eCommerce response
• laser printing technology

Step 5: ensure continual product and promotion improvement

• develop product and promotion packages relevant to different customers
• use the data to change the message and the offer
• build costed models to include all variables – response/media/production

Capturing and analysing customer transaction data can help target different messages and promotions to different customers at specific times through the most cost effective channel. Figure 18.3 provides an example for a mail order web/catalogue business. Anyone who has done this will recognise that it is a complicated task. The key point of the figure is to show the sort of customer analysis that CRM yields. It goes from customer segmenting to targeting in a broad sense (that which marketing of itself can already do) to the more specific targeting to which a marketing incentive can then be applied. All from the data of the individual customer behaviour – recency with both frequency and monetary spend (RFM). This process is at the heart of CRM and it is a continuous one. You will not need reminding that email eliminates print costs and has low distribution costs while the content will be exactly the opposite to the much lamented *spam* as it provides the customer, your customer, with valid and worthwhile information.

Figure 18.3 *Example data capture, analysis and marketing model (mail order business)*

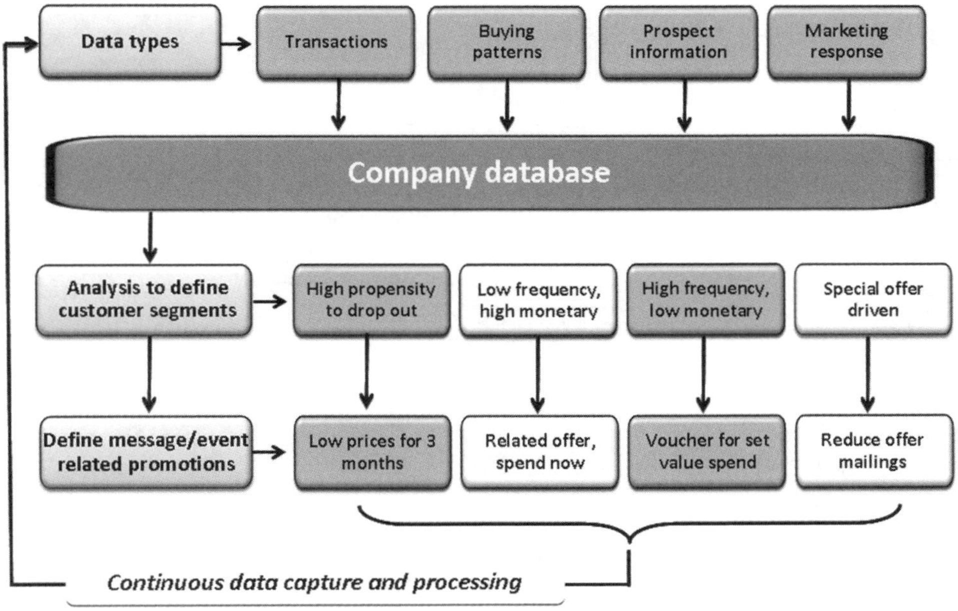

Building a dialogue with customers

It is a great pity that while we can talk to any organisation at any time (and that they have the computer power to know so much about us), that this opportunity is often wasted. For CRM to be meaningful, it is vital to learn to deal with customers as people, and allow the people who deal with customers to be people too.

Built into the human psyche is the need to belong, the desire to be loved and the hope to succeed. We are all individuals who like to be recognised for who and what we are. These Darwinian fundamentals do not change because technology creates new ways of doing things that appear to be quicker and cheaper.

Deal with a customer quickly, cheaply and badly and you will lose them – perhaps not right away but you will. To lose customers is the most expensive thing a business can do, and that is also why every business should work out how it deals with its customers.

This means treating customers as humans and seeing the relationship as a whole from start to finish. The aim is to make friends with your customers (in a professional and business-like way of course). Start by thinking about how a friendship starts, evolves and is then sustained, often through thick and thin. Auto-profiling of customers will enable each customer to have the right script response from the call centre agent and the most relevant web pages opened. Here are some thoughts on the messages to be considered.

Figure 18.4 *Building dialogue with customers*

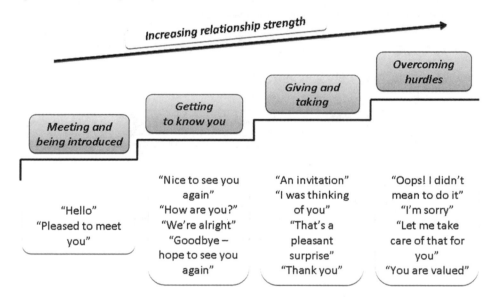

Aim to recognise these circumstances and situations with your customers. Think through how you deal with each of them individually – in person, on the phone or in written form, but before you do, are you sure you really understand the basis of a good relationship?

The secret is mutuality. *I'm OK, you're OK.*

There are just four key considerations concerning a relationship in general:

- we know each other
- we understand and are comfortable with each other

- we trust each other
- we respect each other and don't want to offend or refuse

Now substitute the words 'each other' for 'the customer' and you can easily see how communication can be built up in the context of CRM and lifetime marketing.

Those in business are wrong to call this the lethargy factor. If you're getting things wrong now but not yet losing customers, you will. If you are getting things wrong but trying to put them right, tell your customers – they will understand and are more likely to remain loyal.

In reality, we do not expect much. Just think of the often-heard comments: *"That person is OK because he/she always does what he/she says"* or *"at least he/she understand my point of view or values me"*.

Do not to promise too much. By being realistic and consistent, your delivery should match or exceed customers' expectations. Over-promising simply raises expectations to a possibly undeliverable level.
These are the must-dos:

- do what you say you are going to do
- be realistic
- be consistent
- be pleasant and maintain a mutual outlook even if you have an unpleasant task or message
- understand the other point of view
- keep in touch (not only when you want something)

The reaction you should seek from your customer is to go beyond satisfaction to actually delight them. It is good when nice things happen that we didn't expect – however small and insignificant they may seem. Conversely when bad things happen they need to be dealt with very quickly. If dealt with properly, bad events can turn distressed or angry customers into advocates. Take the gardener's approach – let the relationship grow, and nurture it for best results. Remember also that happy customers tell four to five others of their positive experience, whereas dissatisfied customers tell nine to 12 how bad it was (1).

Bringing these thoughts to your business is not difficult, but it is not easy either.

The first thing you must do is to find out what your customers are thinking and saying.

What is their experience of your business? You will find your own ways to do this.

Then you should consider how to start behaving as a business that wants to build customer relationships.

These critical communication issues are at the heart of making CRM a success, and their recognition is the key to making your marketing and its use of CRM technology a real success. With a high level of customer understanding you will be able to find more like them through skilful selection of 'replica' data sets and then use the range of channel options to reach them more effectively.

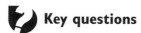 **Key questions**

Here are some key questions to ask when reviewing your marketing strategy. These are the questions you will not get answered from IT or your CRM vendor but they do need answering.

- Have we got the optimum media mix?
- When do we communicate brand or product?
- What is the best way to segment and then profile customers? What's the difference?
- How do we capture their 'condition'?
- When is the most appropriate time for contacting our customers?
- How can we better identify new customers?
- What communication skills to we need to create a dialogue with all of our customers?
- How do we get the best out of our agencies?
- Do we need to restructure?
- What data management and other facilities are needed?
- How clean is my current data?
- How do we build a model to plan activity?
- How much will all this cost?
- Are our competitors gaining an unseen lead?
- Can we quantify the improvements?
- How do we make the most of cross-selling opportunities?
- How do we show that we want to convincingly build customer relationships?

Data is not understanding

So far this entire chapter has been dedicated to analysing and using data to build stronger customer relationships and drive sales. But a watchword to bear in mind is that reliance on intrinsic data alone can lead to tunnel-vision and be risky. Using intrinsic data does not mean that you have fully understood your customer, their needs and why they make the choices that they do. Combining extrinsic customer data with intrinsic data can be even more powerful. For example, customer research can help reveal new targeting variables and data types that could be captured. Research can also help provide a better contextual understanding of the choices that customers make, the alternatives they are considering and triggers and drivers behind those choices. In turn this can help you create stronger propositions as well as more effective promotions.

Now over to you!

 Key points to remember

1. CRM can have far-reaching effects on a business. Make sure you have a clear strategy and financial plan as part of the overall business plan.

2. Board engagement and support is essential for a CRM initiative. Drive from the board down and secure buy-in across the whole business.

3. To maximise the benefits of CRM aim to deliver short-term wins en route to the longer-term vision.

4. Aim to deliver revenue gains as well as cost efficiencies and turn cost centres into profit centres.

5. Remember that implementing CRM will require a significant change within your company. It will need intensive 'husbandry' to make it work. Use management intensity and an integrated inter-departmental approach.

6. Use CRM to measure the effectiveness of campaigns and help plan and re-plan more cost effective activity. Aim to truly understand your customer's attitudes and experience both from intrinsic and extrinsic sources to provide more rigorous and contextual customer understanding and help you make better decisions.

7. Develop specific marketing and sales activity with CRM as the starting point. Anticipate the outcomes to produce targeted communications to customer groups and events.

8. Invest in CRM systems and cultural change only to the degree that is necessary to achieve financial objectives.

9. Pilot CRM programmes either internally or externally to validate CRM business models. Monitor vigorously and regularly report back to the board. Take your time to ensure a smooth introduction. Training and proper administration are vital.

10. Think creatively and aim to develop the brand across all the new channels and media. Think of all the communications, with the customer as part of the relationship.

Customer Channel Management

New Connection – Todd Snider (2002)

In this chapter you will learn:

- *What channels or routes to market are available*
- *How to improve customer channel effectiveness*
- *How to measure and optimise channel effectiveness*

This is where marketing meets the world of technology head on. In the past, distribution simply meant the sales force selling to wholesalers and retailers, and latterly by way of mail order catalogues. The sales function was seen simply as a sub-function of marketing. Yet today we reach the customer through a variety of channels, each with a varying reliance on technology and a different impact on customers and their behaviour. This chapter is about making sense of the multi-channel environment and optimising your routes to market.

The speed of technological change and the exponential growth of the eWorld mean that the specifics of channel management may have changed by the time you read this chapter. This chapter therefore outlines a few guiding principles which you can apply in the context of current technology.

So, what do we mean by channels? They are the means by which you communicate and sell to the customer in certain markets, such as software sales.

The advent of the Internet and using technology to interact with customers coincides with a fragmentation of conventional media. It presents the ability to more effectively target customers who are most likely to buy our products and personalise how we talk to them. So if the maxim of 'half your advertising is wasted' was ever true, it is no longer!

What channels are available?

Figure 19.1 outlines some of the channels available, such as physical channels, telephone, post and the Internet. Within these channels there are many variables, and in the Internet world in particular many new channels continue to emerge including texting, blogs and podcasts. While all channels have their advantages and disadvantages, the new digital channels mean that more accurate data concerning target markets can be accumulated and stored, according to how they have responded in the past.

Figure 19.1 *Summary of channels or routes to market*

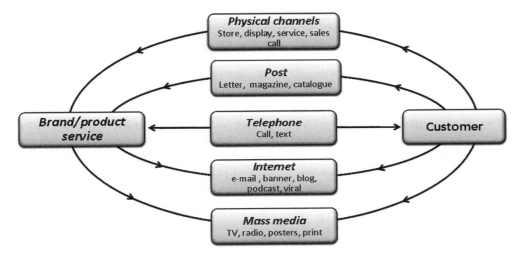

 **Where to start**

The starting point for channel management must be an audit. What information and messages have been used, and through what channel or media? This approach needs to be two-way. Today, many larger multi-channel organisations have created a new role – that of the 'customer experience director' (CED). The CED's task is to create and manage the customer experience across all channels. So the starting point has to be an audit by channel and message, and also by usage of a given target customer group.

The next step is to provide another layer to superimpose on the channel matrix that measures the experience by product and/or brand. Understanding the revelations of the audit will allow you to create more targeted, timely and appropriate messages and sell and distribute products and services more cost-effectively.

Specific accurate data is the key. Comprehensive information on your customers enables you to build a precise profile of them and your relationship with them. This will be based on past behaviour and the information provided when requesting information or logging on to your database. Take note of past behaviour and use it as a model for future buying patterns.

Success factors to improve your customer channel management

Now let's give you a set of principles to apply…

Encourage customer involvement and commitment through careful channel management

By understanding the customer's buying behaviour you should aim to find out how customers think and what the triggers and barriers are to purchasing. This is essential to design the appropriate channel mix. With high value and high perceived risk sales, usually face-to-face interaction is required; conversely, with low value and risk sales, a machine on a wall may suffice. As customers become more familiar with new digital channels, it is likely that more and more sales will take place via this route. Customers who have special interests are already converging on websites, blogs and forums, and brands that cater for these groups can now easily nurture their relationship through these vehicles.

Take the simple example of a complaint. This is most likely to be phoned in. Frequently, the complaining customer is confronted with a premium rate phone number and an automated response menu of options, followed by a wait until an agent becomes available. Would it not be better to give a potential complainant the opportunity to understand the process and be told a good time to call so as to be dealt with more effectively? Better still, offer the opportunity to write complaints online with a 'we will call you back' offer (and make sure you do). Often once a complaint is written down articulately and without pressure, there is less need to get angry with someone.

Configure channel offerings to customers' different channel needs and behaviour

Customers use what they think is the most suitable or available channel for different purposes. For example, they may visit an ATM for fast cash. They may go to a bank branch to solve problems or personal reassurance. In the Internet world, there is a school of thought that recommends making your website 'Marketing Central' – a portal that is hub for all your marketing activity (See Chapter 17 Optimising Customer Communications). While it can be a window into the world of your brand, it should not be seen as a substitute for all aspects of your relationship with customers. Don't think for one minute that if there is a PDF version of a document on a site, it means that a printed copy is no longer required. Service offerings must be relevant to needs – for example, those with busy lives may prefer a printed copy to consider later. **⓱**

The role of a given channel or medium to the whole of your brand communication must also be considered. For example, it is a reasonable strategy to use the most expensive and broad-reaching media simply to establish brand values – a brand umbrella for the panoply of multi-media activity. Inevitably, the campaign to establish the brand will be laden with emotional messages. However, more targeted and two-way channels will be more suitable to communicate rational product benefits and calls to action and generate response to those calls to action.

Data, data and data

The more data you have, the more effectively you will be able to use the channels at your disposal. Many IT solutions offer a marketing dashboard, which you should take advantage of. But do keep your 'marketing' hat on – don't always take data at face value. For example, data gathered from a website drop-down box may simply mean that the respondent has clicked on anything just to continue quickly. There is an emerging theory among data analysts that talks in terms of the 'quantum effect'. This claims that in providing information customers actually change their attitude to the meaning of the data so that the original usefulness is reduced.

The more accurate your data and profiling become, the more you will be able to replicate the responses to your campaigns, convert more prospects and in turn reach them in a much more cost-effective way. Developing your emarketing skills will reduce reliance on external media and costly printing and postage.

Be prepared for interaction

Remember that the new channels are two-way. Send an email and you may receive a reply. Make calls and don't be surprised to be called back. This brings a real responsibility to make sure the channels are open. If you want the channel to be effective, ensure that you have addressed any potential pitfalls.

Tailor messages to channels

You will soon appreciate that not all channels give you the same creative freedom or the means to make a more evocative, emotionally based proposition to the customer. More often than not, the newer the channels, the more rational the message needs to be. The customer may use one channel; say the website, for information gathering, before telephoning or ordering through a different channel.

Aim for a consistent look and feel across all channels

In the 1970s, the call was for integrated marketing. That call has re-emerged in the multi-channel world. However, it has always been the case that the brand is the brand wherever it appears. Many corporate identity manuals do not embrace new technology or how sales or servicing staff should behave. Make sure that yours does.

Maximise your branding, consistent with the limitations of the channels

It is often difficult to sustain the look and feel of a brand given the limitations imposed by screen and software, yet you should strive to ensure that as much of your brand shines through as possible. Consider what you say as well as how it is said. When typefaces and images are used make sure they are fit for purpose and can be displayed on the screen sizes for which they are intended – from desktop to mobile phone or PDA. Make sure you work with professional designers and technicians to achieve this effectively.

Exercise brand controls when using third-party channels

When a distributor or third party gets hold of your brand, beware! There is no easy answer (rather only anticipation). You may need to go beyond creating brand guidelines but create templates or even promotional frameworks to ensure that all communications encounters live up to your brand. Remember too, that there is a fine line between maintaining brand integrity and supporting enthusiastic sales efforts.

Don't underestimate the customer's technical know-how

The facilities available to the individual and their ability to use them are well in advance of many commercial organisations. Don't underestimate the potential of new technologies, such as voice over Internet protocol (VOIP), to better serve and build stronger relationships with customers. Even if the customers don't have this technology, at the very least your image to the customer should be seen as more 'contemporary'.

Try to see the whole picture

It is easy to become preoccupied with activity via a given channel without reference to all the others. As an example, some businesses become carried away with 'pay per click' (PPC) promotions and fail to make comparative checks on other ways of gaining responses. Weigh up the effectiveness and cost of a given channel in the wider scheme of things. For example, a physical sales call can be more effective by selected use of other channels, either mass media, post or an email to promote the brand image or elicit enquiries.

Plan channels by product, brand and customer

The best way to optimise customer promotion, contact and channel usage is to plan in a three-way matrix of customer, product and brand. This will ensure that the right channel is used for the specific message and that the customer has a common, consistent view of the brand, which is always relevant, appealing and distinctive.

Measuring channel effectiveness

There are two prerequisites to measuring channel effectiveness:

Ensure consistent channel measurement

Customers often discard one channel for another if it meets their needs better. For example, the phenomenon of surfing the web means increasingly easy and quicker access. Some will even seek out your brand in new areas. Be alive to the changing dynamics and monitor usage (for instance, the length of stay on a web page) to help manage the process to your advantage and your customers' benefit. Make sure that you set up the means of measuring responses from each channel on a comparable basis.

It is very easy to get carried away with what appears to be a low-cost media. Just because it is there, it doesn't mean you should be wasteful. Even though you can reach many prospects quickly and cheaply, this does not mean that the response should be any less prepared or thought through.

Establish meaningful KPIs

Aim to build up a key performance indicator (KPI) of the actual cost/budget of maintaining contact with an existing customer and the cost of acquisition. This can be cost per thousand, cost per response or cost as a proportion of revenue generated. Setting a goal of driving costs down while improving actual sales performance will be the most illuminating measure on how well you are managing your customer experience in a multi-channel environment.

Key points to remember

1. In this increasingly digital world, there are more and more channel opportunities that could help you build your business. Each one should be seen as more than a sale and distribution opportunity but also an opportunity to communicate and build relationships with customers.

2. Channel strategies should not be planned in isolation. Take a holistic view and plan using a three-way matrix of customer, product and brand. This will ensure that the right channel is used for the specific message and that the customer has a common consistent view of the brand, which is always relevant, appealing and distinctive.

3 Measuring the effectiveness of different channels is critical in order to optimise their role in the mix. Do this by measuring customer value on a consistent basis.

Major Project Planner

20 Leading Projects

Step by Step – Whitney Houston (1996)

In this chapter you will learn:

- *The role of project management*
- *How to lead and manage a project*
- *Project planning tools*

As Peter Drucker, the famous management guru, wrote; "*Management is doing things right; leadership is doing the right things.*" The larger the organisation, the greater the challenge to bring about change, and the more likely it is that project management will be essential to managing that change.

When a new marketing director is announced, it is often with a fanfare from the company and a commitment to growth. However, growth never comes easily. It means change, and change means doing things differently from before. Your fellow employees will have to change and abandon their comfort zone.

As you embrace your role, you will no doubt identify many issues, and instigate many initiatives to catalyse change. The best way to do this, especially if you are operating across departmental boundaries, is to delegate responsibility to someone in your team, and better still initiate and sponsor projects to address the issues in question. Change in organisations comes about through projects. This is a management practice on which you can find a veritable library of textbooks and manuals, software, and even a phalanx of project managers in practice.

Project management has evolved as a separate management discipline, originating with the evolution of IT. The need to bring together a number of complex and critical elements, as well as managing and implementing them at key points along a timeline, demands effective project management skills.

Welcome to project management – a useful and sometimes essential discipline, but be wary of it becoming the objective in itself, rather than the tool to achieve an objective.

Recognise the fundamentals and you will be able to achieve a great deal, at specific points in time, through a number of different people, departments and suppliers.

Most things in marketing tend to be project-based, and therefore a planning application developed in a project management style is an ideal mechanism for you and your department. This chapter is designed to help you establish and lead projects and ensure they are successful.

 ## Where to start?

How do you lead and manage a project?

The first stage is to 'scope' the project. Identify what you need to achieve and, just as important, what is outside as well as inside the scope of the project. Understanding the extent and limitations are key to efficient and effective management.

The second stage is to lay down the timeline, from starting point to when the project needs to be completed.

Third, identify the critical activities and respective deliverables at each stage that contribute to the project. Plot them on the timeline and set their individual completion dates. Do not forget that some activities need others to be completed before they can be finalised – or even started. This is the 'critical path' – the longest path of planned activities to the end of the project, and the earliest and latest that each activity can start and finish without making the project longer (1). Start with the meshing and sequencing of these activities as this is essential to achieving the objectives of the project and completing it on time. If the process is complex, consider using a critical path network. If unsure, ask a colleague in IT but try to restrict them to simple English.

Next, identify the individuals who should be tasked to complete the various activities. Allocate your resources based on capability and knowledge, and allow sufficient time to complete the tasks – then a bit more. Things will not run smoothly or to plan, so make sure you have provision for delays and changes and build this 'wiggle room' into your timeline.

Share and agree your plan with your fellow directors while your project is still at the planning stage, albeit an advanced planning stage. This will enable you to build their ideas to your plan, as well as help you secure any necessary resources from their areas. In turn, this will help you gain their more positive agreement to co-operation and secure their commitment to help you make sure the project is a success.

Your choice of project manager is also an important one – you will need a safe, reliable and credible pair of hands. The job may be something you wish to do yourself, but equally you may be better distancing yourself from this role. Sponsoring rather than managing the project may also provide an opportunity to ensure a more objective approach to the problem. Furthermore, tasking one of your team with the role could present a useful development opportunity by giving them this extra responsibility. Many also use consultants to benefit from their objectivity, project management rigour and tools, as well as the injection of fresh ideas.

Once the plan and process is in place, you will be able to call a meeting to brief those responsible for various activities. You will probably have involved some individuals in the planning process. They can help you 'sell' the plan to everyone else.

Brief everyone comprehensively to make sure they fully understand:

- what the project objective and desired outcome is at each stage, and overall
- what is expected of each individual
- what their deadlines are
- who they need to interact with in order to achieve their goals
- very importantly, the consequences of them not achieving their objectives by the critical dates

Make sure you have buy-in before the meeting ends and make sure everything is clear. They should not be embarrassed to say if they do not fully understand – ultimately, failure is not an option so it's best to solve any misunderstandings at the outset.

Managing the project

Use your plan and timeline to keep a close eye on how the project is developing. Set up a reporting process whereby all contributors can update you on their progress.

If possible, have regular meetings with the project manager or all concerned so that you can quickly identify problems and solve them as a team. Do not let deadlines slip, because missing early deadlines will compound into much greater and potentially disastrous delays later in the project. The outcome will be a project that does not complete on time.

Once the project is finished, review the process. What went well, what not so well? Document the reasons and use these to help you plan subsequent projects more effectively.

Success factors for managing a project

There are eight factors for managing a successful project – but bear in mind that all the advice and processes in the world will not substitute for your judgement.

Be realistic in your expectations

Balance what you want to achieve with what can be easily achieved. If you try to do too much you may over-burden yourself and increase the risk of failure. Ask any government-sponsored IT project leader. Remember, marketing is viewed by management as relatively short-term, so only initiate projects that can be set up, run, completed and implemented in a year or less (regrettably, especially in the UK). Do not get sucked into anyone else's projects with a lengthy cycle, except at the initial stage when you are defining the scope of your project. Better to have quick success than long-term structural shifts.

'Improving customer service' is a project that every incoming marketing director should set up. You do not even have to sit on this particular project group as you can be the sponsor or even encourage the CEO to be involved. You could add *'and reduce costs'* if at first he does not want to do it! When the project team has completed its work, your job will be to use the findings and conclusions that will be agreed to set new standards that the organisation can consistently deliver, and turn this into marketing benefits.

Involve potential stakeholders at an early stage

At the outset, decide who is going to be affected by the change, then consult and involve them in the project. All too often a project fails, either by not being inclusive or because some of the elements of the project are being undertaken elsewhere – and your control is reduced accordingly. Also, make sure that consultation takes place at the scoping stage, as this will enhance the likelihood of a successful final outcome and avoid wasted effort.

Keep the project team to a manageable size

You decide what that is. Remember, *'too many cooks…'*. The project team meetings will be the driving force behind the project (even if you do use fancy project reporting tools). That is why limiting the steering committee to a small number of committed managers who will drive the change is important. You can easily ask the team members to set up sub-committees.

Create a plan and stick to it

The point in creating a plan is to enable efficient, comprehensive yet rigorous analysis of the alternatives and arrive at a conclusion. Don't deviate from your plan of achieving the desired outcome. Remember that 'project creep' (the many and varied things that could and possibly be added to the project scope) will soon lead to 'project paralysis'. To avoid creep, simply note down any identified issues that are outside of the scope of the project. You can then come back to them after the successful completion of your current project. Make it an appendix to the final report.

Manage the critical path

The speed of the slowest activity or participant is the fastest you will go. Most project planning is geared to setting milestones and goals. This is all very well but if one fundamental activity or person is lagging behind then so will the project. That is why it is important to manage the critical path and watch for laggards. Inevitably, there will always be something holding the project back, most likely involving IT or HR. Remember the three Rs: re-prioritise, re-plan or replace the personnel if they are not pulling their weight.

A useful way to manage the critical path is to diarise checkpoint or deliverables meetings on commencement of a project. This can help inject the extra focus and impetus to ensure timely completion.

Keep everyone informed

As well as circulating meeting notes and personal briefings, another way of doing this is to use a Gantt Chart (named after Henry Laurence Gantt, an engineer and management consultant, who first published it in 1910) (2). Gantt Charts illustrate the start and finish dates of key activities within a project (see Figure 20.1 for an example). Some Gantt charts also show the dependency (ie relationships between activities) and the critical path. When using the Gantt Chart as a briefing tool, make a colour key to show progress to date (eg green for completed work), with an update narrative short enough for people to read quickly. Such communication keeps the interest in the outcome alive so it is a good thing to say things like "*we will soon be able to...*"

Ensure effective implementation

Once you have finished the project, it is just beginning for the rest of the organisation. Implementation of the ideas you have developed is critical to maximise the benefits of your work for the organisation as a whole. Plan how you are going to maximise take-up at the start. This is the time when you can make a mockery of the statistics that say things like 66% of projects failed to deliver. It is the time when you will succeed where other managers won't, because you understand the power of communication and

Figure 20.1 *Project plan timing Gantt Chart*

Activity	w/c	Dec 4	Dec 18	Jan 1	Jan 15	Jan 29	Feb 12	Feb 26	Mar 12	Mar 26	Apr 9	Apr 23
Establish project management		▭										
Source and review available research and baseline data (Data mining)		▭										
Kick-start and research planning session		▭										
Communications stimulus development session with team		▭										
Create communications research stimulus		▭										
Develop detailed research samples, discussion guides and questionnaires		▭▭										
Creativity groups (8)					▭							
Telephone and on-line depths (c.30-35)				▭▭								
Qualitative research analysis and insight generation					▭							
Research advisory group review meeting						▭						
Quantitative questionnaire development						▭						
Quantitative fieldwork							▭▭					
Quantitative research analysis and word and PowerPoint document preparation								▭▭▭				
Interactive debrief/workshop											▭

know exactly when and how to use it. View everyone affected by the changes as a customer and communicate to them accordingly.

Use your marketing skills to ensure a successful launch

All too often, a project is completed and then ignored, certainly in terms of making an impact on business forecasts. So make sure you get the organisation to understand the benefits that are likely to come from the successful delivery of the project you have been working on. If it is a project designed for an internal audience, use your marketing skills to launch the project so you command attention, generate interest and get commitment and buy-in to your ideas. If it is a new procedure or system you have created, don't forget to 'test market' or 'pilot' your ideas to ensure they are 'bug free'. And don't forget to invest in proper training in order to overcome potential inertia barriers so your colleagues realise the maximum benefits as quickly as possible. In other words, think about launching an internal project, deliverable in exactly the same way as you would a new product or initiative designed for your customers.

🎯 Tools and techniques

Figure 20.2 shows a simple way to document a project plan. It highlights the objectives at each stage, the key activities to be undertaken, as well as the outputs or deliver-

Figure 20.2 *Project plan activities and deliverables*

Step 1. Research planning	Step 2. Qualitative research	Step 3. Quantitative research
Objectives : • To build a clear picture of individual stakeholder needs, what you know and don't know • To hypothesise issues and communication opportunities to explore with key targeted groups • To put in place the logistics to ensure smooth running of the project	**Objectives :** • To conduct qualitative research focused on key targeted groups • To analyse qualitative research findings and prepare a quantitative questionnaire	**Objectives :** • To conduct comprehensive quantitative benchmarking across 7 states • To analyse and incorporate the quantitative findings into a final research report • To share findings and conclusions in an interactive debrief
Approach • Establish project management • Source and review available research / baseline data • Kick-start and research planning session with key stakeholders • Communications stimulus development session with client team • Create communications research stimulus • Develop detailed research samples, discussion guides and questionnaires	**Approach** • Telephone and on-line depths with key targeted groups in 7 states (4 x 7) • Creativity group discussions with targeted groups in 4 states (2 x 4) • Review meeting with research advisory group	**Approach** • On-line quantitative survey • Analyse and consolidate quantitative findings into a final research report • Analyse findings & develop strategies to maximise stakeholder benefits • Prepare Word debrief document • Interactive debrief and workshop — Present key findings, conclusions and recommendations — Highlight insights & opportunities & provide strategic pointers to meet your objectives
Deliverables : • Agreed hypothesised issues and opportunities, agreed research sample, plan, discussion guides and stimulus	**Deliverables :** • Summary document covering key findings and conclusions from targeted groups and quantitative questionnaire	**Deliverables :** • Document integrating key quantitative and qualitative key findings, conclusions and recommendations

ables at each stage. This is a very simple project timing plan created using Microsoft PowerPoint. This is the same plan as described in the Gantt Chart in Figure 20.1.

Project management software

There is an increasing range of software available to help plan projects. The actual development of software is often as precise and logical as any human behaviour, while the process by which things are done is usually not. And most tasks are not done at the same speed or to the same rigour.

Microsoft Project and Prince 2 are two good starting points. Microsoft Project is an easy-to-use project management tool adopted by many organisations. It has the advantage of interfacing with other Microsoft applications that you use on a day-to-day basis. Prince 2 is used by the government and demonstrates how detailed you can make project management if you have a mind to – this helps provide structure and formality for large numbers of people and departments. In all likelihood, your organisation will have accepted methodology in place and a Microsoft PowerPoint chart or an Excel spreadsheet will more than do.

Key points to remember

1. Establishing a project can address even what may seem to be the most complex of challenges by breaking down the whole into a series of smaller and more manageable activities or steps.

2. Consult and engage the right people at the project scoping stage as this is a powerful way to glean extra ideas, resources and support to address the challenge.

3. A project is only as successful as its implementation. Use your marketing skills to the full at the implementation stage.

21 Creativity and Problem Solving

New World in the Morning – Roger Whittaker (1970)

In this chapter you will learn:

- *How the brain works*
- *How to create a creative working environment*
- *Creative ways to solve problems and generate ideas*
- *Creative tools*

There will be many times in your career when you will face problems; some small and others large. All will probably seem large at the time, but will hopefully pale into insignificance at a later date! Declining sales volume or an inability to create successful new products are problems that befall many. Sometimes problems of this nature are caused by ways of working that are entrenched in the culture of the organisation – *"we should do it this way because we've always done it this way."* Often this is fair, but when a new competitor enters a market and succeeds by changing the rules, it can be a signal that you also need to think and do things differently. Remember the low-cost airlines' effect on British Airways, remember Amazon's effect on WHSmith and Waterstones, Dyson's effect on Hoover and the effect of digital watches on Swiss springs.

As marketing director, the organisation will look to you for a lead. While it will be impossible for you to solve all the problems yourself, you can create the conditions whereby your team can, and through them, the organisation as a whole will also be able to work through problem areas more efficiently. There will be times when enhancements to existing practices will suffice. There will be other times when more radical changes will be required. Different problems and situations will require different approaches to problem solving and more or less creativity.

While creativity gets a bad press in some quarters, there are many myths surrounding what creativity is. These should be dispelled. Creativity is not magic or a wacky art. Nor is it the preserve of the few. Creativity is an ability to make new connections and generate ideas. It is a thinking skill – an ability to think in different ways to solve problems. Creativity can be a disciplined science and can be mastered by all. The purpose of this chapter is to explain how. This chapter is therefore packed full of ideas and techniques to help you solve problems and leverage the creativity inherent in your organisation.

The way the brain works

Being aware of how the brain works is a good starting point. Like we are predominantly right or left handed, 'footed' or 'eyed', we can also be thought of as right or left 'brained'.

The left brain (a *successive processor*) prefers to learn in a step-by-step sequential format, beginning with details leading to a conceptual understanding of a skill. The left side is also often thought of as the logical, thinking side. Left-brained people are thought of as analytical, technical, problem solvers, organised and administrative in nature. Left-brain thinking tends to follow a more linear, logical or convergent path and lead to a more evolutionary outcome.

Conversely, the right brain (a *simultaneous processor*) prefers to learn beginning with the general concept and then going on to specifics. It is often thought of as the creative side of the brain. Right-brained people are imaginative, spontaneous, emotional, dreamers – the artists and musicians of this world. Right-brain thinking is more likely to twist and turn, diverge and make more lateral connections – and lead to a more visionary or radical outcome.

As the two different types of people tend to think in two different ways, it is also possible to combine them in different ways to optimise the creative power of the group. It is also possible to 'teach' people how to think in different ways, so that they can be more creative or more effective at problem solving.

 Ten minute exercise

Here is a short exercise to help you think about your team and assess whether you could organise them to be more effective.

Objective of the exercise:
To help optimise the effectiveness of your team

Guidelines for the exercise:
• Draw up a list of your colleagues and product/brand groups and gauge their problem-solving abilities; then try and categorise each person as a right-or left-brain-dominated person and by level of expertise.

- Consider whether each individual and team is performing above or below expectations.
- If the teams are not working well, ask yourself why?
- Consider whether the team would benefit from a change in mix of expertise or type of person. Also consider injecting expertise from outside the marketing team, perhaps from one of your agencies, or the finance or research and development department.
- Also consider whether specific creative, problem-solving or marketing technical training may be of assistance.

Success factors for solving problems

Empower others first

As a marketing director, there will be a limit to the number of tasks you can do yourself. Remember that a problem shared can be a problem halved and empower your team to work on your problem in the first instance. Being slightly distant from the creative or problem-solving process also means that you will be in a better position to add value. Unburdened by working through the detail, it will be easier to see the bigger picture and help keep your team on the rails. Here are some things to consider when briefing them:

- What's the end business objective?
- What are the boundaries of the problem – what parameters should be considered/not considered?
- What resources are available?
- Who should be involved; has the team got the right mix of experience, knowledge and skills?
- Should a budget be allocated to the task, and if so what is appropriate, given both the potential benefits that could be gained, and the other priorities that you have?
- What's a reasonable timeframe to allow?

Recruit and encourage diversity

The range of skills within an organisation can be a great advantage to the astute leader – especially when co-opting resources for project teams or workshops. Use a combination of left-brained and right-brained thinkers and variety of technical expertise when empowering others to crack a problem. Include people who understand the problem from the customer point of view such as marketers, researchers, sales people and customer service people. Include diverse technical experts such as chemists, computer experts and accountants. While the precise choice of skills will depend on the problem, don't be afraid to go beyond the obvious as this is more likely to inject sparks into the group. A team of up to 8-10 works well, but beyond this there can be diminishing returns.

Create the right environment

Positive emotional energy has been directly linked with creative ability.

Sometimes you may just need to create the right conditions in a meeting or working session, either by leading the group yourself or at least helping to get a project started. Encourage bonding and involvement rather than exclusion which can lead to inhibition and stress. Groups typically go through several stages and paying attention to these stages can help groups become productive. The stages include:

- forming
- norming
- (brain) storming or performing

The first stage involves helping the group to form or coalesce and establishing the guidelines or rules by which they will work. This requires:

- setting the group at ease by orientating the group to the task at hand
- providing them with the necessary knowledge and background to operate effectively
- helping them bond with each other; for example through a round-robin of introductions
- enabling understanding of, and compliance with the rules for running the session. Here are four:
  - all mobiles should be turned off
  - everyone must listen and respect others
  - everyone should be positive in contributing ideas (not evaluate, filter or shoot ideas down ideas) (unless asked!)
  - log any issues and come back to them later (this will prevent issues derailing the creative process yet be captured for later consideration)

Thereafter the group should start to address the task at hand. The leader should maintain harmony and cohesion of the group by listening, encouraging involvement, managing conflict and helping the team build relationships.

Warm-up or energising exercises can be useful to kick-start sessions, especially those interlaced with humour. Ask for example, "what should *not* be done to solve a problem?" The beauty of the question is that it can generate some wonderfully enter-taining responses as well as excellent ideas! Here is a story to help you get the ball rolling.

 Best practice

If you were a cigarette manufacturer involved in a naming session for a new brand, probably the last thing that you would ever call your brand would be 'Death'. However, that is precisely what BJ Cunningham and his 'Enlightened Tobacco Company' did. They made a marketing virtue out of a legally available consumer product, which can kill people when used exactly as intended: "Death cigarettes: for an honest smoke." This act of heresy, though enormously successful with consumers in the 1990s, didn't go down well with the tobacco industry. It eventually landed Cunningham in the European Court of Justice fighting against the might of the established tobacco industry as well as every member state of the European Community.

Many aspects of the creative process can be understood in terms of humour, as creativity and humour are closely related. Developing skills in creativity will help you create humour, and appreciating a wide variety of humour will help develop your creativity. Humour means having fun, and creativity needs a good dose of fun and play. In his book about humour *I am Right, You are Wrong*, Edward de Bono (1) writes: *"Humour is by far the most significant behaviour of the human mind …it tells us more about how the brain works than any other behaviour of the mind".*

Humour is significant because it is based on logic that is very different from classical logic. Classical logic (inherited from the Greeks, and called 'rock' logic by de Bono) involves thinking along very definite paths. While there are potential side-paths, these are temporarily suppressed by the dominant path. If 'somehow' we cut across from the main path to the side-path, the route back to the starting point is very obvious. This move sideways to the main path is the origin of the term 'lateral thinking'.

The 'somehow' when we deviate from main paths or patterns, is the essence of humour, for example, when we say something that is different to expectations.

The significance of humour is that it reinforces pattern-forming and symmetry and works through pattern-switching or asymmetry. The effect can be deliberately recreated in creative thinking by using techniques such as provocation to challenge existing conventions or ways of doing things.

The environment can also contribute to emotional state. Choose an inspirational location. At a mundane meeting level, choose a room with a view and make sure that the arrangement of chairs promotes a relaxed, informal atmosphere. Specifically put the chairs are in a horseshoe configuration rather than a series of rows. There is little worse than a team having to work round a huge elongated table as happens in most boardrooms.

Orchestrate the power of the group

If you've ever participated in a group creative session, you'll appreciate how chaotic they can become. People, being individuals, all think in different ways and considerable amounts of time and energy can be wasted with people talking over each other and at tangents. Choose an experienced facilitator to design a creative session and facilitate the group. The design of the session should take into account the business challenge that you face as well as the personalities of the participants in order to optimise the cultural dynamics and working efficiency of the group.

 Edward de Bono's 'Six Thinking Hats'

Edward de Bono, the pioneer of lateral thinking, developed a creative process to help groups work together more effectively. His 'Six Thinking Hats' (2) is a technique to engage and direct the energies of a group. Helping the group deliberately adopt a variety of perspectives on a subject helps both develop and test the soundness of ideas. Each of the six hats is a colour-coded mnemonic indicating different modes of thinking. The role of the facilitator is to direct the group which hat to 'wear' at particular time. The six hats are:

- White (Neutral): Facts/information – what information do we have/need?
- Red (Fire/Warmth): Emotions/intuition – how do we feel about this now?
- Green (Vegetation/Growth): Creating new ideas – what are some ideas/ alternative ways of fixing this problem?
- Yellow (Sunshine/Optimism): Benefits/positive thought – why is this a good idea? What are potential advantages?
- Black (Devil's Advocate): Judgement/caution – will this work, what are the disadvantages or problems with this idea?
- Blue (Sky/Cool): Control of process/thinking – where are we now, what have we achieved, what should we do next?

Rigorous methods and perseverance

De Bono was a firm believer that great ideas can be generated by conscious, methodical and organised thinking and that creativity is a skill that can be taught. Use an extended and rigorous approach to problem solving rather than a one-off intuitive approach. Not only will this provide more opportunities to look at your problem from a wide range of angles, it will provide more chances to create and develop ideas. While great ideas can sometimes be generated quickly and by chance, there is usually no substitute for rigour, sheer hard work and perseverance. Make sure you stack the odds in your favour.

 Creative problem solving process

This section outlines a general approach to creativity or problem solving (see Figure 21.1), consisting of six steps. This can be undertaken by working collaboratively with a group of colleagues. The steps should ideally be followed in sequence from beginning to end. While following all the steps in sequence will take a longer time, you can be more confident that your approach will be more rigorous, more comprehensive and more likely to generate new ideas. Alternatively, as needs and time dictate, it is possible to conduct just one or more of the steps at any one time.

The approach is loosely based on the Osborn–Parnes Process, which was conceived by Alex Osborn (3), co-founder of the New York advertising agency BBDO, and Sidney Parnes, who is said to have coined the term 'brainstorming' and invested nearly 40 years in teaching and thinking about the creative process. An expanded version of this process is provided in Proforma 21A at the end of this chapter.

Figure 21.1 *Creative problem solving process*

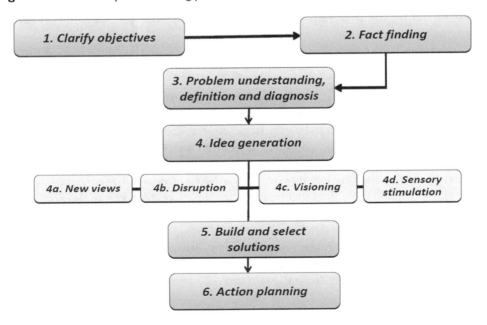

The following section provides step–by–step guidance to using this approach.

Step 1: clarify the business objectives or outcomes to be realised

- Working out the objectives that you must achieve and the constraints that you are operating under provides valuable insight on the problem and thus a clearer focus to address the challenge at hand.
- Some example questions that are useful to ask at each step in the process are summarised in Proforma 21A at the end of this chapter

Step 2: determine or hypothesise all facts that are pertinent to the problem to be solved

- Building a comprehensive understanding of relevant facts at the outset provides a more robust foundation for problem solving and ideation.
- However, time and commercial restrictions don't always make this possible and so there are two possible approaches that can be followed. The first is use who, what, when, where, why and how questions to uncover facts or generate hypotheses. The second is to conduct specific research to uncover relevant facts and insights. As discussed in Chapter 14 on Managing Market or Customer Research, it is usually worthwhile hypothesising issues and opportunities before conducting research, as it is likely to make the research process more focused, productive and cost-effective. **14▶**

Step 3a: define the problem and ensure that the correct question(s) is (are) being asked

- Accurate diagnosis of the causes and effects behind a problem is an essential part of successful problem-solving.
- Check that you are tackling the problem, not the symptoms of the problem. To do this, ask why the problem exists repeatedly until you get to the root of it.
- Where a problem appears to be very large, break it down into smaller parts. Keep on going until each part is achievable in its own right, or requires further research to be carried out.
- Start by writing the problem down on the left-hand side of a large sheet of paper. Next, write down the points that make up the next level of detail on the problem a little to the right of this, and continue until you are unable to write any more. Aim for three or four levels of detail.
- Finally, summarise the problem in as concise a form as possible. Robert W Olsen (4) suggests that the best way to do this is to write down a number of two-word problem statements and choose the best one.

Step 3b: identify the major factors that contribute to the problem

- Next, identify the factors that may contribute to the problem. Draw lines off the spine for each factor, and label it. These may be external forces, people influencers, the product itself, promotional factors, etc. Try to draw out as many possible factors as possible. Try using the fishbone analogy, as seen in Figure 21.2.

Step 3c: understand potential causes behind the problem

- For each of the factors you considered in step 3b, brainstorm possible causes of the problem that may be related to the factor. Show these as smaller lines coming off the 'bones' of the fish. Where a cause is large or complex, it may be best to break it down into sub-causes. Show these as lines coming off each cause line.

Step 3d: diagnose the root cause of the problem

- By this stage you should have a diagram showing all the possible causes of your problem. Depending on the complexity and importance of the problem, you can now investigate the most likely causes further. This may involve conducting further research to verify whether your assumptions are correct.
- Figure 21.2 shows a cause and effect (fish-bone) diagram exploring the reasons behind, and solutions for addressing declining sales for oil-based paint.

Figure 21.2 *Example cause and effect (fish-bone) diagram*

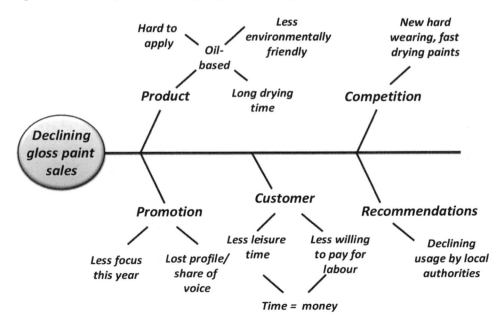

Step 4: generate a long list of ideas to solve your problem

- Having defined the problem that needs to be solved you can now start generating possible solutions.
- Use a range of different techniques and generate as many different ideas as possible. Don't just accept the first one that comes along. Even bad ideas may be the seeds of good ones. Remember, too, that other people will have different perspectives on the problem, and it will almost certainly be worth asking for opinions and ideas from your colleagues as part of this process.

Mind mapping

- 'Mind mapping' is a simple and easy-to-use tool to structure thinking and generate new ideas. It is easy-to-use on your own as well as with others.
- Start by taking a large piece of paper (A3 works well), and draw a circle in the middle of the page. Write the problem to be solved in the circle.
- Each subsequent idea that you generate should be written in a new circle surrounding the middle one. Where a new idea is related to an idea that is already written on the paper, it should be drawn in another circle and connected by a line to the original idea. Figure 21.3 shows a mind map (or spider diagram) for ideas to increase sales of gloss paint.

Figure 21.3 *Example mind map (or spider diagram)*

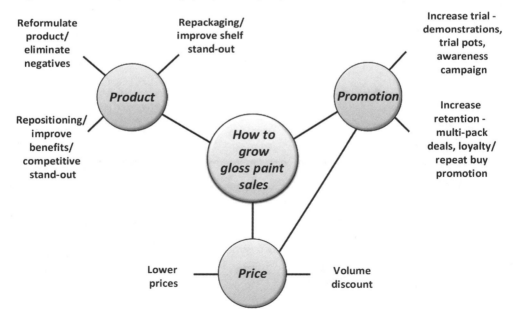

Storyboarding

- Storyboarding has been usefully adapted as a problem-solving tool for use in workshops by The Walt Disney Company (5).
- Once a problem has been articulated, it is written on a card or post-it note on a large wall. The technique has been applied to a wide range of problems in which the introduction of a visual element makes interconnections more readily apparent. Participants in the workshop then generate ideas to solve the problem and write down possible solutions on cards or post-its and stick these to the wall.
- As participants pin ideas to the wall, various alternatives to solving the problem emerge. The benefit of this approach versus traditional brainstorming is that it is highly participatory – participants can see the overall picture emerge and it also enables efficient use of time. There is no limit the level of detail to which the task can be undertaken.

Role of proformas

- Proformas can help focus and direct the idea generation and can be applied to both individual and group creative activities. Proformas should always be designed for a specific purpose eg product innovation, positioning. Example blank and completed proformas for a new service development challenge are shown at the end of Chapter 23 New Product and Service Development. **23**
- A number other creative tools and techniques are described in more detail later in this chapter.
- Some software products are also available to support group creativity. These software products help display ideas to a larger group for all to read. Time can also be saved capturing all the thoughts.

Step 5: select the best idea and develop it into an optimum solution

- This step is always important in later stages of ideation. The aim is to select the best idea and then develop it into the best possible solution. Alternatively, it may be worth examining and developing a number of ideas in detail before selecting the best one.
- In the first instance, your own team will be able to help assess ideas and build on the ideas of others. A number of techniques to do this are described below.
- When making decisions, bear in mind your own, or your organisation's goals. Alternatively create a list of criteria against which to judge the ideas. Often this makes decision making much easier.
- Finally, bear in mind that it is easy to shoot down ideas than develop them. You should be very careful not to be too quick to judge. It is also highly likely that customers, being more objective and dispassionate, will be able to improve on your ideas.

Hearts and Crosses

- Asking team members to vote for their favourite and least liked ideas is a simple way of reducing a long list to a short-list. The short-list can then be prioritised for further development.

'Snowballing'

- It is extremely difficult to create a 'perfect' output in a working session. It is usually better to reflect and iterate the output over an extended period of time.
- In the absence of lots of time, passing the draft output from one person or team to the next will enable others to add to and refine the ideas.
- Alternatively teams should present their ideas to the wider group and solicit challenges and builds.

'Sales pitch'

- Role playing a sales pitch – with teams taking it in turns to play the 'sales' team, prepare and give a 'sales pitch' while the other team play the buyers can also be powerful. It can provide real-life insights on flaws in arguments and flush out executional as well as strategic issues that need to be considered.
- A number of tools for assessing ideas are covered in Chapter 3 Strategy Development. **3**

Step 6: transform ideas into business, marketing and action plans

- Having identified the problem and created a solution to it, the final stage is to implement this solution. This involves not only development of a tangible output from your idea, but a robust plan to ensure that it makes financial sense.
- Documenting a business and marketing plan will also provide a further check that ideas have been thought through and an aid to gaining the necessary approvals. Documenting plans is also helpful in the event that an initiative does not proceed to provide a record of the reasoning should a similar initiative be considered in the future. Business and marketing/action planning is covered in more detail in Chapter 8 From Strategy to Delivery. **8**

 Creative tools and techniques

Four different types of tools and techniques are summarised in Figure 21.4. Once you have a broad grasp of the four types, you'll be able to devise many more tools of your own. Each tool or technique offers slightly different benefits and works best in slightly different circumstances. As a rule of thumb use at least one tool or technique of each type rather than several of just one type, as this will help you look at a problem in different ways and potentially generate more as well as richer ideas. However, the choice is yours, and what's right really depends on the precise problem that you are dealing with!

Figure 21.4 *Creative tools and techniques*

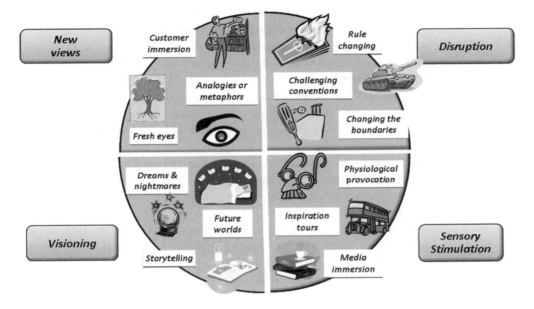

New views or insights on problems

The purpose of these techniques is to help reinterpret and view problems and situations in different and clear ways, thus making them more soluble.

Customer immersion

- From a marketing perspective, enabling creative or problem-solving workshop participants to see issues and opportunities through the eyes of customers is critical, as many have a tendency to revert to their natural 'corporate' types. This can be achieved by immersion in the customers' world through one and ideally more of the following:
  - Reviewing recently conducted customer research in the session itself.
  - Arranging for participants to view research prior to the workshop.
  - Setting participants a pre-task to talk to customers, for example, by phoning a friend or relative.
  - Using tools such as 'need-states and drivers' to help think from a consumer point of view and articulate needs (see Chapter 6 Customer Strategy).
  - Role-playing customers and acting out their lives. **6**

Analogies and metaphors

- WJJ Gordon, the founder of Synectics, developed the use of analogies and metaphors to creativity (6). This method is based on making the familiar odd and the odd familiar. The first step in the technique is to define the problem, and the second step is to re-express the problem using an analogy or metaphor. For example, if the problem is to paint a house quickly, an analogy might be to take a shower, or take the car to the car wash and so on. Steps three and four involve listing the various features of the analogous solutions and then considering how they could apply or be adapted to solve the original problem.
- Looking at problems from the perspective of someone else can help generate new insights and ideas. Consider looking at problems from the viewpoint of:
  - a child; children tend be highly simplistic; how could your problem be viewed and possibly be demystified?
  - a foreigner; what's important to someone from another country may not be the same as what's important to you, as they often have different cultural priorities – this may help shed light on the relative importance or unimportance of an issue as well as possible solutions
  - a person or company that you admire; many companies have a very clear set of beliefs about how to do things. Steve Jobs (Apple) would undoubtedly come up with different ideas to Stelios Haji-Ioannou (easyJet).
  - someone with restricted or enhanced range of senses; how would a hard of hearing or blind person view your problem? What senses could be accentuated to provide a better solution?
  - your own CEO or shareholders; what would ring their bells may be very different from what would ring yours!

Assets and competencies

- Thinking about the assets and competencies of a business is a useful way to generate ideas to grow it. Three steps are involved:
  - First, list all the assets of the organisation or brand (ie physical assets, resources) as well as intellectual or intangible assets such as brands and their associated customer equity.
  - Second, list all the competencies or skills of the organisation or brand.
  - Third, generate ideas for new customer applications for assets and competencies by making connections between the two.

Strengths and weaknesses

- Considering what is truly competitive or weak about a product, brand or organisation can be a powerful catalyst to idea generation (see Chapter 3 Strategy Development).

3

Barriers and bonds

- This technique can help articulate issues and opportunities, and concentrate the brainpower of a group to build stronger customer relationships.
- Firstly, list or create a vivid picture of the barriers that prevent and/or bonds that enable you to build stronger customer relationships.
- Barriers can be either tangible (eg physical product attributes) or intangible (eg customer attitudes) factors that inhibit or prevent products or services connecting with customers. Barriers should be clearly articulated and then they become easier to address.
- Bonds are rational and emotional drivers or triggers that can help build stronger customer relationships. Again, once they are clearly articulated they become easier to apply or leverage. Relationship building is worth considering in context of the customer relationship ladder (Chapter 6 Customer Strategy). **⑥**
- Once the barriers or bonds have been articulated, the energies of the group can be focused on generating ideas to help build stronger customer relationships.

Disruption or rule changing

These techniques help challenge and change the rules or conventions in a market to uncover new opportunities and ideas. They are particularly useful if sales growth has flattened or for those competing in stagnant markets, ie where the competitive dynamics have remained static or stagnant for a long time. They will help you 'zig' when your competitors are 'zagging'!

Rule changers

- Rule changers in other sectors can be a great source of inspiration. Think of some parallel markets to your own and draw up a list of organisations or brands that have succeeded by changing the rules in the market place.
- Then make a list of the strategies they have employed to succeed. Also consider how customers encounter the organisation or brand to provide insights on how their strategies have been executed.

Challenging conventions

- Most markets have an unwritten set of rules by which competitors and customers abide. The purpose of this technique is to articulate those rules, conventions, or deeply held beliefs and then brainstorm potential new conventions or beliefs that could transform the market.

Changing the boundaries

- The purpose of this technique is to fuel new creative ideas by determining and then changing or removing the boundaries or constraints under which you are working. Ask yourself what would or could happen if the boundaries were removed.

Visioning the future and dreaming

These techniques help anticipate and create rich pictures of the future. This is useful to enable longer-term forward planning and devise more 'future-proof' strategies. They are particularly useful for organisations that tend to have a more short-term approach to planning as well as those competing in fast-moving markets. Dreaming or storytelling exercises can be particularly useful in helping to generate rich emotional ideas for positioning products and services.

Dreams and nightmares

- This technique involves using the 'subconscious' to generate ideas. Ernest Hemingway was famed for using this technique whenever he was short of ideas for his stories. By deliberately relaxing and drifting off to sleep, Hemingway recreated a state of dreaming.
- Close your eyes, relax, and drift off into sleep. In the absence of a moderator, to prevent you really drifting off to sleep, do as Hemingway did – hold marbles in your hand and work in a room with a wooden floor!

Future worlds

- This is a projective technique to understand and extrapolate the forces affecting your organisation and use them to imagine alternative views of the future. Building and using scenarios can help explore what the future might look like and likely effects of living in it. Energy companies, more than most companies, need to take a long view of the future, and Shell (7) has been creating global scenarios for over thirty years.
- Initially, create a long list of forces and then cluster them into related groups, ie groups of forces that have similar effects on your business. In undertaking this exercise, you will discover that some forces act in one direction only, eg the ageing population, whereas other forces may have opposing effects – so called 'critical uncertainties'.
- Shell's latest global scenario to 2025 explores the forces of market incentives, communities and coercion or regulation by the state (see Figure 21.5). In this model, the three forces, two wins and one loss, drive towards different objectives: efficiency, social cohesion and justice and security. While all societies often aspire to all three objectives, the forces display elements of mutual exclusiveness. The scenarios created therefore explore the dilemmas involved in pursuit of the objectives.
- Finally, through visualisation of, and immersion in, the worlds you have created, it is possible to hypothesise the effects this world would have on customers, your products or services and organisation as a whole. With a better understanding of the effects of the forces it is then possible to devise strategies to compete in those worlds. For example, in Shell's 'Open Doors' world, they postulate "'Built-in' security and compliance certification, regulatory harmonisation, mutual recogni-

tion, independent media, voluntary best-practice codes, and close links between investors and civil society encourage cross-border integration and virtual value chains. Networking skills and *superior reputation management are essential"*.

Figure 21.5 *Shell global scenarios to 2025*

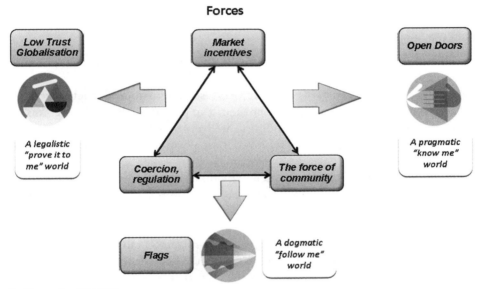

Shell International Ltd 2005

Storytelling or 'imagineering'

- The use of storytelling is an important element of the Disney approach to creativity. According to Walt Disney *"If you can dream it, you can do it."* The beauty of storytelling is that it can engage and unify teams and provide a wonderful catalyst to idea generation.
- Challenged to build a winter ski resort in the sunny climes of Florida, the team turned to storytelling and created a tale based on a blizzard (8). It went like this. 'An entrepreneur came along to build a ski resort. He did very well until the weather returned to normal, melting the snow and turning the ski runs into rushing waterfalls. But the waterfalls were then turned into … water rides for adventurous athletes!' Based on this story the Disney architects created the water park, Blizzard Beach.

Sensory stimulation

These techniques help inspire new ideas by providing new experiences and stimulating the five senses: sight, smell, sound, touch and taste. They are particularly useful for helping to solve innovation challenges.

Inspiration tours

- Shopping or experiential tours; can be useful as a warm-up exercise or to provide rich inspiration for new products, service developments or positioning challenges. Arrange a tour around shops or other places of interest relevant to the task at hand. Touring inspirational businesses can be a powerful catalyst to innovation and culture change challenges.

Media mountain

- Different types of media can also provide a rich source of inspiration for a wide range of challenges. Here are some ideas:
- Films, videos, image boards and Internet-based photo libraries such as gettyimages.com, flickr.com and istockphoto.com can provide additional insight, inspiration and contextual understanding as well as bringing to life desirable (and undesirable) emotions; useful for innovation, positioning and name generation challenges
- Magazines, newspapers, books such as dictionaries and Internet search engines such as Google.com and Wikipedia.org are also useful when generating names.

Physiological provocation

- Sensory stimulus (sight, sound, taste, touch and smell) can be very useful in evoking emotions and in revealing new potential benefits for products and services. Choose stimuli from parallel markets that are relevant to the task at hand. For example, olfactory stimulus can be useful in food and toiletry markets and kinaesthetic stimulus can be useful in fashion and design-led markets.

 Proforma 21A Creative problem-solving process

Here are some questions to help guide your thinking:

Step 1: clarify objectives

- What would we like to accomplish or achieve?
- What are our goals, as yet unfulfilled?
- What would we like to do better?
- What would we like to happen?
- In what ways are we inefficient?
- What would we like to organise in a better way?
- What ideas would we like to get going?
- What relationship would we like to improve?
- What would we like to get others to do?
- What takes too long?

- What is wasted?
- What barriers or bottlenecks exist?
- What do we wish we had more time for?
- What do we wish we had more money for?
- What makes us angry, tense or anxious?
- What do we complain about?

See Chapter 5 Setting Objectives and Measuring Marketing Performance for more insights on setting objectives.   **5** ▶

Step 2: fact finding

Use who, what, when, where, why and how questions to uncover facts or generate hypotheses:

- Who is or should be involved?
- What is or is not happening?
- What evidence do we have?
- When does this or should this happen?
- Where does or doesn't this occur?
- Why does it or doesn't it happen?
- How does it or doesn't it occur?

Step 3: problem understanding, definition and diagnosis
List alternative definitions of the problem.

One principle of creative problem-solving is that the definition of a problem will determine the nature of the solutions. It often helps to think laterally about the problem and find ways to reframe it. In this step, begin each statement with "*In what ways might we (or I)...?" or "How do we (or I)?*"

- What is the real problem?
- What is the main objective?
- What do we really want to accomplish?
- What's stopping us from achieving our goal?
- What is the barrier that we need to overcome?
- What are we really afraid of?

Step 4: idea generation

This is where a variety of creative or problem-solving techniques can be used. Ideas or solutions are freely proposed without criticism or evaluation, for each of the problem definitions accepted in the second stage.

Step 5: solution development and selection

There are five related steps to this stage:

1. List and agree criteria for evaluating ideas/solutions generated
2. The ideas are evaluated (creating an evaluation matrix or proforma – see decision-making in Chapter 3 Strategy Development). ❸
3. One or more of the best ideas are selected
4. Identify any issues that are likely to inhibit the effectiveness of the proposed solution
5. Address the issues one by one and refine the proposed solution

Criteria might include:

- How practical/easy is it to implement?
- How expensive is it to implement?
- Are the materials and technology available?
- Are the costs acceptable?
- How appealing is it to customers; what demand will it generate?
- How much will it build our brand?
- Is it legal?
- How risky is it?

Step 6: action planning

This step involves taking the idea and turning it into a concrete business, marketing and action plan – a plan containing specific steps to be taken and a timetable for taking them. This is covered in detail in Chapter 8 From Strategy to Delivery. ❽

Key points to remember

1. Creativity is neither a wacky art nor the preserve of the few. It can be a disciplined science and mastered by all. It is a thinking skill that can be applied to a wide range of marketing and other problems that are faced by organisations. Creativity should be championed for what it is by the marketing director.

2. Ensuring that your product, brand and project teams include a mix of right- and left-brained thinkers can enable more effective problem-solving.

3. Creativity thrives in the right environment so create the right conditions for success. Allow sufficient time to orientate and help groups work well together. Help them get away from the phones.

4. Group creative sessions need planning and orchestration. Don't allow conflict or mayhem to break out. Choose an experienced facilitator to design and run a creative session. The design of the session should take into account the business challenge that you face and the participants' personalities in order to optimise the cultural dynamics and efficiency of the group.

5. Great ideas rarely happen by magic or chance. Design a rigorous approach to explore problems from all angles and generate lots of ideas. Choose techniques that are best suited to solve your problem and favour using different types of techniques rather than just one.

6. Great ideas need nurturing and building to turn them into great solutions. Challenge and build better solutions by working together as a team, allowing sufficient time and involving customers.

22 Restoring Growth

Think Twice – Céline Dion (1994)

In this chapter you will learn:

- *When and how to get personally involved*
- *How to understand and diagnose problems*
- *How to restore growth to an underperforming product or business*

Most organisations comprise a number of high-performing as well as some poor-performing business units or product lines. As marketing director, you will be responsible for maximising the return on investment (ROI) and sustaining growth from your portfolio as a whole. Occasionally you will need to address underperformance and restore the profitable growth. This is, however, one of the hardest and possibly highest risk tasks you may have to undertake. It will challenge the creative skills of your team and can be a career maker or breaker. So make sure that you think twice. This chapter provides advice and guidance on how to do that.

Why bother?

There are no benefits in working for underperforming businesses. Shareholders require a return on their investments. When these are not forthcoming, this can rapidly lead to cost-cutting demands. Staff morale can suffer, and in turn, this can lead to high staff turnover. This makes growth even harder to deliver and if you are in a team that's losing, you lose. As marketing director you will need to act quickly and expediently to devise a plan to deal with any under-performance.

The transformation process

There are three steps to transforming an under-performing business, shown in Figure 22.1.

Figure 22.1 *The transformation process*

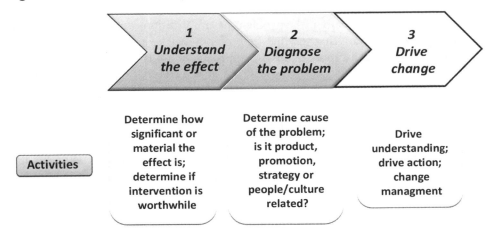

Step 1: understand the effect

The first step is to assess how significant or material the effect is in relation to your portfolio as a whole. As time and resources are precious, there will be a limit to how much time or money should be spent on a product or business that is immaterial in context of the whole. In this instance, do not get involved, or delegate responsibility to deal with the issue. Only if the problem is material for the business should you invest significant time in solving it.

Step 2: diagnose the problem

The second step is to diagnose the cause of the problem as quickly as possible. In the first instance, ask questions and form your own opinion of the cause. In so doing you should also gauge the competence of your team to solve the problem.

Some questions to ask:

- Is the problem a one-off, recurring or ongoing?
- Is the problem caused by an internal operational failure or external market force?
- Is the problem product related, promotion related or strategy related?
- Is the problem people or process related? Does it trace to mismanagement or a cultural malaise?
- What plans do we have in place to deal with the issue?

Your investigations and the nature of the answers to your questions will enable you to assess the degree to which the problem is understood by the management team, as well as their ability to deal with it. The scale, complexity and political sensitivities of the problem will affect the ability of your team to develop a solution. Be aware that they may need help, especially if the problem has implications outside the marketing department. Also be aware that solving the problem may be beyond the capability of your team, in which case a more hands-on approach or alternative resource strategy will be needed.

Consultants can be useful in getting to the root of problems as they tend to be objective and apolitical. They can also be a useful conduit for change and put the problem in a spotlight. You should also consider conducting research among different types of customers as well as potential ones – occasionals, loyals, lapsed customers and those who have never tried your products. Comparing the responses between the different audiences can be a powerful way to diagnose problems (see Figure 22.2).

Figure 22.2 *Using customers to diagnose problems*

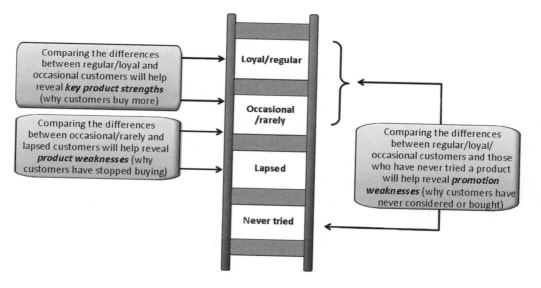

You should also be alert to:

- any mismatches between your product and customer needs – this could indicate that your overall marketing strategy is in need of an overhaul
- the size of the potential customer base – this could indicate that there is limited scope for further growth, and that an alternative strategy should be considered
- issues that go beyond the marketing department, such as the degree to which the entire business is aligned and committed to a common goal, and the degree to which the culture and processes of the organisation help or hinder growth

Step 3: drive change

What you need to do to drive change will depend on the effect of the business problem and your judgement on the abilities of your team to solve the problem on their own. If the problem is less significant, a lighter touch will be more appropriate. If the problem is material, you will need to be more directive. A three-step approach to intervention is recommended:

- Drive understanding – in the first instance ensure that the cause of the problem is understood. Ask your team to prepare a paper or presentation to discuss the issue and recommend options to deal with it. Where there are implications for the organisation at large you will also need a strategy to help the broader management team understand the issues you have identified. Sometimes it will be helpful for them to gain first-hand evidence of the problem – perhaps by observing or taking part in customer research. Inviting fellow board members to respond to questions from discontented customers can be a powerful way to help them understand and start to appreciate the need for change.

- Drive action – if the problem is largely confined within your department, ask your team to create a plan to address the problem. If the problem reaches outside your department, set up a task force or project team. Agree clear objectives and enable clear access to relevant senior management. Ensure the plan is properly documented to facilitate discussion and agreement to action.

- Strengthen management – if the problem is beyond the capability or experience of your current managers, they may need to be replaced. Alternatively, second or co-opt other managers on a project basis. If you plan to set up a task force, include representatives from relevant functional areas.

Success factors to restore growth

Pay attention to staff concerns

Being the closest to customers, your people should have a good idea of what is really going on. There may be many reasons beyond the obvious why the business is failing, and you owe the business as well as your staff a duty of care to understand them. Be aware also that, if a business or product line is failing, the staff may have low morale and be concerned for their own wellbeing. Intervene as little as possible, or as much as needed, to effect change without disempowering or demotivating the team.

Ensure robust understanding on which to base investment decisions

Make sure you understand the reasons behind a performance decline from the end customer and trade customer point of view. Use research to fill any gaps in knowledge.

Use research to explore upside potential and opportunities at the same time both to save money and time.

Beware of diagnoses that suggest only promotions are at fault

Poor performing promotions can cover up more fundamental problems such as the products themselves. Long term performance decline is more likely to result from more fundamental elements of the mix and changes in competitive relativities. These variables need to be understood.

Manage the short term and the long term

When the pressure is on, make sure you manage the short term, otherwise there won't be a long term. Promotion and price activity will normally be the fastest means to boost short term sales.

Focus on the best trade as well as end customers as these will be the ones that you have most to lose by losing. Use creativity to avoid creating a hostage to fortune. Devise loyalty initiatives to prevent lapsing and help protect revenue. This will also help alleviate any issues and buy time to create better and longer lasting solutions.

Bear in mind that if a business or product line is failing, further promotion investment may not deliver long term return. Sometimes it is better to cut your losses rather than be held back by, or correct, previous mistakes.

Challenge 'sacred cows'

Dealing with long-standing decline is likely to be harder and may require more far-reaching and deep-rooted change. Fresh eyes are often needed to both spot and slay sacred cows (something considered to be exempt from criticism). As a new marketing director you will be best able to do this. Alternatively, transfer colleagues from other areas or bring in outside help.

Consider all the alternatives, from doing nothing to re-launching, repositioning and divestment. Consider new business models, as well as practices and procedures.

Only when you are confident that you have a great product is it usually worth substantial promotion investment to generate a trial and kick-start renewed growth. Test your way to higher investment levels to ensure that your efforts deliver the necessary returns.

Key points to remember

1. Sustained profitable growth is the lifeblood of most organisations. This is a key role and a necessary preoccupation of the marketing director.

2. Invest your time on maintaining the health of the overall business and don't spend disproportionate time or money in arresting the decline of minor lines.

3. Ensure a proportionate response to dealing with problems. The larger the problem, the more deep-rooted it is likely to be. Establish task forces to deal with significant problems. If the problem goes beyond the confines of the marketing department, co-opt representatives from other functions to help diagnose and then solve the problem.

4. As the key creative department in the organisation, it is your responsibility to think the unthinkable in order to identify possible solutions and address the problems you have identified.

5. Pay attention to managing the short term and seek out quick wins to maintain sales and profits. Remember, if you don't manage the short term there may not be a long term. Whilst promotions may not help you manage the long term they can buy you time to manage the short term.

6. Make sure your product or service is competitive before you invest in building significant trial and sales. Test your way to higher investment levels.

23 New Product and Service Development

Step It Up – Stereo MCs (1992)

In this chapter you will learn:

- *The benefits of product innovation*
- *Pitfalls to avoid*
- *The strategic role for innovation*
- *Alternative innovation strategies and types of innovation*
- *How to create a successful new product or service*

According to research conducted by the US Product Development and Management Association (PDMA) between 1990 and 2004, new product development success rates have consistently been in the region of around 58% (1). On another measure, the 'best' performing organisations in new product development are twice as successful as the 'rest'. The best performers require only four ideas to generate one winner compared with over nine for the rest. So for those marketing directors who want to 'step it up' and ensure greater new product development success, this chapter is designed to help you.

Why bother innovating new products?

Innovation is a key driver of growth and can play – and has played – a substantial role in restoring or maintaining the growth of many organisations. Research by Kuczmarksi and Associates (2) reinforces the role of new products as a growth driver. In a study of 11,000 products, the strategic roles of the products were rated "important" or "very important" in the following order:

- attract new customers or a market (93%)
- gain or maintain competitive advantage (91%)
- retain customers (88%)
- fill a growth or profit gap (73%)
- arrest margin erosion (56%)
- utilise a new technology (31%)

It is also significant that respondents did not see strategic advantage in merely adopting a new technology, only when they could also attract new customers.

Pitfalls to avoid

Understanding what the enemies of innovation are will help you anticipate and deal with them:

- Lack of customer understanding – when analysing the reasons for new product failure in 1992, US innovation expert Dr. Robert G. Cooper (3) identified that insufficient or faulty market or customer research was evident in 75% of cases. In a further 55% of cases, he also identified that test marketing had not been undertaken or had been done poorly.

- Lack of brand understanding – both real and perceived brand strengths can provide a basis for competitive advantage, as even unreal or latent strengths are true in customers' eyes and can be nurtured and developed. Products that ignore their inbuilt strengths may not only fail to stand out but may fail to resonate or connect with consumers.

- Lack of discipline – while some rely on an intuitive approach to new product development, this is extremely and increasingly high risk, both financially and for the executives concerned. Moreover, the power of innovation is not in the thing, but in the process. At diversified technology company 3M, for example, innovation is defined as a process that creates products that *create a new basis of competition*. Successful innovation requires a deliberate, planned and rigorous process to guide product development from beginning to end.

- Procrastination or lack of drive – as a result of increasingly fickle customers, and in increasingly fast moving markets, product life cycles and are getting shorter and shorter. Those that take too long over product development or fail to grasp opportunities when they appear will lose out to those that move quickly. Effective management is essential to maintain momentum in new product development.

- Cultural impediments – most organisations tend to evolve 'ways of thinking' and 'doing things' over time. While initially beneficial, they often become 'hard wired' into business processes and can eventually become a liability. Potential cultural impediments include the size and nature of an organisation. Some large organisations are centralised, overly controlling and bureaucratic, thus making decision making unwieldy and slow. Other organisations may be run by autocrats, or spawn fiefdoms. In these organisations, good ideas can be overlooked or stifled through the force of personality or cultural myopia. Think how many times you've heard the mantra – *"we've always done it this way."* Thomas Watson, chairman of IBM, was famously myopic in 1943, when he said *"I think there is a global market for maybe five computers."* The film industry was equally so about embracing video technology in the 1980s. The lesson is that cultural impediments are sometimes hard to spot and overcome from within an organisation. Sometimes an external force is needed to spot and facilitate change, and as Abbie Hoffman (4) said, *"Sacred cows make the tastiest hamburgers"*!

- Lack of creativity – it is very difficult to generate good ideas and far too easy to kill ideas at birth. To a point, successful product development is a numbers game. Success requires disciplined creative thinking (see Chapter 21 Creativity and Problem Solving) and the creation of sufficiently large numbers of ideas, and to make allowance for some ideas that will fall at some hurdles. It also requires effort to be placed on nurturing ideas to ensure that enough will reach later development stages. **(21)▶**

- Lack of time – this means lack of thinking time. While ideas can be generated in short time periods, it is likely they will be paid scant attention, or masked by the pressures of business as usual. Bear in mind that great ideas always take time to form and flourish. 3M, for example, took four years to develop and bring to market their now ubiquitous 'Post It' notes. Push back on pressures to succeed overnight, and manage and set realistic expectations.

- Fear – risk averseness is often embedded in organisational attitudes and processes (see Chapter 27 Culture Change and Brand Delivery). The nature of risk in itself can also lead to emotional rather than rational debate, and less rather than more considered decision making. Consider how to embrace rather than fear risks – devise rigorous processes to help assess and manage risk through product development processes. **(27)▶**

Strategic role of innovation

The role that innovation plays, or should play, in your organisation will depend on the industry sector in which you compete as well as your aspirations and capabilities.

For example, in fast-moving consumer goods – FMCG – and technology markets innovation plays a significant role. Products in these categories eg toothpaste and software, have a short life span, and a high proportion of brand sales are attributable to new products. Figures 23.1 and 23.2 summarise the types of innovation strategy that can be employed.

NEW PRODUCT AND SERVICE DEVELOPMENT **293**

Figure 23.1 *Innovation strategies*

Alternative innovation strategies	Implications
First mover vs follower	First movers have the first chance to attract and retain consumers; however, they must also bear the costs and risks inherent in creating the market. It is therefore important to try and protect the product to maximise the time available for exclusive sale and ensure excellence in implementation. Followers can often 'piggy back' on the product development work and investment borne by the first movers. Positioning is critical for followers. Positionings can be devised to cannibalise the first mover brand or to attract new users and create new market segments (probably most important if you own both brands!)
Existing or new brand name	As discussed in earlier chapters, products and brands must be distinctive and appealing to drive purchasing. Launching 'new to the world' products under a new brand name is likely to enhance stand-out. 'Me too' products, especially if part of a range, are likely to be more competitive if launched under the umbrella of an existing brand.
Step change vs incremental change	Innovation can be considered on a scale from modest or incremental change to large or step change. It can also be considered in terms of continuous change or not. There are benefits in adopting all of these strategies and they are not mutually exclusive. Step change innovation usually presents a greater challenge to an organisation, especially if it involves being a first mover and represents a step change in a market. Equally the rewards can be commensurately greater. Incremental change usually involves lower cost and risk. The pace of change in some markets, such as FMCGs and technology, demands continuous innovation. It is important to anticipate or unlock future consumer needs in order to try to develop products and services that will remain competitive in the foreseeable future.

Figure 23.2 *Types of innovation*

Type	Benefits	Examples
New to the world	Sits at the tip of the innovation continuum; new to the world products often comprise new technologies or packaging and offer a competitive advantage over alternative products.	Launched in 2000, Creative's Zen portable media player pre-empted Apple's iPod by one year. Apple is nevertheless outright market leader, largely through effective marketing, and despite disputes over some US patent rights (which are based on a first to invent, not file, basis.)
New to the organisation	Carry an additional risk to the organisation concerned as they demand additional resources, skills, systems and know-how.	Mars' entry into ice cream was high risk but ultimately very successful. Risks can be mitigated by using third-party producers.
Line extension	At the lower end of the risk scale, line extensions can simply add new variants to a product range. At the higher end of the risk spectrum, they can take brands into new categories.	While Caterpillar started out as an earth-moving equipment manufacturer, the brand has now extended to clothing and footwear. The unusual nature of the extension underlines the benefits of building a brand and how values can be transferred across categories.
Product renovation or improvement	Renovation can take many forms (eg new formulae, packaging or design) from the simple to the more complex and costly.	Software almost continuously adds new features to improve functionality and usability.
Brand repositioning	Promoting new benefits can attract new consumers and help enter new markets.	Milton Sterilising Fluid, used for sterilising baby feeding utensils, is now promoted and used for surface cleaning and in food preparation.
Process improvement	Sits at the bottom of the innovation continuum; finding better ways to produce products can contribute to customer benefits and reduce costs.	Many South East Asian economies, often characterised by low labour costs, have created a national competitive advantage in copying Western products.

Team questions

To help determine what the strategic role of innovation currently is and should be in your organisation, consider the following questions.

- Thinking about your current position relative to your competitors; are you in a position of advantage or disadvantage? (If you are market leader you probably have most to gain by leading the market and most to lose by not doing so)
- What's your innovation track record?
- What innovation competencies/skills/technologies/resources have you got?
- What proportion of your annual revenue and profit comes from new products?
- Is this higher or lower than your competitors?
- What is the typical lifecycle of your products?
- How does this compare to your competitors?
- Is there a shared understanding and belief about the role of product innovation?
- If at a disadvantage, what could you do differently?
- Should you be a first mover or a follower?
- Should you be truly unique or an imitator ('me-too')?

 Success factors for innovation

There are a number of criteria for developing successful products and services. These are born of both experience and accumulated research evidence.

Ensure products meet a need

The most vital consideration is that new products must meet a need. For new to the world or step change products and services, needs may need to be entirely new or unmet by existing products and services. Sometimes, new needs may simply comprise several different but not previously related needs.

When new technology products fail it is often because they do not meet a need. So often, new technologies are simply new features trying to find a need. For example, the Sony Walkman was initially rejected by consumers because they could not see the need for a portable tape recorder when they had one at home. It was only when the product was positioned to help change consumers' moods or environment that it unlocked a new need and then sales took off.

Ensure products stand out

Research conducted by Booz Allen in 1992 revealed that 98% of products that were clearly superior and delivered a unique benefit, ultimately succeeded. While this fact

Best practice

The story of how Lockheed Martin developed the US's first operational jet fighter at the time when the US were being drawn into World War II provides inspiration on how to organise effective innovation teams (5). The now famous Skunk Works® was created in 1943 and they created a prototype fighter in just 143 days. This compares with the more usual ten years for aircraft and cars today. What allowed Skunk Works® to operate so effectively and efficiently was a young engineer called Clarence L 'Kelly' Johnson's unconventional organisational approach. He broke the rules, challenging the current bureaucratic system that stifled innovation and hindered progress. His philosophy is spelled out in the '14 Practices and Rules' his team followed. Many of these rules are still considered valid today. These are reproduced below.

Figure 23.3 *Clarence 'Kelly' Johnson's 14 Skunk Works Rules*

1. The Skunk Works manager must be delegated practically complete control of his programme in all respects. He should report to a division president or higher.
2. Strong but small project offices must be provided both by the military and industry.
3. The number of people having any connection with the project must be restricted in an almost vicious manner. Use a small number of good people (10-25% compared to the so-called normal systems).
4. A very simple drawing and drawing release system with great flexibility for making changes must be provided.
5. There must be a minimum number of reports required but important work must be recorded thoroughly.
6. There must be a monthly cost review covering not only what has been spent and committed but also projected costs to the conclusion of the programme. Don't have the books 90 days late and don't surprise the customer with sudden overruns.
7. The contractor must be delegated and must assume more than normal responsibility to get good vendor bids for subcontract on the project. Commercial bid procedures are very often better than military ones.
8. The inspection system as currently used by the Skunk Works, which has been approved by both the Air Force and Navy, meets the intent of existing military requirements and should be used on new projects. Push more basic inspection responsibility back to subcontractors and vendors. Don't duplicate so much inspection.
9. The contractor must be delegated the authority to test his final product in flight. He can and must test it in the initial stages. If he doesn't, he rapidly loses his competency to design other vehicles.
10. The specifications applying to the hardware must be agreed to well in advance of contracting. The Skunk Works practice of having a specification section stating clearly which important military specification items will not knowingly be complied with and reasons, is highly recommended.
11. Funding a programme must be timely so that the contractor doesn't have to keep running to the bank to support government projects.
12. There must be mutual trust between the military project organisation and the contractor, with very close co-operation and liaison on a day-to-day basis. This cuts down misunderstanding and correspondence to an absolute minimum.
13. Access by outsiders to the project and its personnel must be strictly controlled by appropriate security measures.
14. Due to the fact that only a few people will be used in engineering and most other areas, ways must be provided to reward good performance by pay not based on the number of personnel supervised.

is a re-expression of basic marketing principles, many fail to remember this simple point!

Executional excellence

In highly competitive markets it is increasingly difficult to capture attention let alone prompt purchasing. Products and services can fail to connect for a myriad of strategic and executional reasons. The devil is in the detail. Pay attention to product positioning and communication nuances as well as product functionality or design. All elements of the promotion and product mix must signal this new product is distinctive and appealing to generate interest, trial and repeat purchasing.

Institutionalise innovation

The most successful innovators, including Diageo, Procter & Gamble and Lockheed Martin, have instituted very rigorous processes to manage innovation. Some also manage innovation separately from the day-to-day business or employ champions to drive innovation through their organisations and ensure that it is given the necessary attention and resources.

 ## Success factors for service innovation

Services are very different to products and three additional factors will help ensure successful service innovation.

Make the intangible tangible

Services are different in being intangible – they do not have a physical form. It is therefore even more vital to bring them to life, in other words, make them tangible so consumers can react to them. Stimulus that summarises the offer – and its benefits in writing and with pictures – is vital.

Create service packages to simplify the complexity

There are typically many more variables involved in service innovation than product innovation. Variables usually include a variety of detailed characteristics, features and benefits, as well as personality traits. Dealing with this additional complexity is a significant research and development challenge. It can be overcome by designing services as packages or 'bundles' of elements to meet the differing needs of various customer segments. This reduces the complexity into manageable and comprehensible offers. Expressing and visualising the offers in packaged form also enables the relative appeal to be assessed and the key drivers to be identified.

Identify and highlight differentiating features

Service features also play a crucial role in differentiating an offer, and a mechanism is needed to decide which should be put in the spotlight. Importance needs to be given to creating, exploring and understanding the relative appeal of a potentially large range of individual features, as well as the role that they play in the overall service package. Creating lists of features (Figure 23.8) and assessing the relative appeal of the different ones can be useful to sort the wheat from the chaff. The list should comprise brief descriptions of all of the component parts of the offer and the benefits that they offer customers. Customers can then assess the relative appeal of the components by ranking or rating them on a predetermined scale (6).

 **Innovation process**

A rigorous process is vital to manage new product development risks and help ensure product success. Another survey of new product development conducted by the PDMA in 1991 found that for every 100 serious ideas or concepts, around 73 are screened out at an early stage in the development process and just 27 enter the more costly development process. Of the products that are developed, 12 are launched and nine succeed. Viewed this way (Figure 23.4) those products that have been success-fully developed and nurtured through a rigorous product development process have a much greater chance of success, with around three quarters of products being launched in contrast with around 58% overall. Of course, as costs mount throughout the product development process, risks clearly increase. It is therefore very important to manage the risks throughout the process and invest in the early stages in order to identify ideas that merit investment and screen out those that don't.

Figure 23.4 *Attrition rate of new product ideas*

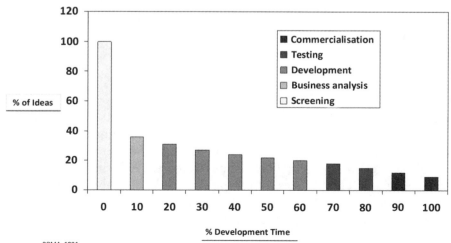

PDMA 1991

Let's now look in more detail at a process to develop new products (see Figure 23.5). Throughout the process there are gates at which certain criteria must be met in order for products to move onto the next step in the process. Strict adherence to the gates and associated qualification criteria are essential to manage the risks involved in developing new products. While this is presented as a linear process of 12 steps, this is often far from the reality. Expect more 'to-ing and fro-ing'. Think about the process as a funnel with screens or filters at each stage. Aim to generate lots of ideas in the early stages so you can ensure that a handful of them are funnelled through to the end. Use this process as a checklist to challenge your own in-house processes or even create one from scratch.

Figure 23.5 *Example innovation or gate process*

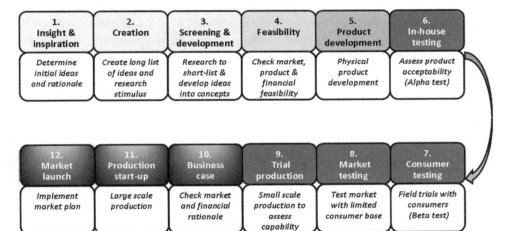

Let's go through the steps in turn:

Step 1: insight and inspiration

This initial stage involves committing resources to identify insights and inspiration for new products. In other words you need to identify initial new product, service or business ideas, and obtain sufficient evidence that there is genuine demand potential for the idea. There are several possible start-points for innovation although these should ultimately converge:

- insight-led innovation – whereby innovation is inspired by identifying a new or unmet customer need
- brand-led innovation – whereby innovation is needed to build a brand (ie reinforce brand competitive advantage or image)

- technology-led innovation – whereby a new technology or ingredient provides the basis for a unique or 'protectable' new product or service

Chapter 14 on Managing Market or Customer Research elaborates on techniques that can be used to identify insights. Proformas are useful to articulate insights as this ensures they provide a robust foundation for ideation. Proformas 23A and 23B at the end of this chapter summarise the information that you should be looking to identify.   **14▶**

Step 2: creation

This step involves taking the insights generated at step 1 and using them to generate ideas. As it is far too easy to shoot down ideas it is vital to consider and explore all the nuances inherent in ideas at this stage. Chapter 21 on Creativity and Problem Solving outlines some ways you can do this.   **21▶**

Ideas should be developed or nurtured away from the stress of a workshop situation and over a period of days and weeks rather than just a few hours. Empower multiple teams to provide extra creative brainpower. After at least two or three weeks have elapsed, the teams should then be combined in a working session to share and build ideas. By the end of this stage you should aim to generate a significant number of ideas in the form of rich stimulus, say, a hundred at least.

It is also important to bring the ideas to life as stimuli, as this helps make them more concrete and comprehensible. In turn, this enables the ideas to be explored, scrutinised, challenged and developed with your colleagues and ultimately customers. Figures 23.6, 23.7 and 23.8 illustrate three types of stimulus and the benefits they provide.

Figure 23.6 *Example research stimulus – product/service descriptions*

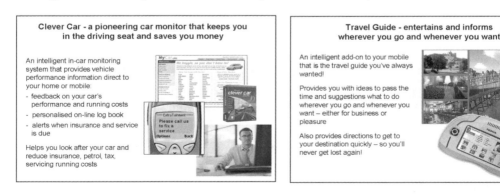

- Rough visuals and brief descriptions of what the product or service does and what makes them different – they are useful to gauge relative product or service appeal and stand-out and understand what drives or inhibits appeal. These need to be produced in a comparative form and clear so they can be easily understood and assessed.

Figure 23.7 *Example research stimulus - 'brandcepts'*

- 'Brandcepts' – akin to simple press or poster advertising – are useful to express and explore emotional territory that products or brands can occupy and help verify that insights on which products are founded are sound. This stimulus is very powerful in exploring and determining optimum combinations of rational and emotional benefits as well as tone of voice – all of the key constituents of brands.

Figure 23.8 *Example research stimulus – feature lists*

List of Features

1. Available to play Monday to Friday
2. Play on your mobile phone
3. Play on the radio
4. Play through the Internet/email
5. Play with your favourite newspaper
6. Play via red button on tv
7. Chance to win £1k every day
8. Jackpot rolls-over and increases if it isn't won

9. Playing everyday guarantees a win once a week
10. More times you enter in the week the greater prize you can win
11. Enter once a week with a chance to win something every day
12. Two chances to win; every day and also at the end of the week
13. Chance to win cash and non cash prizes eg cars, holidays
14. Themed around special occasions eg the World Cup, Valentines Day
15. Themed around celebrities
16. Linked to a daily TV game show

- 'Feature lists' – long lists of product features – are useful to explore and gauge the relative importance of features and provide insights on which 'bundles' work best.

Step 3: screening and development

Once the product stimulus has been created, creative customer research (see Chapter 14 Managing Markets or Customer Research) can be conducted both to develop and screen ideas. This will help refine and turn the ideas into more robust concepts, as well as potentially generate more ideas. Using research to develop rather than just evaluate ideas is really a 'no-brainer' – it shouldn't cost any more money. You just need to choose your agencies with a little more care and find those who can add value throughout the process.

14

Step 4: Feasibility

This step involves assessing the broad feasibility of the idea. This should cover customer needs, market gap and opportunity, product technical assessment and financial potential and risk. The customer research should confirm whether there is customer need or want for the new product and how competitive it will be. Market and competitor analysis should confirm the nature of the market opportunity. The product technical assessment should confirm whether the product can be built and if so at what cost. Combining the customer, market potential and cost data should enable you to assess initial financial potential and risks.

Step 5: product development

The product development stage is potentially the most time-consuming step of the process and more expensive in involving resources outside the marketing department. A favourable feasibility study should enable you to justify the commitment of resources to develop the actual physical product and make a more informed assessment of risks that may need covering at a later stage.

Step 6: in-house testing

Once product samples become available, they should be tested in the safe and relatively low-cost confines of your organisation. Try the product yourself, as well as seek inputs from a diverse range of colleagues. In this respect, your colleagues act as proxies for customers. Approach the task of gleaning feedback from your colleagues in the same way as customer research, for example, through a mini questionnaire. This will help ensure that your findings are as rigorous as possible. Both first impressions, as well as insights arising from regular usage, will be useful. At a later stage in the process it will be useful to compare and correlate the data generated with the results of larger-scale customer testing. Creating a database with information accumulated over a period of time will provide extra confidence in what you are doing or provide an earlier alert to potential issues.

Step 7: customer testing

Larger-scale product testing using customers is essential to provide confidence in the quality and performance of your product. Again, establish a procedure that will compare results across products. Double blind trials – comparing the reaction to two unbranded products, say, your product and the market leader – are a good place to start. Many standard or proprietary methodologies exist for this type of research but it can be better to develop your own, to maintain confidentiality in the findings as well as a degree of competitive advantage.

This type of research can also be conducted on elements of the marketing mix, such as positioning and communications, to provide an additional confidence gauge. Again, many proprietary methodologies exist and some derive a notional sales estimate, for example, AC Nielsen's Bases (7) and Acupoll (8).

Step 8: market testing

Once you are confident in the results of your work to date, all aspects of the mix can be brought together for a real in-market test. This should check that all elements of the marketing mix will work as planned to drive customer awareness, trial and retention. These key statistics, together with all product costs, promotion costs and selling price information, will be needed to generate a robust estimate of return on investment (ROI).

Step 9: trial production

At around this time you should also plan a limited production run or pilot to verify that you will be able to produce the product to plan. You should also ascertain what quantities of product can be produced by your plant and if so, what capital expenditure is needed for large-scale production.

Step 10: business case

Once steps 8 and 9 are completed you should be able to finalise the business case for the new product. This should contain all the necessary evidence to explain how and why your investment in your new product will generate a return. It should also provide a candid assessment of the risks and how these will be mitigated. In Robert G.

Cooper's investigation of common factors behind why new products failed, he found that a detailed financial analysis was omitted or inadequate in half of the cases where new products failed. This is the critical gate to determine whether to proceed and the quality of the decision will depend on the quality of all the work that has taken place so far.

Step 11: production start-up

With approval to proceed, it will be possible to make the necessary investments in resources to produce your new product.

Step 12: market launch

The final stage in the process is to implement the marketing plan and launch the new product. There are mixed views on whether changes to implementation plans should be allowed post the test market. Some companies have policies to ensure that full launch plans should be identical to those in the test market in order to avoid risks. While there always likely to be arguments that improvements can be made, changes should only be made with caution. In so doing, every effort is made to isolate and verify the effect of every individual variable.

 Proforma 23A Example Offer Proforma

Insight & application of insight	*Insight Summary:* Summary of profound understanding on a consumer or his/her circumstances. Has to be expressed as a consumer need, want or belief to ensure that it is something that genuinely matters to consumers. *Application of Consumer Insight:* how could this consumer need, want or belief articulated by this insight be acted upon or applied to benefit the business.		
Consumer proposition/ promise	Summary of what the product, service or brand offers consumers and why it is different and appealing		
Target market	Description of target consumer	**Occasion**	Description of when the consumer could use the brand
Rational benefits		**Emotional benefits**	
Summary of the rational benefits delivered by the brand		Summary of the emotional or self image benefits delivered by the brand	
Offer features / supports (reasons why)			
Summary of the key product, service or brand features that make this claim credible and believable			
Differentiators	Summary of the key differentiating benefits (and possibly features) relative to competitors		
Personality style and tone	Description of how the product, service or brand talks to consumers Some times helpfully described in terms of dos and don'ts		

Proforma 23B Completed Offer Proforma

Insight & application of insight	Most companies, especially those who are forward looking want to reduce purchasing (and selling) administration complexity and costs and utilise in their expensive human resources on more added value activities in order to maximise profits		
Consumer proposition/ promise	A new easy-to-use web-based trading service to help your business to buy and sell products and parts with extra confidence and efficiency		
Target market	Efficiency seeking companies	Occasion	24 hours a day/7 days a week
Rational benefits		**Emotional benefits**	
Ease, speed of use Cost efficiency, security Process management and control		Trust Control Forward thinking	
Offer features / supports (reasons why)			
Secure/confidential purchasing/trading environment Easy-to-use/search purchasing system Multiple supplier catalogues/listings Supplier guarantees Flexible purchasing processes and information Data import and export functions		Extensive product catalogue with detailed and easy-to- read product specifications and prices (with more than basic office supplies) On-line and telephone help	
Differentiators	• Awareness and reputation of parent company, trust, reassurance • Comprehensive business service, not just purchasing • Not just another web portal		
Personality style and tone	• Clear, concise, to the point, intelligent • Dynamic, forward looking		

Key points to remember

1. Innovation can be a key driver of growth. Understanding the role of innovation in your category as well as your own organisational strengths and weaknesses are essential inputs to deciding what the strategic importance and role of innovation should be in your organisation in the future. Get buy-in to your strategy for innovation from your top team in order to secure the resources that you will need to succeed.

2. Successful product innovation requires the adherence to a rigorous process whereby products must fulfil strict qualifying criteria at each stage. The front end of the process is particularly important to weed out poor ideas, develop the good ones and avoid waste at potentially more costly later stages.

3. Successful new products will always meet a customer need and offer distinctive benefits versus possible alternatives.

4. Ideas can easily be shot down in flames. Make sure you develop enough to compensate for those that will fail to meet early stage criteria. Make sure you explore all the nuances inherent in an idea to give each one the best chance of success. This requires a disciplined approach, skills and techniques to make new connections, as well as sheer hard work.

5. Develop and agree a robust business case for new product initiatives before making substantial commitments, including necessary investments, ROI and an honest assessment of risk.

6. Products can fail through poor strategy or poor execution. Pay attention to both. Work with consumers to help provide insights and guidance to ensure executional excellence.

24 Marketing and Digital Technology

Check This Out – LA Mix (1987)

In this chapter you will learn:

- *Digital technology trends and their applications in marketing*
  - *Marketing performance measurement and planning*
  - *Marketing processes*
  - *Customer contact management and sales force planning*
  - *Brand and communications management*
- *How to deliver a new technology project*

Every part of our life is affected by new digital technology and marketing is no exception. It underpins how many things that we take for granted will work, for example, computers, cable tv and 3G phones. In television and radio, digital transmission is also transforming the quality of viewing and listening experiences up and down the UK and analogue television switch-off is currently scheduled to be completed by 2012. In turn, this switch-off will free up more of the electromagnetic spectrum and enable it to be reallocated to more powerful applications.

The environment is rapidly changing, and as a result every day poses new opportunities and threats. As marketing director, you need to be aware of those in order to avoid falling behind your competitors or to help stay one step ahead. This chapter is designed to provide inspiration concerning the burgeoning range of possibilities there are out there, as well as encourage you to seek out opportunities that are relevant to your business.

What is digitisation?

Let's start with a simple definition. *'Digitisation is the transmission and translation of information from analogue into digital signals'*. In simple terms this means that instead of data being transmitted as a continuously changing signal it is transmitted in a form of binary code, as a series of ones and zeros, equivalent to the turning on or off of a switch. In turn this enables more information to be packed into signals as well as making those signals clearer.

Digital technology trends

Here are some key ways that digitisation and digital technology affects marketing:

- Convergence – the increasing convergence of the worlds of communication, computing and telephony is enabling increasing connectivity between electronic devices. This means that the transmission of information in digital form can be almost instantaneous and limitless in distance whilst retaining the quality of the original message.
- Processor power – improvements in semi-conductor technology means more and more data can be stored, and on smaller and more portable devices. According to Moore's Law (1), almost every measure of the capabilities of digital electronic devices (processing speed, memory capacity, even the resolution of digital cameras) is improving at (roughly) exponential rates. This has dramatically changed the usefulness of digital electronics in nearly every segment of the world economy. Moore himself, however, has accepted that this process cannot continue indefinitely (2).
- Open source development – the increasing availability of software source code on the Internet and free redistribution licences has enabled more 'open' and collaborative software development. This is fuelling both more and faster development of new software applications.

Application of digital technology in marketing

Only your imagination is likely to be the limiting factor on the range of potential new applications of digital technology to marketing. Here are three key benefits that technology can bring to the marketer:

- a new means of collecting, storing, analysing and using information
- a new means of automating marketing processes to save money as well as put control in customers' hands
- a new means of communicating with customers and building relationships with them (see Chapter 18 Customer Relationship Management and Database Marketing).

18▸

Figure 24.1 *Application of digital technology in marketing*

Marketing performance measurement and planning

Chapter 5 Setting Objectives and Measuring Marketing Performance discussed marketing performance management. A set of metrics will of course provide many diagnostic and analytical benefits but the data can be equally applied to enable more effective planning and more reliable forecasting. **5**

There are, of course, many IT and software suppliers who could help you produce a 'dashboard' (an indicator of all the key marketing measures on one screen). Start with what you want to know and then discover what you know from the sources that are available.

Our purpose here is not to provide a list but to outline some of the principles that you should follow. In answer to how to create the data for a management dashboard, a representative from one of the top marketing automation software companies once replied, "*It's your company's data…*" So, the starting point is to define what you need and what you have. Here are a few areas you should consider in the collection and management of information:

From the top down, it is essential that the overall objectives and application of data is understood and clear. Often, the consequences of marketing activities and decisions made over the long term may not have been considered when your performance indicators were first established. So beyond defining the indicators, define how they should be used and interpreted. The data can be configured – for example, made comparative, turned into moving annual totals or shown in relation to budget/forecast. Your aim should be to monitor performance and then create, where possible, a predictive model. (You can read more detail about CRM implementation and setting up and managing data in Chapter 18 Customer Relationship Management and Database Marketing)   **18**

Also try and ensure that all discrete areas of marketing activity can be measured independently. For example, all web-based activities will readily generate their own stream of data.

From the bottom up, look at all the data and extract and use what is meaningful and relevant. Consider which activities generate their own data – this can in turn provide insights that provide an in-built competitive edge. Think about the following points:

- What data could you collect that could give you an edge?
- How could you capture it?
- What is the best way to store it?
- How can you analyse the data, use it to drive growth and make predictions?

In its early days, marketing was lucky in that it could hide behind such third-party measurements as cost per thousand readership and viewing figures. However, luck will always run out in the end and now is the time to re-think.

Those who create data as part of a transaction, such as banks, utilities, mail order and telephone companies, can accurately rely on it and have historically been at the forefront of the measurement revolution. If you have to undertake other marketing activity to create it, it is going to be more costly to collect and be at a level removed from the original customer. However, the rise of activity that generates its own data (as a spin-off – reliable, specific, fast, confidential) means that marketing automation and management dashboards can now be reasonably considered by all.

As a result of this evolution consumer goods companies, as well as many others, are embracing this new world. Cosmetic companies are gathering information from in-store consultations in order to recommend products based on an understanding of skin types and colours. Likewise, baby product manufacturers are gathering data on babies so they can build lifetime relationships and target products based on age.

In defining your needs, you should seek ways to control, monitor and predict the effectiveness of media and promotions, integrated marketing communications, customer satisfaction and brand equity, expenditure and of course demand and profitability.

These sets of data, clearly presented, will improve the efficiency of your marketing activities and provide a proper comparative record for future planning and forecasting. In doing so, you will need to integrate data from multiple sources – for example, your accounting systems and sales ledger, as well as customer sales and media sources. This is where you will need help from your IT department, as well as other colleagues.

Marketing processes

While many marketing activities and processes are ad hoc by nature, many are or could be both systematic and repeatable. In 2005, the very useful web portal *MarketingProfs* conducted a research study to show the extent to which companies were using technology to automate their in-house processes (3).

Figure 24.2 *Application of digital technology to marketing processes*

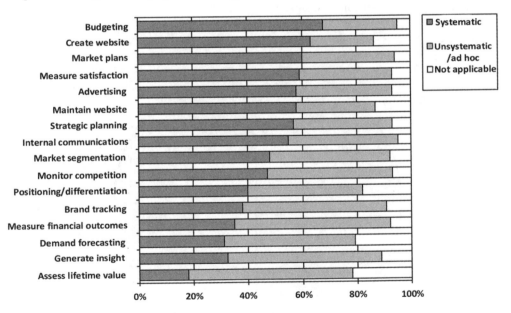

From a marketing director's point of view, automating in-house working processes provides two potential advantages – potential time and cost savings and embedding procedures (introducing procedures that set the standard and are consistently and correctly followed).

Of course, the same logic can also be applied to customer processes. There may be significant time and cost savings to be realised by creating online customer registration or purchasing procedures for your products and services. The watchword here is to make this as easy and engaging as possible in order to maximise click-throughs.

Customer contact management and sales force planning

This is partly dealt with in Chapter 18 *Customer Relationship Management and Database Marketing* but new digital technology and its principles have an even wider application for sales force planning. Customer contact management tools such as Goldmine and Act have continually updated themselves and been joined by a flurry of online remotely hosted solutions, led by Salesforce.com. ⓲

There are two key benefits from a marketing perspective; first, to manage the sales pipeline in relation to marketing spend and second, to control the quality and effectiveness of the sales presentation.

Some of the key applications are show in Figure 24.3.

Figure 24.3 *Application of digital technology to sales force planning*

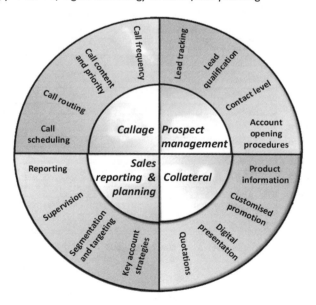

All of this information can be achieved at various levels of regional and territory granularity. It can also be very beguiling but a word with your sales director counterpart or indeed report will soon tell you that the salespeople who are best at completing data entries are not necessarily always the best performers.

Brand and communications management

Digital technology can also be an asset to control your brand and produce promotion materials, enabling brand standards to be maintained and campaigns to be created centrally and then distributed for local adaptation and production. It can even facilitate the customisation of messages to customers.

By setting up a brand asset management database of all images (which your IT experts will call 'digital assets') you will be able to produce materials for all channels and media, and for all customers around the world, at the touch of button. Figure 24.4 shows how a major supermarket controls the images of supplier products.

Figure 24.4 *Application of digital technology to customer communications*

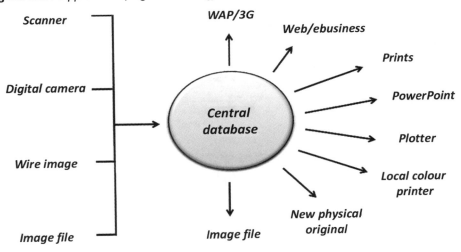

Digital asset management (DAM – get used to the TLA-three letter acronym!) is growing in importance and various forms of publication management can be added to it, which can in turn be used to publish advertisements and literature in both printed and web form. Some systems allow local adaptation from centrally developed campaigns, others speed the design and production of catalogues. Others also facilitate brand understanding and behavioural consistency.

Where to start?

Be it campaign management, data management and analysis, brand asset management and publication systems, or a simple dashboard of your key performance indicators (KPIs), whatever technology you employ plays an important in the improvement of the marketing function.

For a healthy start, Figure 24.5 shows a sequence of activities to undertake.

Figure 24.5 *Planning to introduce new digital technology*

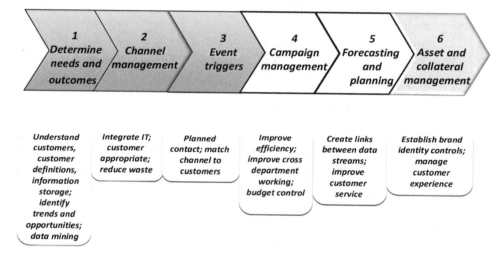

 Success factors for delivering digital technology projects

Develop a robust understanding of the potential benefits

Before initiating a digital technology project, you should develop a clear understanding of the benefits that the project will bring. The inevitable return on investment (ROI) statement will need to be completed but do avoid the notional savings that are difficult to measure, like time saved. Moreover, focus on more tangible measures such as direct costs, number of staff or the external purchase cost of buying in the same activity.

Look closely at any case histories and if possible try to see the technology working in real time rather in a PowerPoint presentation.

Make sure the scope of the project is realistic and close

The main problem with any technology is the desire for more than is practical. Adding extras adds significantly to cost and time, not only at the initial planning and implementation stage but also at later stages as this may render any supplier upgrades unusable. Defining a detailed and clear set of needs at the outset can help prevent this. More time spent pre-planning will mean a better project delivery, both in terms of speed and expense.

It's a fast-moving world. Digital technology changes so rapidly and you should do as much to ensure that you future-proof the project. You'll hear phrases like 'best of breed' and 'fit for purpose' but be aware at least of the major shifts. At the time of writing, these include the moves from big databases being held centrally to 'hosted' or 'on-demand' online services.

Strong project management

Far too many new technology projects overrun on both time and budget. A sizeable number fail completely. This is partly because needs are not specified at the outset or change throughout the course of a project – this occurs when the procedural implications are properly understood at the outset. Beware of the pitfalls and do what you can to manage the project tightly and closely. Come down heavily and early on any slippages and slip-ups or you risk further regret if progress continues to be slow and the project becomes more costly in the long run.

Train, train and then train some more

Training and on-the-job practical help are key components to ensure successful adoption and implementation of new technology. Make sure this is included in your need specification before it is agreed and make sure you actually experience a training session yourself in order to ensure that it is fit for purpose.

So much capability is wasted. Features so enthusiastically sold and bought can end up lying dormant and unused by all but a few. There is always this danger, so make use of the aforementioned few by getting them to become your ad hoc trainers and unofficial helpline. You may find that they will do or know tricks that even the salesman who sold you the package in the first place may not be aware of.

 **Pitfalls to avoid**

Bear in mind that data and its use is advocated by the people who create the means to have it. IT and software companies have long seen marketing as purely marketing communications. The drive for marketing automation comes unnaturally from this source – it often has non-sequiturs built in and many incorrect assumptions about effectiveness and response measurement Moreover, the lingua franc and acronyms are being set by those who literally do their marketing by numbers. One important advantage you can give yourself is to learn the lingo, at least to help you distinguish a 'blue sky idea' from a 'low hanging fruit'. However, beware of using it to try and confuse rather than clarify a point, as this could backfire on you.

There are a number of TLAs that you should be familiar with. One of the most important is SLA, which stands for 'service level agreement'. Just what service standards are going to be set and what are the penalties for them not being reached? Equally important is what are the costs associated with the support.

With the widespread availability of data and the consequent ability to target and measure, accuracy often seems to override content. The creation of the resultant message is often poorly and simplistically done. The challenge in a data–rich company is to improve the content of the message, while the rest of us must decide what data we need to reach the optimum decisions.

Many who work in mobile phone or financial services, for example, will probably scoff as they consider UE (user equilibrium) modelling in the context of NEG (new economic geography), all in the context of MPS (marketing performance solutions) of course. All of this is very desirable if, and only if, you have the relevant data. The ability to predict 'churn' (the number or percentage of lapsed or lost customers), for example, is as important in pricing terms as service quality, so that the balancing act is between potential customer dissatisfaction and profit. It will not always be that way as the market matures and customers become savvier.

The future

Technology continually evolves and in the future will enable increasingly rich promotion opportunities and an increasing variety of new routes to market. But bear in mind that technology does not always deliver what it intended and the user will find new ways to use it unintended by the developer. Having the vision to interpret customer behaviour remains a core skill of the marketing director and nowhere will that skill be more important that keeping apace and anticipating the twists and turns of the digital revolution.

 Key points to remember

1. Embrace digital technology – if you are good at it, it can make you even better, and if you're not, it'll certainly help you to improve.
2. On the other hand, beware! A great deal of so-called marketing automation and software has been designed by IT companies for their own existing clients. Start by building consensus on your needs, understanding what benefits this will bring you and drawing up a clear specification of all requirements, desired uses and applications.
3. Use customer and expert understanding to remain at the leading edge of the curve and anticipate and plan for the future.

25 Mergers and Acquisitions

Two Become One – Spice Girls (1996)

In this chapter you will learn:

- *How marketing can add value to the M & A process*
- *M & A assessment tools*
- *Pitfalls to avoid*
- *The importance of people*

Companies must expand. To stand still is to fall behind the competition. Such growth is the core of marketing but to achieve rapid growth, a merger or acquisition is seen by over half of companies to be preferable to organic growth (1). While the CEO and shareholders are constantly seeking to add value, merger and acquisition (M&A) success rates are not high. There have been many well-publicised disasters and research suggests that around two-thirds of companies say that they actually lost value through such activity (2).

While the deals may have been logically sound, mergers go sour for many reasons – poor strategy, personality problems at the top, cultural differences, poor employee morale and incompatible systems. However, the main reason for failure is the inability of management to integrate the two entities. In haste, and under pressure to do the deal, executives often fail to install effective tracking and monitoring processes and fail to manage the people side. The marketing director can play a key role in understanding behaviour as well as communicating and motivating people.

To ensure success, expansion must be planned, fit strategically with the company's mission statement and competencies, and be affordable. So as marketing director, you can play a key role both in ensuring proper strategic justification for a merger or acquisition as well as contribute to a more successful outcome. There will, however, be times when you may feel sidelined by the accountants. This chapter outlines the areas where you could add value.

The role of marketing

One current school of thought is that the title of marketing director should be changed to 'director of growth' – it is in this context that you should be able to add considerable value. M&As are not an activity but more a strategy for growth and because of this the impetus should emerge naturally from your business strategy.

Ensuring justification for an acquisition

Strategic

In the course of planning for growth, you will already have identified attractive market expansion opportunities and profit pools (see Chapter 3 Strategy Development), and this is the place to start.

3

There are seven strategic marketing reasons to consider an acquisition – your understanding of the market, the customer drivers, channels to the market, brand shares and strengths and weaknesses (including your own) will help confirm or otherwise that this is the case.

The seven reasons are:

- increasing market share or moving share to critical mass
- expanding into new markets, such as filling a geographical gap
- providing new products or services for current customers or to extend or strengthen a brand positioning; sometimes this may involve acquiring new people skills or technical capabilities
- strengthening relationships at trade and retail levels
- adding a new channel capacity or a new route to market, such as via the Internet
- elimination of a competitor, or preventing opportunities for a competitor
- adding customers, or accessing a new customer base.

As a matter of course, you will be regularly monitoring the marketplace and be aware of the performance of your competitors. It could be that certain brands have dominance in certain sectors, be they geographical, by customer group or by channel to market. Moreover, you will understand their positioning and the impact of your competitors' advertising. You may even know of a few cases where you could do a better job if you got your hands on them!

Financial

An acquisition must make sense in financial terms. The potential gains in relation to the price that is paid will be a critical part of the value judgement. To justify an acquisition in marketing terms, you should be able to forecast increased sales and brand shares, and calculate improvements in production, distribution and media efficiency. This information is readily transferable to a potential target feasibility report.

To meet any of these objectives, the cost and time of achieving them organically can also be calculated. It will therefore be possible to make a robust comparison of the alternative scenarios.

While marketing may well be the key ingredient in the decision to acquire and merge, economies of scale or a requirement to improve return on capital employed in the business are also of great significance. Most of this activity is, of course, driven by and controlled by accountants.

In practice, the forces that drive M&As often lie outside marketing and may be as the result of other actions in the marketplace. For example, a competitor may wish to divest some of its portfolio – it may be over-geared, undervalued in a sector or under pressure from predators or venture capitalists. However, wherever the idea is instigated, formal financial needs will call for due diligence reports.

Marketing can contribute to this process. Indeed, you may well have already modelled the marketplace and be ahead of the accountants, as part of developing your own marketing strategy. If so, you are in a strong position to assist the CEO and board at this time.

Shareholder value added

The key to success is to acquire companies with low earnings multiples, and convert this to a higher earnings multiple. Aside from the supply side savings, a merger or acquisition should really present new growth opportunities over and above the new revenues that you will inherit. This is usually a City expectation and the most successful M&As are those that create extra shareholder value by unlocking and exploiting synergies.

The ongoing exploration of the environment in which your company operates may well have highlighted new opportunities but this is where your creativity and the creativity of your team can play a key role. So, dust off your market research on any competitor brands and look for ways to improve or market them more effectively. Review the potentially enlarged portfolio and identify areas where you could quickly rationalise or launch new products. Review relative channel strengths and search out instances where additional competence could help drive extra growth. For further inspiration on ways to add value, Chapter 16 Brand Management and Positioning contains a useful section of managing brand portfolios. Chapter 23 New Product and Service Development is also worth a look. 🔟⑯ ㉓

Risk management

Managing the risks calls for thorough due diligence and this is where your accountants will also be involved, not least in dissecting your target's financial accounts. It is an area where marketing can also play a key role through your knowledge of the market, contacts and research skills.

Other areas to check are:

- Key employees – who are they and have they any skeletons in their cupboards? Spend time on a search engine of your choice, and any trade portals. Check out the company's website as well as business networking sites such as Linked In. Speak to other people in the industry, especially ex-employees.
- Products and brands – try them to assess the quality, talk to customers and the trade to find out what they think of them, look at review sites such as Ciao and news sites such as Google News. Also check for patents and trade marks owned (more information on these in Chapter 30 Marketing and the Law).   **30▸**
- Agency relationships – who are they, and what do they think of their client?
- Customers – how many are there, and are they loyal to the companies' products or not? With a company that relies on a small number of large clients, seek assurance in the continuance and future stability of revenues, as this could be a deal-maker or breaker. Interview the target's customer base to verify the position.

🔧 Tools and techniques

Judgements on 'fit' – organisational, strategic and cultural – can be partly instinctive, borne out of deal experience and business acumen. However, the most important principle to follow is the ruthless pursuit of value.

It is likely that some market modelling may need to be undertaken at this stage in order to verify opportunities that add value. There are also a number of strategic models that can give a useful framework for assessing opportunities, risks and 'fit':

- Ansoff's (Strategic Growth Options) Matrix (Chapter 3)   **3▸**
- Boston Consulting Group Growth-share Matrix (Chapter 3)
- Porter's Five Forces (Figure 25.1)
- Shell Directional Policy Matrix (Figure 25.2)
- Kaplan and Norton's Balanced Scorecard (Figure 25.3)

However, bear in mind that all models have certain advantages and disadvantages. They are often simplistic, two-dimensional, only true at one point in time, usually generalisations, and merely an aid to decision making (that is still up to you).

However, the very nature of M&As is complex, and models do help make this more understandable. They can also be a great aid for communicating points to others.

Figure 25.1 *Porter's Five Forces of Competitive Position*

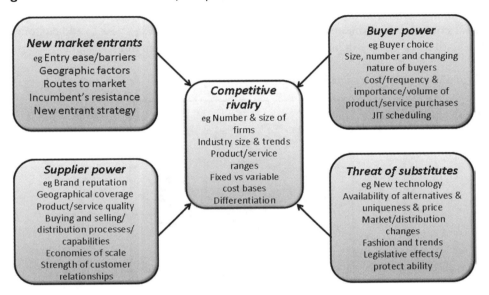

Porter's Five Forces (3) helps evaluate a market and your place in it as a consequence of merger and acquisition opportunities. Every business aims to drive down costs and improve product performances – Porter sets them in the context of overall business and the means by which you can defend or attach a given strategy. Porter identifies 'five forces' – an excellent framework for understanding a market or competitor (or acquisition target). It is also helpful to determine where a company's strengths lie, or could lie, by focusing on a particular market segment. However, do bear in mind that it is important to recognise this as primarily a marketing tool and as such it is best suited to determining markets and product areas to focus on, rather than the status of a potential target per se.

- Supplier power – what is the relative bargaining power? High if raw materials are in limited supply and controlled by one or two companies. Low if your company has the advantage of economies of scale or product uniqueness.

- New market entrants – what is the threat from new entrants? High if new competitors can set up in competition at low cost. Low if you have the advantage of economies of scale or product uniqueness.

- Product and technology development – what is the threat from substitutes? High if substitutes are currently being developed that have technical or price advantages, otherwise medium or low.

- Buyer power – what is relative bargaining power? High if over 50% goes to two or three major customers, otherwise medium or low.
- Competitive rivalry – what is the level of competition? This depends on the level of market fragmentation and comparative market shares.

What Porter underestimates, however, is customer power. It is a wise to add customers as a sixth force when you have to contribute to the management report.

Figure 25.2 *Shell Directional Policy Matrix*

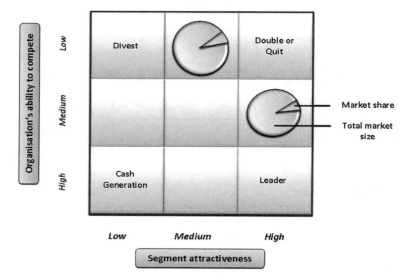

Shell developed this nine cell matrix to add more directionality to policy-making (4). Their model combines the criteria in Ansoff's Matrix and the BCG Growth-share Matrix and is useful to analyse strategic options that have been generated both for existing and new product markets. The technique examines strategic alternatives against two sets of criteria:

- segment attractiveness: which sectors look like winners?
- ability to compete: in which sectors can your organisation compete strongly?

Businesses operating in attractive segments with a strong ability to compete will be best placed to grow and establish leadership positions. Businesses operating in unattractive segments with low ability to compete will be most suitable for divesting.

Here again, in practice, the simplicity of the model needs modulating. For instance, growing market share can be expensive and a declining market may contain considerable potential profit. This is particularly the case when operating in a market that is mature and the only way to expand sales may be by acquiring a competitor. Be careful, too, not to focus entirely on becoming bigger and better in a market that is getting smaller and smaller, as it could lead to disaster.

Figure 25.3 *Kaplan and Norton's Balanced Scorecard*

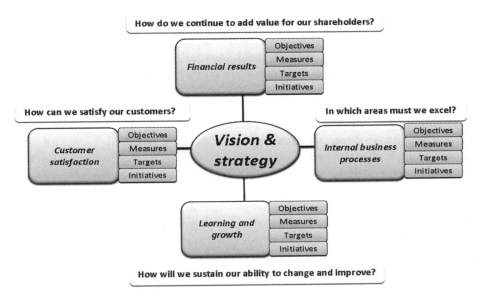

Kaplan and Norton's balanced scorecard (5) is useful when the current information is unreliable or unknown, as it may be in the context of a newly acquired company. In 1992, when Kaplan and Norton introduced it, they described it as the dials of an aircraft cockpit. The balanced scorecard is a move away from the traditional preoccupation with financial and market-based metrics as being the only true indicators of business success. True strategic progress, they argued, results from a balanced contribution of other strategic activities, for which targets should be set and measured.

The balanced scorecard shows the other performance areas which should be measured in addition to financial results, as these are also value-adding areas. These are namely the internal business processes, customer satisfaction and learning and growth.

As each area represents a chain of elements, a direct link is forged between the vision and strategy of the company and performance measurement. Each one is detailed by objectives, measures, targets and initiatives. Incorporating the main elements of an organisation and intertwining them serves as a way of making sense of strategy and measuring the performance.

The tool is useful in a number of ways: to provide a 'big picture' overview of the organisation, as a checklist and as a means to articulate strategy into a set of measurable outputs across the activities of the organisation. In this way, strategy becomes part of the daily agenda, it goes beyond short-term quick fixes and is powerful in helping to manage post-merger implementation.

Of course, your marketing-biased proposals will have to be put forward within a framework required by overall management. These will include management fit, technology compatibility, economies of scale and, above all, business value. (If you are into software then there are many forms available to create balanced scorecards.)

Inevitably, the decision will rest or fall on the financial implications of any proposed deal. In recent years there has been an increased recognition of not only the cost of marketing, but its value too. This has resulted in the now accepted practice of brand valuation, the calculation of which in itself may well contribute to the deal-making decision process. For more information on brand valuation, see Chapter 16 Brand Management and Positioning.   **16**

If the marketplace is large and information-rich, you may consider the science of 'urban economics', as used by the mobile telephone companies. This takes into account labour efficiency, education, technical knowledge and preparedness to commute. All are used as indicators in establishing the unknown effect of a service on a given territory.

Contributing to a successful outcome

Once the deal has been planned and justified, the next stage will be to agree the deal and make it happen. There are a number of pitfalls to avoid. While as marketing director you may not be front-line in the deal-making process, many of these pitfalls are worth bearing in mind as they can be assuaged at the deal-making stage.

All of these will either have been dealt with or mitigated at the planning stage. If necessary, encourage your colleagues to conduct a risk assessment to help ensure that all risks are identified and have been addressed.

Beyond the logic and negotiation of the deal, there is also a need for robust integration and implementation plan. This is also where many mistakes are made. At the same time, there are several key areas where marketing skills can also play a vital role to ensure success.

Figure 25.4 *Pitfalls to avoid*

Pitfall	Mitigation tactics
Over-paying	• Due diligence on the numbers • Careful negotiation and agreement • Linking revenue and profit estimates to the deal price
Objectives/synergies not well understood	• Due diligence on company research and potential
Poor strategic fit	• Rigorous strategy development process, boardroom buy-in
Inability of management to integrate the two entities, realise the economies of scale and add value	• Careful negotiation and agreement to roles and responsibilities • Linking to deal price • Effective customer marketing and communications
Incompatible cultures	• Due diligence on the people and culture • Careful assessment through the deal-making process
Clash of personalities/egos	• Agreement on job titles/roles • Linking roles to deal agreement/price
Poor employee morale, leading to loss of talent	• Agreement on location for company HQ, brand name • Staff retention incentives • Link staff retention to deal price • Effective staff marketing and communications
Loss of productivity	• Linking productivity to deal price
Incompatible systems	• Due diligence on systems
Changing market conditions	• Due diligence on market potential and customers • Effective customer marketing and communications

Marketing to manage the people side

Many of the pitfalls to avoid have a human component.

Times of change mean times of uncertainty. A takeover or merger can lead to a considerable increase in staff turnover or simple absenteeism, dependent on the dominant culture. At the planning stage, use your communication skills – help your CEO and fellow directors see the overall picture, potential risks and the key aims and benefits of the proposed deal right from the outset.

Keeping everyone informed, showing the benefits of the changes and introducing new people and new ways of working will smooth the transition. Some of the expertise in change management may be found among your HR colleagues, and your HR director could be a valuable asset. Post-merger communication planning plays a vital part. Start by laying down the basic frameworks so that if a merger or acquisition does take place understanding and systems are already in place.

Also ensure efficient means are in place to communicate with staff. This means identifying ways that will motivate them and that they will respond to, not just the means that are the lowest cost. Seeking cultural compatibility is important. Communications should be specific and related to the exact circumstance. Consider creating a campaign linked to brand values and with success as a leading theme. This can be used to bring all the elements and people involved together. Consider creating a newsletter, using corporate portals and all department events. A conference, although expensive, has the advantage of bringing people together and ensuring everyone sees and hears the same important message. Chapter 12 Team Motivation and Development and Chapter 13 Managing the Board and Business as a Whole are packed with ideas that can help you manage the people side. **⑫ ⑬**

Marketing to maintain customer service and drive growth

The group that requires the most attention is the customer. Before finalising the deal, a practical integration and marketing plan should already be in place. However, sometimes this is not given sufficient thought until the ink on the legal documents has dried. Everyone will be under pressure to realise the benefits as quickly as possible – you can help by cranking up the marketing machine to capitalise on the new opportunities!

The first three months are critical in any acquisition. Play an active part within the management team during this key period, both to integrate the organisations and devise and implement marketing plans to add value. Chapter 1 Getting Started, Chapter 26 Rationalisation or Downsizing and Chapter 27 Culture Change and Brand Delivery are all packed with ideas that can be applied in this situation. **① ㉖ ㉗**

As well as fulfilling the objectives you want to achieve, a merger or acquisition also provides the opportunity to encourage lapsed customers to return and to attract new ones. Take a look at the customer data and the way in which customer records are held, and look for ways to bring the structure and weighting into line. This activity will help you assess opportunities to communicate with the customer base – both to reassure current, new and acquired customers of the benefits of the change, as well as to reveal opportunities to cross-sell other products or services.

Consider creating a promotional event to make sure you communicate the advantages of the enlarged organisation to all. Make sure that each customer is communicated with at this key time. Even if no change of message or channel is planned, the level of service needs to be stepped up. Consider using offers and promotions which are consistent with the brand positioning to maintain the relationship with the customer. Naturally everyone craves the reassurance of continuity of service or supply, yet the change offers the opportunity to do more.

Consider introducing special pricing for a limited period, and sector-specific offers. If necessary, offer incentives to get your sales people in front of your customers and able to tell the whole story. In B2B and key account relationships, many of the accumulated negative practices ("*they don't stock that size*" etc) that grow up between sales and customers can also be swept away with real positive effect.

Take the marketing lead

Finally, there may also be some jostling for positions that could affect your role. It is important to show leadership and be, and be seen to be, confident. The enlarged organisation will lead to consideration of departmental restructuring and potentially new methodologies. As soon as you know a merger or acquisition is in the offing, this is an unusual opportunity to take the initiative and potentially accelerate your career. So develop a marketing action plan and make sure it lands on your CEO's desk first.

 Key points to remember

1. If marketing is about growth then that growth can successfully come from M&As. This is an important element of being a marketing director. Go grow!
2. Rigorous market research and planning will show you where the merger and acquisition opportunities lie. Much of the information needed to facilitate the right decisions will be available from normal marketing practice.
3. Establish the value by understanding what will be achieved through M&As. Assess the comparative and added value versus your base business plan.
4. Be aware of the many pitfalls that can cause the failure of mergers and acquisitions. Devise plans to mitigate the key risks and address as many as possible through the process of, and in advance of, agreeing the deal. It should be possible to mitigate some of the risks by agreeing solutions and building these into the terms of the deal.
5. Facilitate good communications – cultural fit is critical to success so act quickly and use your marketing skills to help bring it about.
6. Create a practical marketing plan to drive growth – establish a plan for the first three months and act quickly, using sales promotion to bring forward or accelerate sales.
7. Above all it's a people thing and the winners in M&A make sure that the people gel and the businesses gel. Use all your marketing skills to make it happen successfully.

26 Rationalisation or Downsizing

Bright Eyes – Art Garfunkel (1979)

In this chapter you will learn:

- *Pitfalls to avoid*
- *Alternative strategies and implications*
- *How to make the best out of a downsizing*
- *How to make redundancy choices*
- *What to do if the worst happens*

Rationalisation or downsizing is increasingly commonplace in the corporate world, either as a result of a takeover, sales or profit decline or sometimes an office relocation or new CEO. Most likely downsizing will be driven by the broader business requirements and from the board downwards.

There are many risks in downsizing, from falling foul of employment legislation to causing lasting harm to the corporate culture and business. While the HR director will have the key role play to ensure that mistakes are not made, the marketing director can also help pre-empt potential issues and help ensure a successful outcome.

Pitfalls to avoid

Employment legislation has a critical bearing on how to go about downsizing and most businesses will be paranoid about putting a foot wrong. In this situation it is easy for managers unfamiliar with the law to go 'off-record' and prompt litigation from aggrieved employees.

Downsizing for the sake of cost reduction alone has also been castigated by some as shortsighted and neglectful of what resources will be needed to increase future revenue streams (1). Others do not question the sense of downsizing, but argue that time spent on restructuring and re-engineering is better spent on determining core competencies and relating those competencies to the external marketplace.

The most profound effects of downsizing can be in culture change (2), not saved costs or productivity gain. For example:

- power shifts away from rank-and-file employees in the direction of top management/ownership. This causes a shift in emphasis away from the wellbeing of individuals towards the organisation as a whole
- working relationships change from being 'familial' to being more competitive
- employer-employee relationships move from being long-term and stable towards being more short-term and uncertain

Much research (3) has documented the harmful effects downsizing can have on 'survivors'. The effects have been described in terms of lower morale, high stress and anger, envy and guilt. Working relationships can also become strained. These can involve backstabbing, conflict, placing of blame and overt failure to co-operate. Links between perceived fairness of the layoffs and survivor commitment to the organisation have also been shown. Communication effectiveness can also affect commitment. Perceived unfairness and the breakdown of orderly communications can fuel gossip and resentment as well as uncertainty and fear. If these issues are not pre-empted or dealt with at an early stage they can cause lasting cultural damage.

 ## Where to start

There are extremely difficult decisions to be made when downsizing. No one looks forward to it and that's why it is often handled badly or put off until it is too late. In formulating plans to downsize, consideration must be given to the legal prerequisites as well as the knock-on and long term and short-term consequences. HR (and possibly legal counsel) must play a critical role to ensure everything is done by the book. There are two broad approaches you can follow:

Figure 26.1 *Alternative downsizing strategies*

Downsizing strategy	Implications
Fast, reactive to circumstances eg takeover, sales or profit decline or need to pacify shareholder concerns	Risks negative perceptions, associated with organisation decline and can have a detrimental impact on the culture; while a one-off cut may be better than a series of cuts, the effects can still be long-lasting; care needs to be taken to anticipate and avoid laid-off employees feeling angry and surviving employees feeling helpless and demotivated in order to help the organisation recover as quickly as possible
Planned, proactive, usually integrated with a wider set of objectives to improve organisational efficiency, productivity, and/or competitiveness	Less chance of being perceived as a 'fire sale'; more chance of maintaining management and business credibility; can help businesses be more competitive in the long run

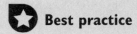 **Best practice**

Faced with increasing retail trade pressure and eroding margins in the early 1990s, Procter & Gamble worked hard to reduce management layers and streamline operations while introducing everyday low pricing (EDLP) to better align prices with consumer perceptions of its products' value. This strategy not only helped increase shelf space and market share but helped the company achieve its highest profit margins in twenty years.

Downsizing strategies

There are many different ways of planning to downsize, ranging from secretive sessions to open discussions and solicitation of ideas from employees. There are also different protocols for termination notices, from relatively harsh same-day terminations, to more generous 90-day or longer notice periods. Clearly providing more generous financial packages than just the legally required minimum is more likely to assuage.

There are also differences in intent, for example, with reductions planned to smooth the transition from the past to the future or planned to be deliberately disruptive to the status quo. Figure 26.2 (4) assesses downsizing practices by whether they tend to reinforce (or leave alone) the existing culture or destabilise it. Methods that are less disruptive and/or give employees more of a sense of control are categorised as reinforcing the current culture. Those likely to induce pain (particularly among those who are asked to leave) will be destabilising. Of course, the degrees of cultural reinforcement or destabilisation vary depending on the nature of the culture of a particular organisation.

Figure 26.2 *Culture reinforcing and culture destabilising practices*

Culture reinforcing	Culture destabilising
Voluntary reductions (eg attrition, buy-outs, job sharing)	Involuntary reductions (layoffs)
Advance notice	Sudden termination
Shared pain (eg cuts across all levels)	Winners/losers (eg executives get big bonuses while cutting others' positions)
Explicit criteria for 'who stays, who goes'	Criteria are secret
Transition assistance for those who depart involuntarily (eg outplacement)	Little or no assistance
Transition assistance for survivors	Little or no assistance
New 'rules of engagement' between organisations are made clear	Reductions treated as exception or something that does not require explanation
Consultation and involvement in both the process and direction setting at all levels in the organisation	Goal setting done at top without input

Success factors for achieving culture change and downsizing

How can an organisational leader know how to steer an appropriate course? This is not an easy task but dealing effectively or ineffectively during a downsizing situation can set you out as a great or a poor leader. Here are some ideas and rules of thumb to lessen the pain and hasten the gain:

Prevention rather than cure

While the marketing department will not be the sole contributor to corporate overheads, do what you can to keep the size of your department in check in the first place. Don't build or be seen to build an empire and don't throw people at problems. Consider hiring people on contracts and paying them through the marketing budget rather than payroll or using consultants to provide short-term resource to solve particular problems.

Make the easy cuts first

Cuts may be inevitable, so make the easy ones first. Take a hard look at all your marketing expenditure – media, promotion, product development and then staff. Consider putting off projects until the end of the year and consider not replacing staff who have just moved on. Be realistic and black and white about the level of cuts needed, and decide where savings will have least impact on the business. If you use sub-contractors in your business consider opportunities to transfer staff and out-source key functions.

Ensure redundancy choices are entirely objective

If you have to make redundancy choices, this is where your HR Director must be a first port of call. In the first instance you will need to set criteria against which you can judge all of your team. This is covered in more detail later in this chapter. It is also advisable to trail the process and consult widely so that the process of making choices is, and is seen to be, totally transparent and entirely fair. Consultation is also a legal requirement if the number of redundancies exceeds twenty in the UK.

Be as open as you can and manage the people side

Gossip and rumour will be rife and both leaving and surviving colleagues will naturally be uncertain and wary about their future with the company. It is also reasonable to assume that all defences will be up, and that mistrust will be widespread in expectation of the worse. The individual manager, as well as the organisation as a whole, can make the situation much better or much worse through what is not said, as well as through what is said, and how people are treated. It is barely possible to under-communicate during a downsizing. Speak to all staff either as a group or on an individual basis and be as open as you can about the end game without compromising the business. Be as financially generous as you can with the leavers as this will also have a bearing on those that remain.

Be visible and available to leavers and survivors

Both survivors and leavers will be feeling a range of emotions – hurt, anger, uncertainty, fear, loss of livelihood and so on. Leaders need to listen and show compassion and understanding. As a human being, you may also discover personal benefits in being able to help both leavers and survivors grow and gain as much as possible from this difficult situation. Many will have questions or just want to talk and seek reassurance from you. Make a point of going out of your way to be visible and available and don't take things personally when the going gets tough.

Show dignity and respect to leavers. There is much debate about when and how to tell and talk to future leavers. Some swear by holding a meeting at the end of the day. Others suggest that holding the meeting at the beginning of the week to allow time to get a CV prepared. Everyone will have different needs and only you will know them best. Most important is to help leavers get through the 'shock' phase and to channel their energies positively – through creating an action plan, arranging outplacement, and reviewing and updating CVs. This can be greatly aided by trailing the process before-hand. Most will appreciate the opportunity to talk and gain advice and support. Some may be delighted to 'escape'. Some will appreciate follow-up support, either face-to-face or by phone or email. Generally, it is unhelpful to escort people out of the door – this certainly won't help the attitudes of those left behind.

Motivate the survivors – they are equally likely to be feeling pain; some may have close friends who are leaving and may be considering leaving too. They may have lost some of their self esteem and will need reassuring of their worth. Some may have lost faith in the organisation and may need help and motivation to step up to a new challenge. Critical will be to reassure that the vision and strategy for the organisation is sound, and that the business is in good hands.

Emphasise a motivating vision of the future

A key challenge will be to turn the negative impact of the downsizing into a positive force. At a corporate level, a senior manager should be appointed to oversee both internal and external communications, and marketing can contribute to shaping that message. You can play a key role to help the team understand that the organisation has a rosy future and gain their commitment to help ensure that the organisation is reborn in stronger and fitter form. At a departmental, if not wider level, spend time explaining the end-game and painting a picture about the future to energise the team.

Challenge and incentivise your team

Challenging and incentivising the survivors can also help them feel valued and appreciated. Consider resetting objectives and providing new financial incentives to reward and recognise. It may also be an opportunity to put new people in new roles to invigorate and motivate.

Improve processes

Downsizing can be a catalyst to review old procedures and traditions eg to eliminate unproductive meetings or approval processes. Look at ways to get the company as whole closer to customers in order to add value. Initiate process reviews to eliminate activities that do not add value. Involve the whole of your team in this process.

Plan to build morale

Downsizing is a time when the organisation will never have felt worse so devote energy and resource to build morale. Consider empowering the team to investigate ways to ensure that good comes out of hardship. Allocate a budget and then withdraw and let them get on with it. Task them to look at ways to overhaul long-standing traditions and introduce new ones. Task them to look at ways to improve working relationships. Task them to make people 'smile'. An example might be to establish a lunchtime forum for subjects that people really care about or launch a communications vehicle to update on progress and good news.

Making redundancy choices

To comply with UK law the criteria used to select jobs for redundancy should objective, fair and consistent (5).

In a redundancy situation, it used to be common practice to make part-time workers redundant before full-time workers. However, the automatic redundancy of part-time staff is likely to be illegal on two counts. First, it could infringe the regulations to treat part-time workers less favourably than their full-time equivalents. Second, since many part-time workers are women, it is likely to be seen as a form of unlawful sexual discrimination. Different treatment of full-time and part-time workers is only legal if it can be justified on objective grounds.

Figure 26.3 summarises some alternative strategies for determining redundancy candidates. Strategies that reflect the organisation's priorities and needs as well as motivating staff are likely to be the most effective. An example of best practice is also described.

Figure 26.3 *Alternative redundancy strategies*

Redundancy strategy	Pros	Cons
Based on objective scoring system such job performance reviews or sales results	Compliant with UK law; fair	May not reflect business priorities
Across the board cuts in all departments	Potentially compliant with UK law	Adverse impact on culture; may not reflect business priorities and needs
Last hired, first fired	Potentially compliant with UK law	May not reflect business priorities and needs
Seniority	Potentially compliant with UK law	May not reflect business priorities and needs

 Best practice

Here are two examples of scoring systems used to make redundancy choices

1. To help make redundancy decisions across an entire organisation following a merger, a scoring system was devised based on two criteria. Firstly, a measure based on end of year job performance appraisals, and secondly a measure on the business criticality of the role.

2. To make redundancy decisions in a sales-force following declining sales of the key product in their portfolio, a company assessed each individual on a points score out of fifty covering three criteria. Twenty five points were allocated based on sales performance versus target with five of those points allocated for consistent performance. Twenty points were allocated based on skills and capabilities as derived from their last performance review. And finally, five points were allocated for a 'clean' disciplinary record, with this figure reducing if 'disciplinary' action had been taken in the period under review.

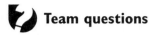 **Team questions**

When developing your own downsizing strategy, use the questions below as a checklist for discussion with your senior management colleagues. The 'smell, tell, bell, sell, swell' test was devised by Thomas A Hickok (3) and is intentionally short and simple to aid recall.

Figure 26.4 *The Hickok 'Smell, Tell, Bell, Sell, Swell' Downsizing Test*

SMELL	Is the company being decent to its employees? Or will, over time, the stench of fish left out too long become apparent?
TELL	Has the essential condition, which may lead to some difficult decisions, been communicated to the organisation's employees? Have the employees been able to provide input?
BELL	Have we carefully thought through the consequences for those 'for whom the bell tolls'? How will this affect those who may lose their jobs? How will this affect those who remain?
SELL	Are we prepared to announce and explain our/my decisions to multiple stakeholders, including shareholders, the media, community activists and politicians?
SWELL	Does the plan for change, of which these decisions are a part, offer the organisation the opportunity to achieve better results in the future?

Joining an organisation that has just retrenched

First, consider yourself lucky that you've not had to make the hard decisions in the first place. The key is to market yourself as an asset that the company needs in order to function successfully (6). Take time to listen and understand at the outset. Again, here are some ideas to consider:

Get actively involved in the company

Be versatile – take the initiative and show interest in the success of the company along with what it does. An employee should be proud of what he does for an average of 40+ hours per week. A career is like marriage – if you don't put any thought and effort into it, you may be left with nothing one day.

Stay calm

If the re-sizing has already occurred or is in the midst of occurring, stay focused and concentrate on your job. Discuss what you can do to help with your boss.

Look on the bright side

If the worst comes to the worst and you are involved, look on the bright side. Losing your job does not mean the end of the world. It can often open doors to better opportunities. Now is the time to look into all those dream jobs you once yearned for! Consider sending a press release to the trade press and make sure you can be contacted when needed.

 Key points to remember

1. Keep your marketing team lean in the first place. Don't throw people at problems and don't build an empire. Consider using consultants to address short-term challenges and outsourcing to address longer term resource issues.

2. Downsizing or making redundancies can have adverse consequences. Used sparingly and with planning, downsizing can be an organisational lifesaver, but when layoffs are used repeatedly without a thoughtful strategy, it can destroy an organisation's effectiveness. It is vital to think through the long- and short-term consequences and plan ahead to ensure a fundamentally sensible approach is followed.

3. Don't under-estimate the costs and time involved in down-sizing. It is an expensive process and will take a lot of time and energy.

4. How you treat people really matters – both the people who leave and the people who remain. How downsized employees are treated directly affects the morale and retention of those who are not downsized. Engage in appropriate dialogue with both leavers and survivors.

5. Key outcomes of downsizing must be to preserve the organisation's intellectual capital and enhance the corporate culture. Offer employees and shareholders alike a realistic vision for the future of the organisation.

6. Have a ready explanation for downsizing that is true for all stakeholders. There are dangers in making 'macho' management style announcements to the financial community, as these will also be seen and heard by colleagues in the business.

27 Culture Change and Brand Delivery

Power to the People – John Lennon (1971)

In this chapter you will learn:

- *What organisational culture is*
- *Types of organisational culture*
- *How to increase economic value*
- *How to change a corporate culture*
- *Culture change models*

Changing an organisation is a messy, complicated business. A landmark study by Kotter and Heskett (1) indicates that culture change becomes tougher as organisations become more established and successful. The basis for an organisation's initial success can be hindrances to future success if circumstances are different from those which existed previously. The study also suggests that those companies managing their cultures well saw revenue increases of 682% versus 166% for the companies that did not; stock price increases of 901% versus 74%; and net income increases of 756% versus 1%. The purpose of this chapter is to help provide a better understanding of the role and types of culture in organisations, and how you can initiate change to maximise competitive advantage from your own culture.

Organisations, like all groups of human beings including tribes and countries, tend to evolve a culture over a period of time. Some cultures resist change by enacting laws to preserve and protect traditional values and put up barriers to alien ideas and things. For example, the French government has forbidden the commercial use of English words for which there are French equivalents. In contrast, some cultures are very receptive to change. The People's Republic of China has been adopting Western technology and culture in everyday life for the past two decades. In 2003, the Chinese government made the decision that all children in their country must learn English, beginning with the third grade of elementary school. This is likely to accelerate Westernisation.

Definition of organisational culture

As discussed in Chapter 8 From Strategy to Delivery, Daft (2) defines culture as *"a series of values, standard interpretations, insights and ways of thinking that is shared by members of an organisation and passed on to new members"* **8**▶

In other words, culture is *"the 'glue' that provides a common understanding to focus and motivate people to deliver the organisation's vision."*

Looking at this in more detail, organisation culture can be divided into four levels (see Figure 27.1). At the top are 'artifacts' – those aspects (such as dress codes) which can be easily identified yet are hard to understand. Beneath artifacts are 'institutions' – the established structures of an organisation, such as the design and processes by which an organisation operates. Underneath institutions are 'behavioural norms' – the basic ways that employees behave towards one another as well as towards those outside the organisation. These are often enforced by written rules or guidelines in the form of strategies, goals, philosophies and codes of conduct. Finally, underpinning all of these elements are the 'beliefs' of the organisation, the accepted truth or opinion on the things that are considered important. These may be difficult to discern because they exist at a largely unconscious level, yet they form underlying attitudes and beliefs by which the organisation operates – thus they provide a key to understanding why things happen the way they do. They can include deeply held beliefs, for example, about how relationships work and how things get done. They can include shared values such as respect for the individual and belief in the power of teamwork.

Figure 27.1 *Components of organisational culture*

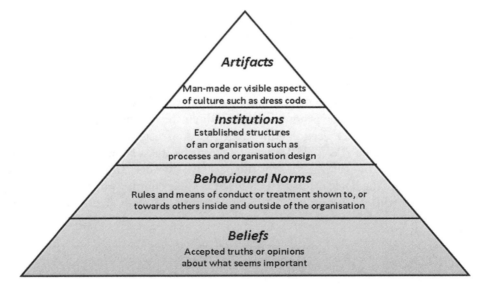

Types of organisation culture

The organic, fragmented and yet interdependent nature of cultures, and myriad of institutions and variables that shape them, means they are ever-changing and hard to define. The shared history of a group helps shape its future. It is usually easier to make observations and statements concerning individual cultural components rather than culture in its entirety.

Based on interviews conducted with businesses across a range of sectors in 2003 (3), the most successful cultures focus on customers and also on delivering a distinctive offering (ie brand) to customers. The same study also revealed two other variables that are useful in describing and delineating organisation cultures:

- size and influence of individual personalities, and
- the nature of control/empowerment mechanisms

Figure 27.2 illustrates these variables in the form of a matrix. Different types of organisation culture are characterised in each quadrant. While successful organisations are evident in each, there can be a tension in achieving the right balance between controlling or directing the organisation and empowering or motivating the people to deliver. These tensions are often only evident as organisations experience 'pain' or market dynamics change.

Figure 27.2 *Types of organisation culture*

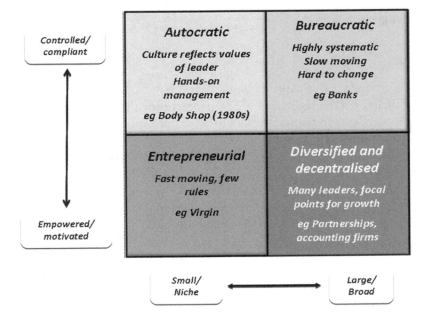

In order to help you understand your organisation and recognise potential cultural issues and opportunities, the following section brings to life the types of organisation culture in each of the quadrants.

Autocratic

These organisations are small and directed and managed by a leader who is very directing or 'hands-on'. As an example the Body Shop in the 1980s and 1990s, when controlled by Anita Roddick. The Body Shop achieved initial fame as an 'issue' brand – its mission was to foster social and environmental change as well as deliver profit. The problem was that the organisation became 'blinkered' and it became difficult to deal with new competitive pressures and replicate the business model outside the UK. This was overcome by franchising, and more recently, by changing senior management.

Entrepreneurial

These organisations are fast-moving and driven by entrepreneurs who also empower others to be entrepreneurial. Virgin is a good example of a brand that owes much of its success to its charismatic leader, Richard Branson. However, as Virgin grew, some entrepreneurial attempts to extend the brand were less successful than others eg cola. Virgin then realised that its real business strength was in starting up businesses and that the brand strength was its 'attitude', in particular, in challenging the 'establishment'. Today, Virgin has redefined itself as a venture capital organisation and established a centralised brand team, charged with adding more control and cohesion to build the brand.

Bureaucratic

These organisations are like super-tankers – hard to manoeuvre. Examples include many large PLCs, particularly banks. The problem for these organisations is that systems and procedures initially instituted to help control and make decisions can also stifle entrepreneurial flair. Employees start to fear challenging the status quo and become risk adverse. This means that the organisations tend continue to follow the assumed business wisdom and be slow to react to changes in the marketplace. Senior management change, the acquisition of new customer-facing skills and reducing organisation layers are strategies that have been employed to deal with these problems.

Diversified and decentralised organisations

These organisations have many units and leaders. Examples include partnerships such as accounting and legal firms, and diversified multi-nationals. The problem with these organisations is that individuals managing their own business units can become too self absorbed to the detriment of the whole. This problem is being dealt with in some firms by creating centralised brand teams, installing management systems and introducing planning processes to enhance control.

 Team questions

Asking where your organisation is on the various axes will help you start to uncover new strengths, weaknesses and opportunities and threats facing your organisation.

Considering what aspects of your culture inhibit your ability to compete to help you determine and prioritise any issues you may need to deal with.

The importance of culture

An aligned and motivated workforce is essential to meet the organisation's objectives. Dissent and/or malaise can dissipate resources, cause employee defections and impede or derail progress.

 Best practice

US retailer Sears famously turned its business round by aligning and motivating employees to deliver customer satisfaction by tracking employee's attitudes and behaviour through to customer satisfaction and financial results (4). The data generated showed that a 5 percentage point improvement in employee attitudes drove a 1.3 percentage point improvement in customer satisfaction, which in turn drove a 0.5% improvement in revenue growth.

An empowered and forward-looking organisation is also essential to anticipate and see off potential threats or problems before they have a serious impact. In increasingly fast-moving markets, it is naïve to assume that business models that work today will automatically work tomorrow. In order to adapt to changing market, customer and competitor dynamics, employees need to be the eyes and ears of the organisation and take the initiative to recommend solutions to deal with problems they see.

Joseph Pine and James Gilmore (5) argue that we are entering an experience economy, in which experiences are as different from services as services are from products (see Figure 27.3). In restaurants such as the Hard Rock or Rainforest cafés, for example, the food is merely a prop for the entertainment experience. As customers experience good service in one area they expect it in the next and as a result even traditional service businesses are becoming more experiential. Moreover there is more economic value to be found. Employees are essential for the delivery of these experiences and what they believe and how they behave is founded in an organisation's culture and values.

Figure 27.3 *Increasing economic value*

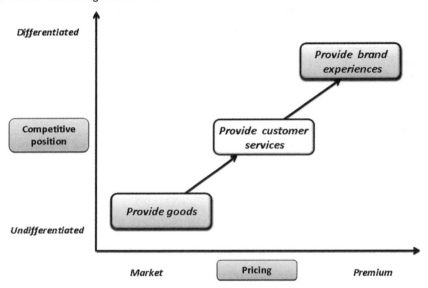

Hardwiring attitudes and beliefs into ways of doing things can have a profound impact on brand stand-out and competitiveness.

 Best practice

Footwear, apparel and accessory brand Nike has evolved an innovative and highly competitive corporate culture to 'just do it'. As Nike's founders say, "*Our mission has always been to provide a competitive edge, to help athletes perform better. We climb inside the athletic mind. We feel every beat of the athletic heart. We flex, bend, twist and torque every inch of athletic sinew and muscle. It's not easy, but it's natural for us. We're athletes.*" This manifests in the nature and pace of product innovation. In turn, it reinforces the very dynamic and competitive brand image.

Where to start

Culture change involves changing the basic beliefs and norms in an organisation to improve organisational performance. It is a form of organisational transformation, that is, both radical and fundamental.

The status quo inherent in organisations usually results when forces resisting change are in balance with the forces pushing for it. In order to shift the balance in favour of change, the status quo needs to be unbalanced. In other words, employees have to be rocked out of their comfort zone so they will realise the need for change. Organisational theorists including Kurt Lewin (6) and Chris Argyris (7) have insisted upon the need for a destabilising element or 'burning bridge' to catalyse change. 'Destabilisers' or 'burning bridges' include:

- Sales or profit decline – particularly if the consequences hit employees' pay packets. In this instance, culture change can be positioned as a means to stave off more deep-rooted cost-cutting, such as downsizing.

- Downsizing – even under circumstances where departures are voluntary. Downsizing signals that the 'psychological contract' between employers and employees has changed (see Chapter 26 Rationalisation or Downsizing). The message is that the employer can no longer offer job security and that management has decided who 'has a future' with the organisation and who does not. The 'new' psychological contract being marketed is conditional employment, (potentially with training and development opportunities to help keep employees 'employable'). The message is 'if you want to continue to work here, you will have to work harder eg be more responsive or more of a team player.' **26**

- Merger, acquisition or joint venture – the combination of two different cultures can often lead to confusion or conflict (see Chapter 25 Mergers and Acquisitions). Cultural mismatches are a key reason why mergers fail. This can present an opportunity to refresh the culture or create a new hybrid. It is likely that the both partners will have something to gain from the other. **25**

- Location change – the events involved in the move all combine to symbolise the dumping of unwanted baggage and a fresh start. The review and abandonment of old files, tools, IT systems, working locations and team allegiances can extend to working practices and behaviours.

 Culture change process

The complex nature of cultures and far-ranging causes and effects means that culture change is very complex. In order to effect change, we recommend a three-step approach along the lines of the strategy development process outlined in Chapter 3 Strategy Development:

❸

- Step 1: Understand the culture now
- Step 2: Define the desired future culture
- Step 3: Develop culture change plans

Step 1: understand the culture now

Due to the multi-faceted nature of cultures, it is important to take a holistic approach to studying cultures and the environment in which they exist. Culture change programmes are best conducted by multi-functional teams including HR and marketing or the corporate brand team. This will help ensure the focus is on addressing the business problems of the organisation.

A mix of qualitative research and quantitative tools and techniques should initially be used to understand the culture and start to generate alternatives:

- self-completion questionnaires, including a list of adjectives to describe the culture; can be used to involve the entire organisation and benchmark perceptions across departments and potentially other organisations
- one-to-one interviews (useful for senior staff, to protect confidentiality, understand causes and effects and uncover responses to sensitive, potentially personal responses; can also be therapeutic for respondents to get issues off their chests)
- group discussions (useful to explore commonalities and differences in opinion among particular work groups or departments as well as devise solutions to problems by utlising the creativity of the group)
- observation of group language, customs, traditions, and interactions

An impartial moderator can help desensitise issues, protect confidentiality and encourage more open responses.

Some questions to ask include:

- What are the business problems that we need to overcome?
- What are the causes behind the problems and, if we are to address this problem, what do people need to do differently?
- In what areas do we need to prioritise investment to generate the desired returns?
- What would cause resistance to change at an individual level and how do we overcome this?
- What adjectives describe the culture now and how we'd like it to be in the future?

Step 2: define the desired future culture

- Once the current culture and associated causes and effects have been fully understood, it will be possible to start to define a desired future culture as well as methods to effect change. This is likely to be an iterative process and the aim should be to create and agree a draft definition by consensus.

- Ideally the process to draft the desired future culture should ideally reflect some aspects of the desired culture itself, for example, by empowering a cross-functional team – this can be a powerful signal of desired change in itself. Equally, you may feel bold enough to open up the challenge to the organisation as a whole in the form of a competition.

- However, ultimately all levels of the organisation will need to be involved, in order to secure buy-in.

- The document that defines the culture should also be unique to the organisation concerned as it will also be an embodiment of the culture itself. Some ideas and models are described later in this chapter.

- Here is a checklist of questions to ask when defining a desired culture. If you can answer yes to all of these, you may not go far wrong.
  - Are they compatible with our business goals and strategies?
  - Do they reflect what makes our organisation different and better in the customer's eye?
  - Do they reflect what we want people to do?
  - Do they reflect how we want people to behave?
  - Is what we want people to do credible, believable and achievable?
  - Is the manner in which we propose to document (and ultimately disseminate) the culture consistent with the culture itself?

Step 3: develop culture change plans

- The complexity of culture change inevitably means that a multi-faceted approach will be needed to effect change. Employees need to buy into the vision and also see personal benefits in change. Both carrots and sticks will be needed here. Bear in mind that culture change takes time and research supports the idea that a multi-year effort is required.

- Here are a number of tools and techniques that you could use:
  - The full range of internal communication vehicles (departmental meetings, job reviews, notice boards, publications, Intranet, email etc) are essential to ensure that ideologies are understandable and convincing. Communicate widely and repeatedly and encourage others to join in.

- On the job learning, peer-coaching or local learning community based methods are practical and enable each member to be held accountable to behave in a manner that adheres to the desired type of culture that an organisation wishes to cultivate.
- Themed workshops or working sessions that involve self discovery and discussion of issues and opportunities are more powerful than presentations and telling or selling alone. Such sessions also work harder when:
  - messages are customised to specific working groups eg functional areas
  - working groups share the same discovery experiences
  - working groups are empowered to develop their own change plans and take these back into the work place
- The full range of HR tools, including job recruitment processes, job performance measurement and remuneration and reward procedures are essential to any change programme.
- Social activities – the primary ways that people learn their cultures is through the social experiences. Think laterally how you could modify existing social activities or introduce new ones to accelerate change.

Success factors for managing a culture change programme

Find and cultivate innovative leadership

Leadership must champion change and reinforce commitment to the new culture, otherwise it will be undermined. If leadership is unaware and inconsistent then confusion can ensue. If leadership does not lead the culture then you risk being buried by it. Empower change champions throughout the organisation to help accelerate the process of diffusion and change.

Carrot AND stick approach

Employees at every level must be committed to making imaginative contributions to organisational success. They need to be empowered to take responsibility for the organisation and will do so more readily if this is linked to their own destiny. Write culture change behaviours into contracts and performance review procedures. Include both incentives (carrots) to reward positive contributions, and disincentives (sticks) to discourage negative contributions.

- Treat people like you want them to treat customers; unless employees experience desired behaviours for themselves, they are never likely to understand or be motivated enough to use the same approach in their dealings with customers.

- Institutionalise change; at every stage, the change process is under threat though forgetfulness, omission, abandonment or return to an earlier stage. After successful implementation, hard wire processes and procedures to reinforce the benefits and embed learning.
- Measure, monitor and feed back progress; measure change and look out for quick wins – both at an organisational and individual level. Gathering information will help identify areas that require most attention so you can fine tune the change programme. It will also help generate stories that reinforce positive learning. Make sure the stories are well publicised in order to embed learning into the culture.
- Creative refreshment to maintain momentum; people can easily become bored and it is important to avoid the danger of the change programme becoming 'this year's initiative'. Use creativity to refresh and refuel the change programme with new activities.

 Best practice

When Citibank underwent a major change programme in the 1990s, employees were promoted, trained or let go on the basis of their performance on two measures – meeting their job objectives and living the new customer-focused culture. Those that met both were promoted. Those that failed one were retrained and those that failed both were let go. Consider hiring new employees or seconding employees from, or to, other departments or companies to infuse new skills and ideas.

 **Pitfalls to avoid**

'Initiativitis'

According to recent research in the US, two thirds of the Fortune 100 (and probably an equally significant proportion of small and medium-sized companies) claim to be in the middle of change programmes designed to improve the behaviour and skills of employees (8). Change programmes abound under many names – Total Quality Management (TQM), Six Sigma, Customer First, Living the Brand and so on. While all are potentially worthwhile, beware of instituting too many initiatives – the effect of a series of disconnected initiatives can cause scepticism, loss of credibility and comprehension among employees. Ultimately it can undermine their very purpose. Make sure your change programme evolves in a cohesive fashion over time.

'Sheep dips'

It has become popular in recent years for change programmes to centre around one-day or one-off workshops. While these workshops may be relatively low cost and offer benefits, they have been discredited by some as 'sheep dips'. It is very unlikely that a one-off initiative will deliver long-lasting culture change. Take this into account in your planning.

Mismatches between behaviours inside the organisation and outside perceptions

Customers, as we have discussed, are increasingly discerning. While a customer may be attracted to an organisation through its brand image, loyalty will be won and lost by their personal experience of the organisation. If the customer experience falls short of expectations that have been created through advertising and promotion then confidence will be undermined.

Statements of 'motherhood and apple pie'

There is a danger in designing cultural values that are both obvious and the same as the next organisation. This too can undermine credibility. Try and articulate distinctive values that help enhance brand stand-out. Also use distinctive communications and vehicles such as symbols, rituals and stories to reinforce your desired cultural values.

🎣 Tools and techniques

In this section we describe three related models to help define cultures – each contains a different level of detail. What's most important however is that the format chosen is appropriate to your own culture, and fit for the purpose that it is intended.

Figure 27.4 describes current and desired cultural values in a similar format to the Brand Strengths or Muscles described in Chapter 16 Brand Management and Positioning. This is designed to aid clarity and comprehension when the two models are used together. The additional benefit of this model is that the desired culture change shift is very clear.

16

Figures 27.5 and 27.6 explain the desired cultural values in more detail.

Figure 27.4 *Current and desired cultural values*

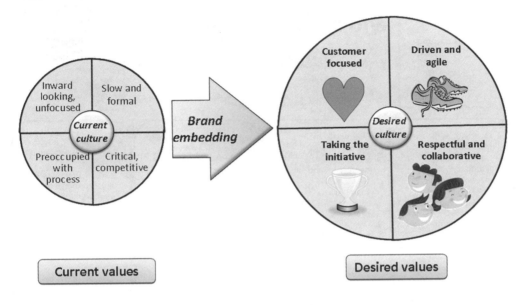

Figure 27.5 *Desired culture and values Model 1*

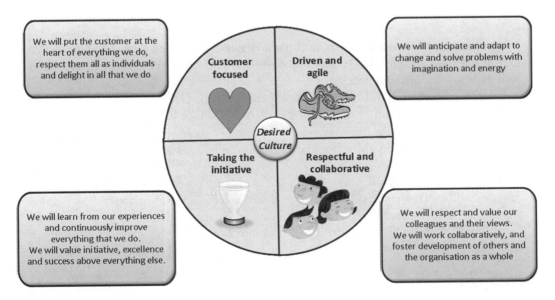

Figure 27.6 *Desired culture and values Model 2*

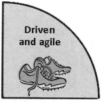

Customer focused

Taking the initiative

Respectful and collaborative

Driven and agile

- Customer at the heart of everything we do
- Understanding, anticipating and meeting customers' needs at all times
  - Being welcoming/ accessible
  - Recognising customers as individuals
  - Being expert in all we do
  - Going that extra mile to delight

- Learning from experiences
- Valuing initiative, excellence, and success above all else
- Taking personal responsibility to solve problems
- Valuing and empowering others to take initiatives and deliver results

- Valuing and respecting our colleagues and their different opinions
- Believing in the power of teamwork to generate better solutions
- Fostering the development and well being of others and the organisation as a whole

- Anticipating, adapting to and responding to change
- Solving problems with energy, imagination and urgency
- Overcoming road-blocks and never taking no for an answer

 Best practice

The mobile phone retailer Carphone Warehouse is widely regarded as a great experience brand. It has achieved this by institutionalising its focus on meeting customer needs. The Carphone Warehouse culture is defined by 'five fundamental rules'. The rules speak for themselves and need little embellishment. They apply not just in stores but also in call centres and support functions. They appear on the reverse side of the business cards of all employees and are lived and breathed by everyone within the company. The rules are set out below:

1. If we don't look after the customer, someone else will.
3. Nothing is gained by winning an argument but losing a customer.
4. Always deliver what we promise. If in doubt, under-promise and over-deliver.
5. Always treat customers as we ourselves would like to be treated.
6. The reputation of the whole company is in the hands of each individual.

Application of the rules starts with recruitment – only people who 'love customers' are hired. All pay and benefits are linked to customer care and it is even in a director's job description to listen to customer care telephone calls. Carphone Warehouse also invests four times the average on training – all employees are required to attend a two-week induction programme, where half of this time is spent on customer care and half on technical training. They also invest in 'fun nights out' to engage and reward emotionally.

By contrast, a major financial services company produced a set of values and distributed these to employees on cards. In this instance, the words were quite formal and authoritarian as was the manner with which the cards were dispensed. Unfortunately, the cards became a company joke and this undermined the credibility of the initiative. This serves to underline the point that successful culture change requires more than a few snappy words. It requires fundamental behaviour change and leadership by example to direct and empower all of the people in the organisation.

 Key points to remember

1. As customers experience good service in one market, they increasingly expect it in another. It is imperative for organisations to strive for continuous internal improvement, as this impacts on how they behave towards, and are perceived by, customers.

2. Organisation cultures play a fundamental role in aligning and motivating employees to meet an organisation's objectives. Successful cultures and culture change programmes can be vital to sustain and increase organisation value, and reinforce competitiveness and stand-out in the marketplace.

3. The difficulty in changing an organisation's culture should not be underestimated. The business as a whole, and in particular, HR and marketing or central brand teams need to bring people together to effect change.

4. The most successful organisations have cultures that are highly customer-centric.

5. Delivering a unique customer or brand experience that goes beyond plain service is an increasing differentiator. It is something that you should aspire to achieve.

6. Throughout a culture change programme the marketing director and the rest of the leadership team need to be highly visible and lead by example. Any inconsistency in behaviour will undermine the efforts to achieve change.

7. A full range of communications and HR tools will be needed to effect sustained and lasting change. Expect that it will be a multi-year effort.

28 Crisis Planning and Management

Bridge over Troubled Water – Simon and Garfunkel (1970)

In this chapter you will learn:

- *How to create a disaster management plan*
- *How to conduct a risk assessment*
- *What to do if and when a crisis occurs*

Even the most successful, efficiently run organisations can sometimes encounter crises. Disaster can strike in any place and at any time, including within the next 24 hours, so it's important that you are always well prepared. Problems can occur through fire, flood, a terrorist or pressure group attack, computer system failure and many more unforeseen circumstances. They can cause serious interruption to essential aspects of your business. They can also ultimately cause loss of customers, intellectual property, revenue and much worse. It only takes one unforeseen disaster to occur, one disgruntled customer to go to a newspaper, one aggrieved employee to post something on the Internet, and the reputation and future of your organisation could be damaged forever.

The key to handling such a crisis effectively is to put plans in place before it actually happens. This chapter is designed to help you anticipate and prepare in order to prevent or mitigate the effect of possible disasters as well as take action should disaster strike.

 Crisis planning process

Although all disasters and crises are different, the process of planning and setting effective procedures can follow a universal format. Having this already in place will reduce any potential negative effects. You can become well prepared by following a simple step-by-step process, which will help you identify the things that could go wrong and set a plan to prevent or counter them when they do. Here is a six step process to help you:

- Step 1: Starting out

- Step 2: Risk and impact assessment
- Step 3: Develop a disaster recovery plan
- Step 4: Test the plan
- Step 5: Staff training
- Step 6: Maintain the plan

Step 1: starting out

- It is vital that the organisation as a whole takes the development and maintenance of the disaster recovery or business continuity plan seriously. Responsibility for some critical areas will lie with the marketing department – it is not one of those tasks that can be left until everyone has time to deal with it.
- The contingency plan needs to be developed by a team representing all functional areas of the organisation. If the organisation is large enough a formal project needs to be established, which must have approval and support from the board.
- Appoint a disaster recovery manager. This should be someone with good administration and implementation skills, and who has the respect of colleagues.

Step 2: risk and impact assessment

- One of the first tasks to undertake in contingency planning is to prepare a comprehensive list of the potentially serious incidents that could affect the normal operations of the organisation. This list should include all possible incidents, no matter how seemingly unlikely their occurrence.
- Proforma 28A provides an initial list of risks and areas to be considered.

Proforma 28A Risk assessment template

Risk	*Questions to ask*	*Risk mitigation plans*
Buildings	What are the risks to the buildings from floods, fire, theft, vandalism or invasion by pests?	Regular and documented building maintenance; define locations of, for example, water and electrical supplies, stopcocks, fuse boxes, isolation valves and systems; plan for alternative accommodation/control centre from which to manage disaster recovery operations.
Care of staff	How do we ensure the security, safety and wellbeing of staff, or deal with the aftermath of potential disasters?	Establish plans for providing necessary food, water and medical care; establish plans for counselling support;

Communications	What are internal communications risks and needs? How can we communicate with all of our staff quickly and effectively? What are the external communication needs and risks? How do we deal with the press?	Maintain up-to-date records with staff contact details; assign clear responsibilities for communications; prepare short press releases for potential eventualities.
Data	What are the risks from loss of data?	Regular data back-ups; staff data access policies.
Emergency suppliers and equipment	What external resources are needed to help overcome the disaster eg data recovery firms, PR companies?	Establish a list of contacts, including provision for out of hours support; establish contacts and procedures for rapid replenishment of stock or other supplies that may be needed in an emergency.
Emergency services	What emergency services could be needed?	Establish contacts with key services and create a list of contact details, including for out of hours support.
Equipment	What are the risks through equipment failure?	Regular and documented equipment and building maintenance; define salvage priorities.
Fire	What are the fire risks and escape procedures?	Regular fire hazard checks, fire drills and installation of warning and prevention equipment.
Health and safety	What are the health and safety risks?	Clear health and safety and evacuation policies.
Infestation	What are the risks of infestation?	Regular checks for signs of infestation.
Insurance	What's the scope of current insurance? What other risks can be insured?	Comprehensive insurance, process for alerting the insurance company and gaining authority to spend money if needed; investigate the cost of insuring for consequential loss.
IT	What are the risks from computer attack or malfunction?	Install appropriate anti-virus software and arrange alternative systems; determine priorities for restoring IT; arrange clean start-up discs for systems.

Procedures	What are the risks through loss of staff eg illness, injury etc?	Document all key procedures and disaster recovery plans; avoid allowing key staff to become totally indispensable – even in the short term; make appropriate arrangements for staff cover.
Security	What are the risks from break-ins or theft, vandalism, bomb attacks and arson?	Staff policies and use of security equipment, security patrols and checks.
Staff responsibilities	Who does what in the event of a disaster?	Assign a clear chain of command and responsibilities for all aspects of disaster planning and recovery; ensure effective training.

- Consider how each incident could affect the organisation as a whole, staff, customers as well as the reaction of the media. Against each item listed, the project team or manager should allocate a probability rating. Each incident should also be rated for potential level of severity of impact. From this information, it will become much easier to frame the plan in the context of the real needs of the organisation and the impact of any disaster on it.
- Use specialist experts to advise on the nature of risks and how they can be mitigated or overcome eg fire, IT etc.
- Then consider all the possible media that might report on your business and assess the damage each could cause. List details, keeping this information secure.

Step 3: develop a disaster recovery plan

- Once the assessment stage has been completed, the plan can be established. This should detail the range of activities to mitigate the identified risks as well as milestones to move the organisation from its disrupted status back to normal operations.
- The first important milestone is the process that deals with the immediate aftermath of the disaster. This may involve the emergency services or other specialists trained to deal with extreme situations.
- The next stage is to determine which critical business functions need to be resumed and in what order. The plan will be detailed, and will identify key individuals who should be familiar with their duties under the plan.
- During the planning stage, it will also be important to establish clear lines of communication with employees, key customers and suppliers, and the media. The last of these involves appointing a press spokesperson. It's a good idea for the spokesperson to establish a good relationship with local and trade journalists before any crisis occurs. It is also helpful to prepare procedures to be followed and draft statements to deal with potential eventualities.

Step 4: test the plan

- Once the plan has been developed it must be subjected to rigorous testing. This should be carried out in a suitable environment in order to reproduce authentic conditions in so far as this is possible.

- The plan must be tested by those persons who would undertake the activities in question if the situation being tested occurred in reality. The test procedures should be documented and the results recorded. This will help obtain feedback so that the plan can be fine-tuned.

- Equally, audit both the plan itself and the contingency arrangements supporting it. Do not take any short cuts just because it is a test.

Step 5: staff training

- This stage follows on from the development of the plan and the successful testing and audit of activities.

- All staff must be made aware of the plan and its contents and their own related duties and responsibilities.

- It is also important that staff take the disaster recovery planning seriously, even if the events that would trigger the event seem remote. Obtain feedback in order to ensure that responsibilities and duties are understood, particularly those *that require dependency on actions being taken by third parties.*

Step 6: maintain the plan

- The plan must always be kept up to date and applicable to current business circumstances. This means that any changes to the business process or relative parts must be properly reflected within the plan.

- Someone must be assigned responsibility for ensuring that the plan is maintained and updated regularly and should therefore ensure that information concerning changes to the business process is properly communicated.

- Any changes or amendments made to the plan must be fully tested. Staff should also be kept abreast of such changes insofar as they affect their duties and responsibilities.

What to do when a crisis occurs

First, don't panic! The detailed actions that need to be taken will depend on the nature of the crisis and the local situation. However, if you have followed the planning and procedures process and this is properly documented, these should provide a framework for managing the crisis. It should be noted at this point that the plan must cover what to do both during and outside working hours – alerting key management personnel, contacting emergency services and other necessary parties. Make it clear under what circumstances any building should be evacuated.

Procedures for initial action on discovering disaster

- alert the emergency services as necessary
- alert the disaster reaction manager, disaster reaction teams and press spokesperson
- assess the damage and scale of response needed
- establish a control centre from which you can co-ordinate and direct your response to the disaster
- communicate and brief staff as documented in the disaster recovery plan
- implement disaster recovery plan
- ensure all media communications are directed through the communications manager/press spokesperson (make sure no-one else speaks to the press)

Success factors for dealing with a crisis

From the perspective of the marketing director and/or corporate communications director, here are a few key areas to pay attention to:

Ensure proactive and positive communications

- Given the likelihood of confusion, fear and possibly panic, there is likely to be a risk to your brand reputation. Considered, proactive and positive communications will be vital both within the organisation and to reassure the public at large.
- Stay calm and communicate. Inform staff, customers and suppliers of problems where possible, rather than leaving them to discover the news in the media.
- Provide a short statement. If journalists call, your spokesperson should never say "no comment". This will make your business appear at fault, even if it is not. If more time is needed to consider a response, suggest when the spokesperson will call back or send an extended statement. Keep to this and try to answer questions as honestly and briefly as possible. If you're not comfortable with the press (and many people aren't), consider some media training.
- Put a positive spin on a crisis to neutralise its effect. Good news is often 'no news' to a journalist. You might be able to help people being made redundant to find new local work or could be closing a factory but moving the business online to serve the online global market.
- Be proactive rather than reactive when you have foreseen potential bad publicity,

such as job losses. Stress the positive. Even if you can't control the media, you can do your best to influence it.

- Follow up with positive actions, changes and news. After a crisis, emphasising positive stories – such as improved practices and community involvement – will help to restore your reputation in the longer term. You can turn bad publicity round by listening to customers, assessing where improvements can be made and by finding creative solutions to turn the negative into a positive perception of your company. Think proactively, prepare and communicate and you'll ride out the storm.

Act swiftly to recall affected products

History is littered with brands that have been damaged by failing to act quickly to protect the public from risk. Err on the side of caution and the best interests of staff and customers at all times to maintain goodwill. Determine what batches of products are affected and prepare clear recall notices. Be clear about the level or risk. Go out of your way to make good any damage caused. Remember that dealing with these situations can help cement customer relationships for life and that failing to deal with them can have the reverse effect.

Ensure speedy stock replenishment

Also act quickly to ensure that supplies are replenished. It will be helpful to have contingency plans that can be enacted in the event of a sudden need.

Manage interruption to service

Experience has shown that initial public concern and sympathy following a disaster rapidly wears off if services continue to be out of action for any length of time. Therefore, the disaster recovery manager must deal with the long-term effects while simultaneously maintaining an acceptable level of service to customers. Regular progress reports will help retain the support of customers and senior management. The disaster recovery manager should continue to keep the communications manager informed as long as the media remain interested in the story.

If staff levels permit, it is best to have two separate teams – one to deal with recovery and the other with service continuity. It is possible, depending on the scale of the disaster that both teams will need to operate out of temporary accommodation. This will be a difficult time for staff, particularly if the recovery period is a protracted one. Staff must be kept busy, motivated and informed if their morale is to be maintained beyond the immediate recovery period.

Care for staff

Do not underestimate the impact of a disaster on staff. The recovery phase can take much longer than initially anticipated, and the impact on staff morale can be long-lasting. In some cases, staff counselling may be appropriate.

Learn from the disaster

Every disaster should lead to a re-examination of an organisation's policies and procedures to make sure that lessons are learned and that the likelihood of the same disaster occurring again is kept to a minimum.

Each time the Disaster Recovery Plan is implemented, the procedures followed should be analysed and a report written, which assesses the success of the operation and makes recommendations for any necessary changes. Fresh risk assessment exercises should also be undertaken for relevant areas and activities. Any lessons should be documented in a Revised Disaster Recovery Plan.

Disaster-specific pointers

Here are a few pointers to deal with specific types of disaster:

Dealing with terrorist threats

If you are given a telephone warning, do not cut off the conversation, keep the caller talking and obtain as much information as possible. For example, where a bomb is located? What time will it go off? What are the motives of the terrorist? Can you get more details on the identity of the caller (who does he/she represent, accent, background noises etc)?

Suspect objects and packages

Do not move or touch suspect packages in any way. Evacuate the building (the procedure should be part of your Disaster Recovery Plan) and inform the police. Where possible, leave doors and windows open in the vicinity of the package. The person who first discovered the package should be made available to the police.

IT

Recovery from an IT-based disaster may be a matter of restoring the system from back-ups. However, where theft or vandalism or other damage to hardware has occurred, new hardware may need to be ordered and assembled before backups can be used. Ordering of new hardware may be delayed by negotiations with insurers. Make sure that your plan takes account of how to minimise any such delays. Local procedures for service continuity may have to be implemented for the intervening period.

Insurance claims

In all situations, lists of materials, equipment and furniture damaged in the disaster will need to be itemised so that insurance claims can be prepared. Order replacement items and equipment as soon as local circumstances allow (eg insurance payments). Inventories will have to be updated to reflect losses and new purchases. In extreme disaster situations (eg if your building is destroyed by fire), you will most likely get an unsolicited visit from a 'risk assessment adviser' offering to maximise the claim from your insurer. These advisers prey on people who are in distressed states and not thinking clearly. They do not work for nothing and will want a hefty percentage of your eventual claim. Do not make any commitments on the spot. Tell them you will only make a decision when you have had time to fully assess the company's position.

Cash management

Procedures should also be put in place to ensure that post is received and invoices processed. This may be critical to the long-term health of the organisation. Make sure that your bankers are aware of or even part of your plan.

 Key points to remember

1. Disaster can occur at any time and in any place. Remember the problems that have befallen brands including Coca-Cola, Hoover, Perrier, Persil, Ratners and Railtrack. The corporate communications or marketing department is likely to be responsible for maintaining customer and media communications, as well as sales and services, and will be at the centre of any disaster that strikes.

2. Creating, testing and honing a robust disaster recovery plan is essential to mitigating the risks of possible disasters, as well as helping return the business to normal. Get board agreement and support for such a plan.

3. Do not underestimate the importance of proactive and positive staff, customer and media communications to maintain goodwill, and your brand reputation. Prepare responses to potential eventualities.

4. Practice responding to emergencies to help pressure-test your plans and identify any weaknesses that should be reflected in them.

Communicating with Other Audiences

Message to the World – David Cassidy (1990)

In this chapter you will learn:

- *The benefits of communicating with different audiences*
- *Who are potential audiences and their needs*
- *The importance of corporate social responsibility and key messages*
- *How to create an effective communications plan*

Sometimes the marketing director must also play a key role in co-ordinating communications to multiple audiences. There may be several reasons for this.

First, as part of a plan to drive growth, there will be a need to communicate with and motivate all internal as well as external audiences. For example there may be a need to influence political audiences in order to create conditions for growth. Second, where the brand is concerned, it is vital to manage communications in order to ensure a consistent take-out across all audiences. Third, with increasing demand and pressure for greater corporate social responsibility through more stringent corporate governance standards, as well as customer demand, there is an increasing need for internal company practices to improve. Furthermore, as companies rely on local communities, both for employees as well as customers, there is an increasing needs to build connections with local communities. This chapter is designed to provide insights and advice to help you communicate effectively with other audiences.

 Where to start?

Where the customer and channels of distribution are paramount, the marketing function should be seen as setting communication guidelines and providing the creative frameworks for all company communications.

How often have you seen tiniest detail inhibit otherwise good work? Consider the email layout and typeface with no company protocol or agreed signature, or the HR advertisement produced with only the lightest but barely visible corporate identity.

A period of growth can be best kick-started by a re-launch. Whether full blown or soft, it gives the whole organisation the opportunity to look to the future with fresh eyes.

Success factors for managing company-wide communications

Create a 'brand-based' communications plan

For each audience, develop a simple but separate communication strategy and set of templates based on the brand values agreed with the appropriate director.

For those organisations that are multi-national or dominant in a country, the role of communicating with other audiences is driven by what has become known as corporate social responsibility (CSR). In the UK, there is now a government minister of CSR, and a business as well as a financial review may well become a statutory requirement. Naturally, many organisations have already embraced CSR and taken many voluntary steps to improve the quality of life for employees and their families as well as for their local communities and society at large.

Every business should, of course, act responsibly. The major social concerns are fair trading and employment practice, the environment and the local community. As a prerequisite, marketing should embrace the communication issues in the context of the brand. Moreover, if your brand is large enough, the practice of social marketing should be considered. The basis of both CSR and social marketing has to be the brand and its positioning. The stronger it is, the easier that task is. As an example of best practice, Tesco has the strapline 'Every little helps' at the heart of its annual report to shareholders.

Create an easy- to-use style guide

Start by preparing an easily accessible style guide with examples. Consider making this available on the company Intranet with downloadable and easy-to-use templates that can be customised to a range of needs, for example HR guidelines or PR releases. This is so much more effective than the dry manual followed by many design agencies. Consider including a glossary of 'brand words' or 'useful terms'.

Provide implementation support

Help select and create a roster of designers and producers for all communication materials. Create the necessary procedures to ensure that all communications are checked for accuracy, completeness, brand building and risk avoidance. For example, as and when it is relevant, ensure that all communications are signed off by the legal/compliance, marketing and channel representatives.

Keep communications records and undertake regular reviews

Ask for a copy of everything and keep an up-to-date file or log. Keeping PR releases/clippings can be useful and interesting reading material for reception areas. In the Internet age, the media is monitored by the likes of Factiva (part of Dow Jones – News International), a company that monitors messages and how they are covered and then indicates the most influential media as well as the actual journalists. Undertake regular communication reviews to keep a track on the performance of your communicators, communications and effectiveness. This helps keep the messages on track and the targeting as precise as possible.

Be ready for disasters

Chapter 28 Crisis Planning and Management provides more in-depth insights on this subject – a summary is provided here. Make sure that you have in place a complete plan that is ready to roll out immediately if disaster strikes. Disaster can make or break any brand. If a disaster strikes, embrace it and show that your brand or company can deal with such situations positively, fairly and effectively. That way you and your brand will emerge stronger (this takes planning specialists and another book). Make sure you have a company spokesperson who is trained and prepared for all media. **(28▶)**

Defining the audiences

The target audiences beyond customer and distribution are shown in Figure 29.1. Don't forget that the overall beneficiary will often be the customer.

Staff and their families

Work with HR to provide an accessible means of communication concerning the company handbook, history and career guides to name a few. Establish an 'open day' or create a 'reach-out' programme so that all can be involved once or twice a year.

The board

Keeping your fellow board members abreast of and involved in what you are doing is vital. This can also help you build your relationship with them and support the growth agenda. This is covered in detail in Chapter 13 Managing the Board and Business as a Whole. A summary follows: **(13▶)**

Figure 29.1 *Corporate social responsibility audiences*

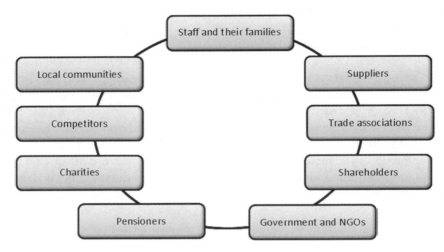

- use your marketing resources to prepare key presentations
- develop brand value-led motivation programmes and 'off the shelf' training schemes
- customise communication to reflect and strengthen your own brand
- instigate new employee 'communication vehicles'; consider internal magazines, events, competitions, blogs and the Internet for your colleagues to communicate to their staff and the business as a whole and do the same for all management teams.

Suppliers

Probably the most under-utilised resource any organisation has is its supplier base.

Strengthening ties and more proactive supply chain management can help your company realise many additional benefits, for example, better terms, first refusal on new products and more insightful intelligence as well as a more stable supply line.

Marketing's remit can involve simple communications through to joint funding of activities. Consider using meetings or conferences to establish guidelines as well as supplier awards to enhance relationships and margins.

Trade associations

Trade associations fulfil many purposes from providing a stronger voice on issues and opportunities through to the provision of intelligence and helping lead and develop industries and professions. The value of a trade association will probably depend on the industry you are in or association to which you belong. Whether you see lots or little value in membership, it is important at least to maintain a minimal presence so you can become further involved whenever it may be necessary.

Shareholders and the city

If your company is publicly listed, you probably have a fellow director of corporate affairs who will be responsible for the city relationship. However, you do have the chance to have some influence.

Shareholders, as well as the professional investment community and the associated media, can often be easily encompassed in an overall consumer campaign and benefit from your investment in other media, especially the financial press.

Equally, these audiences will comprise highly influential and opinion-leading consumers who can be powerful advocates of your products and services. The corporate report is a powerful vehicle to communicate your corporate as well as brand messages. Consider setting up shareholder benefit schemes and offering incentives to increase trial, familiarity, purchase, usage and endorsement of your products. However, also bear in mind that not all investors are the same, and a 'one size fits all' approach to communications may miss the mark. Use your marketing and research skills to understand the needs of the different audiences so you can better target messages that will meet their needs and inspire.

The increasing presence of investment and share-dealing websites and related online discussion boards provides a powerful vehicle for both one- and two-way communications. Keeping an eye on these boards will enable you to learn how both you and your competitors are perceived, as well as provide the opportunity to set the record straight.

Government

We used to be almost afraid of politics but with green issues and carbon footprints increasing in both public and political importance, your marketing strategy must embrace both the ethical and environmental issues beyond legislation so that it becomes publicly endorsed.

Pensioners

Legislation now mandates that pensioners must be provided with an annual update on the performance of the pension fund. As one-time employees, this audience will be potential advocates and opinion leaders of your brand. Use your annual update as an opportunity to provide them with information to help sell your brand, products and services.

Charities

Carefully selecting and supporting specific charities related to the overall direction and role of your company in society can enhance the company's reputation and its legacy for the future. These same criteria should be used in the choice of educational and scientific support.

Devising a policy that helps build your brand will help you focus your investments as well as save precious time and resources in dealing with requests for donations.

Competitors

Work with your fellow directors to establish strategies to collaborate with your competitors where it is in your mutual interests, and vice versa. There may be some areas where collaboration would be opportune, for example, to enable free trade across borders, and some areas where there is a particular risk of divulging commercially sensitive information. With increasing Internet threats from hackers, viruses and phishing, this area of your business may merit particular attention. Within the business, in addition to the protection afforded by the usual door security, signing in measures and non-disclosure agreements, some companies enforce strict clear desk policies at the end of the day to avoid sensitive information falling into the wrong hands.

Local communities

Building strong links with your local community can work to both your advantage and theirs. You may already view your local community as a ready pool of qualified labour and customers. Equally, your local community may see you as a source of employment and support for the local economy. Unless you are a pollutant (air, noise, smoke, smell, traffic, light etc.), you may rightfully expect them to be already on your side. Some may also be brand advocates. You should therefore take advantage of the many opportunities to 'oil the wheels' and facilitate goodwill. This can be achieved in many ways, for example, by investment, sponsorship or the loan of talent to support schools, and community or sports associations. Choose areas that support your brand. Where there are issues, it will also be in your interests to set up joint working groups with the local community to address them.

Defining the messages

The principles and sequence of activities that underpin a company's reputation are described in Figure 29.2 below.

Figure 29.2 *The path of corporate social responsibility*

Having defined the key audiences, identify and develop a specific contact strategy for each one. This can then roll up into an overall plan.

The key messages will largely be dictated by the company's mission and the influence of the brand(s). From these will stem the fundamental business principles on which the business is founded so that a policy can be established on the key areas of CSR, not only in the recognition of the law but also how the company will actually implement the policy. In operational terms, this will ultimately impact on:

* the environment – what are your policies to minimise carbon emissions and maximise sustainability?
* staff – what are your policies to protect and ensure the safety of your workforce and visitors? What are your policies to ensure diversity and equality as well as training and development?
* procurement – what are your policies to your suppliers to maintain your business as well as your ethical reputation?
* the community – what are your policies to support the community as a whole; both as customers and neighbours, and as a catchment pool for labour?

What messages do you drive through to the target audiences? How green are you? How responsible?

There are two things that, as a marketer, you can do. The first is to express communications in terms of the brand, and the second is to set some standards and provide some measurement and evidence of improvements.

These standards, while they may well be part of the overall management controls, also need to be presented in the form of a CSR review on an ongoing basis, to prove that the correct standards have been achieved or that relevant progress is being made.

Keeping on track using knowledge management

Creating the messages and responding to issues of public, government and media concern can be greatly aided by knowledge management.

The demands of keeping tabs on all the activity of a large organisation and filing and retrieving all the information have brought the previously doubted skills of librarianship to the fore, now in a new guise, coupling the art of taxonomy with the understanding of cyberspace. Taxonomy is the practice and science of classification. Having a company information manager is a must for every organisation needing to produce accurate corporate responsibility reviews. Of course, there is much more that this function can undertake such as helping to build and manage 'communities of practice' and facilitate interdepartmental communication and understanding.

 Key points to remember

1. The media, public interest and the law itself are all extending their reach into trading organisations – this means that communication with a range of audiences over and above the consumer is an increasing and essential part of doing business.

2. Whether or not your organisation has a specialist communications function, you should ensure that marketing structures, thinking and communication plans are framed to ensure that the brand really benefits.

3. To build a reputation as a good corporate and socially responsible citizen, set out your policies to do this, report against them and demonstrate sustained progress to meet the aspirations you have set.

4. Creating the messages and responding to issues of public, government and media concern can be greatly aided by knowledge management. This is a role that fits well with that of the marketing director and as part of your 'early warning radar', so work with, or help create, this function in order to remain alert to opportunities and threats in the marketplace.

30 • Marketing and the Law

Right Thing to Do – Carly Simon (1973)

In this chapter you will learn:

- *Key laws that govern the marketing profession*
  - *Consumer protection*
  - *Competition*
  - *Environment*
  - *Copyright & patents*

Marketing maintains the public face of a company so it goes without saying that you should aim to stay within the law in all you do. In practice the larger the organisation the more there will be in terms of structural support, from company secretary to company lawyer and risk manager. The starting point should not necessarily be the law as much as the good practice laid down by the industry bodies, both trade associations such as the Institute of Sales Promotion and organisations such as the Advertising Standards Authority which will give valuable advice to avoid any possible transgression. These organisations also issue codes of practice for you to follow – often easier to understand that the law.

Yet we live in an evermore ordered world, and the law will inevitably impinge upon your work.. In fact the government and the European Union (EU) have introduced many laws that affect the relationship between business, consumers and increasingly, the environment. Research by the Chartered Institute of Marketing (CIM) indicates that the majority of marketers fail to have a good understanding of the laws that govern the marketing profession (1). This chapter summarises some of the main areas to be aware of and legal devices that should be used to protect business assets.

Legislation also changes continually and contains many nuances that are open to interpretation until challenged in a court of law. At that point, courts may make a ruling that sets a precedent and effectively updates the law.

You should therefore always refer any potential issues to your own solicitor to be sure you are aware of the latest legal situation. Maintaining good relations with your solicitor is also important as he or she can be an important ally in helping you legally maximise the benefits from your marketing activities.

The main purposes of these laws affecting marketers are:

- to protect consumers from unfair practices
- to make sure there is free competition between businesses and that they do not gain an unfair advantage over their rivals
- to protect the environment
- to protect inventions and intellectual property.

Consumers and the law

To prevent businesses from making misleading claims or selling faulty products or services, there are a number of laws designed to protect consumers.

Trade Descriptions Act 1968

This makes it a criminal offence to describe goods and services incorrectly. If a watch is described as water-resistant to 50 metres and made in Switzerland, then that is exactly what it must be.

Sale of Goods Act 1979

When you buy a product you enter a legal contract with the seller, meaning that it is the seller and not the manufacturer who must deal with any complaints a consumer may have. The seller must make sure that the goods are 'fit for purpose' and of 'merchantable quality'. They must do what they are supposed to do and not be damaged or defective in any way.

This Act was also amended in 1994 and 1995.

Supply of Goods and Services Act 1982

This has the same purpose as the *Sale of Goods Act* but applies to services.

Weights and Measures Act 1985

This makes it illegal for a business to sell short measures or goods that are under-weight. A pint of beer should be a pint of beer and 1 kilogramme of sugar should be 1 kilogramme of sugar. Inspectors have the right to test weighing and measuring equipment to ensure it is correctly calibrated.

Consumer Protection Act 1987

Businesses are liable for any damage that their defective goods might cause. The Act ensures that goods are safe to use and not likely to cause injury or loss of life eg faulty gas heaters.

Food and Drugs Act 1955

It is a criminal offence to sell food or drink that is unfit for human consumption, or on which the labelling wrongly describes the contents or misleads people about the quality or nutritional value of food.

Consumer Credit Act 1974 and 2006

This Act states that any business giving credit must be licensed. Consumers must know how much extra they are paying in interest, and there must be a 'cooling off' period during which goods bought on credit can be returned.

In 2006 the 1974 Act was updated to extend to consumer protection and to allow lenders to compete on a fair and comparable footing. It provided for the introduction of the Financial Ombudsman Service (FOS) scheme for dispute resolution and the introduction of the Unfair Relationships Test.

Unsolicited Goods and Services Act 1971

Businesses are prevented from delivering unordered goods and then demanding payment.

Fair Trading Act 1973

This Act established the Office of Fair Trading, the main aims of which are to:

- inform consumers of their rights
- prosecute businesses that break the law
- recommend to the Monopolies and Mergers Commission (MMC) any businesses that need to be investigated.

Most consumer legislation is enforced through local councils' Trading Standards and Environmental Health Departments. By introducing these laws, the government is forcing businesses to accept their responsibilities to consumers. Compliance with these laws will lead to increased costs for businesses but will also ensure they maintain consumer satisfaction by providing quality products and high service standards.

Unfair Commercial Practices Directive (May 2008)

This new EU Directive will prohibit misleading or aggressive commercial practices, including advertising and marketing. The aim of this Directive is to harmonise protection throughout the EU. It will be introduced in the UK in the form of the *Consumer Protection from Unfair Trading Regulations*. This will replace most of the Trades Descriptions Act.

A commercial practice will be deemed unfair if it is a misleading action, omission, or aggressive. A misleading action will include information that is erroneous or 'likely to deceive the average consumer, even if the information is correct'. Misleading omissions will include those omissions that hide material information or make such information unclear or ambiguous. A commercial practice that is aggressive will impair a consumer's freedom of choice, coercing him or her to make a transaction that would not have been made otherwise.

The regulations are designed to protect consumers from unscrupulous traders and protect small businesses from unfair competition.

The regulations list 31 specific practices which are banned, for example:

- faking credentials
- exhortations to children to buy products
- pestering consumers by phone, fax and email

The regulations are to be enforced by the Office of Fair Trading, Trading Standards officers and Ofcom, and anyone in breach of this will be subjected to a potential unlimited fine or imprisonment for up to two years.

Data Protection Act 1998

This is a large and complex act. It defines a legal basis for the handling information relating to living people. It is the main piece of legislation that governs the protection of personal data in the UK. Although the Act does not mention privacy, in practice it provides a way in which individuals can enforce control over information available about them.

It has eight basic principles:

- Data may only be used for the specific purposes for which it was collected.
- Data must not be disclosed to other parties without the consent of the individual to whom it relates, unless there is legislation or another overriding legitimate reason to share the information (for example, the prevention and detection of crime). It is an offence for 'other parties' to obtain this personal data without authorisation.

- Individuals have a right of access to the information held about them with certain specific exceptions (for example, information held for the prevention or detection of crime).
- Personal information may be kept for no longer than is necessary.
- Personal information may not be transmitted outside the European Economic Area unless the individual to whom it relates has consented or adequate protection is in place, for example, by the use of a prescribed form of contract to govern the transmission of the data.
- Subject to some exceptions for organisations that only do very simple processing, and for domestic use, all entities that process personal information must register with the Information Commissioner.
- Entities holding personal data are required to have adequate security measures in place. These include technical measures (such as firewalls) and organisation measures (such as staff training).
- Compliance with the Act is overseen by an independent government authority – the Office of the Information Commissioner (OIC). The OIC maintains guidance relating to the Act.

Competition and the law

The main legislation influencing the conduct of businesses is competition policy. These laws and controls ensure that businesses are run legally and fairly.

Restrictive Trade Practices Act 1976

Businesses are prevented from:

- agreeing to fix prices with a competitor
- restricting output, which in turn would reduce supply and artificially inflate price
- dividing the market eg supermarkets agreeing to stay out of each others' areas.

Resale Prices Act 1976

It is illegal for manufacturers to fix the price at which retailers can sell their products. Manufacturers can recommend a price but not enforce it, ie supermarkets are allowed to sell jeans at prices less than those recommended by the manufacturer.

Fair Trading Act 1973

This act set up the Office of Fair Trading (OFT) and the MMC. Their roles are to ensure that competition takes place between businesses and to stop restrictive practices. The MMC investigates businesses that wish to merge and to prevent a monopoly being created. A monopoly situation is defined as one where one business controls 25% of the supply of products or services in a market and would be judged to be against the public interest.

When many nationalised businesses, such as British Telecom, were privatised, they had monopolies in particular markets. As a result, the government set up regulators to monitor those businesses and deal with any complaints from consumers.

Role of regulators

In the UK there are many regulators, such as Ofcom (communications) and Ofwat (water). All have regulatory powers delegated by government. They are also obliged to have a consumer panel (an independent body to ensure that the views of the consumers are reflected in the regulator's decision-making).

The environment and the law

Today, the government, consumers and businesses are much more aware of the environment and how we are damaging it. There are currently two acts that help protect the environment.

The Environmental Protection Act 1990

Under this Act, businesses must ensure that they are using those methods that will best reduce the amount of land, air and water pollution.

Clean Air Act 1993

This controls the emission of smoke from factories and homes.

Intellectual property and the law

There are a number of laws designed to allow ownership of intellectual property (IP) in the same way as owning physical property. This enables the use of IP to be controlled; it generates rewards and is designed to encourage innovation and creativity.

The four main types of IP are:

- copyright: protects material such as literature, art, music, sound, recordings, films and broadcasts

- designs: protect the visual appearance or appeal of products
- patents: protect the technical and functional aspects of products and their processes
- trade marks: protect symbols or logos that can distinguish the goods and services of one trader from another

IP also covers trade secrets, plant varieties, geographical indications, performer rights and so on. Often, more than one IP may apply to the same creation.

Copyright, Designs and Patents Act 1988

This gives the creators of literary, dramatic, musical and artistic works the right to control the ways in which their material may be used. The rights cover the broadcasting and public performance, copying, adapting, issuing, renting and lending of copies to the public. In many cases, the creator will also have the right to be identified as the author and to object to distortions of his or her work.

Copyright arises when an individual or organisation creates a work, and copyright applies to a work if it is regarded as original and exhibits a degree of labour, skill or judgement. When an idea is fixed, for example in writing, copyright automatically protects it. This means you do not have to apply for copyright.

Interpretation is related to the independent creation rather than the idea behind the creation. For example, an idea for a book would not itself be protected, but the actual content of a book would be. In other words, someone else is still entitled to write their own book around the same idea, provided they do not directly copy or adapt someone else's to do so.

Names, titles, short phrases and colours are not generally considered unique or substantial enough to be covered, but a creation such as a logo that combines these elements, may be.

Design right is also a free, automatic right available when someone creates an original design. It gives that person the right to stop anyone copying the design for up to 15 years. Registered designs mean that no one can copy the design in the UK for up to 25 years.

Patents law

Patents law also consists of a number of acts, rules and directions that set out legal rights, duties and procedures for patents. These are designed to provide a complete code of patent validity and protection against infringement. They codify the law of property in patents and patent applications, and provide for procedures operated by the Patent Office in granting and revoking patents, granting compulsory licences, determining inventorship and ownership and other such matters.

A granted patent must be renewed every year after the fifth year, for up to 20 years' protection.

Trade Marks Act 1974

Trade mark legislation in the UK consists of acts, rules and statutory instruments that set out legal rights, duties and procedures relating to trade marks. The Trade Marks Act (1974) covers the registration of trade marks and the protection of registered trade marks in the UK.

The UK's membership of certain international conventions and treaties also gives rise to obligations to protect patents originating in other member countries.

A registered trade mark must be renewed every ten years to keep it in force.

Registering designs, patents and trade marks

For advice and application forms to ensure that your IP is registered and protected, contact the UK Intellectual Property Office (the operating name of the Patents Office). A number of companies also specialise in helping companies register their IP.

 Key points to remember

1. The law is complex and changes continually so work closely with your legal counsel to stay on the right side of the law while still pushing the boundaries to their limit.

2. As a first port of call work with the appropriate trade bodies to ensure you stay within the law and trade codes of practice.

3. In order to protect products and brands from infringement and copy-cat activity, make sure you own the necessary, relevant copyright, design, patent and trade mark protection, specific to the countries that you wish them to cover.

Appendix 1

References & Further Reading

Introduction
References
1. Arrowsmith, David *AccountingWEB website* (www.AccountingWEB.co.uk), August 2007
Recommended Reading
1. Wilson, A *The Marketing Audit Handbook*, 2002

Chapter 1 Starting Out
Recommended Reading
1. Directors' responsibilities – Companies House website
   (www.companieshouse.gov.uk/about/gbhtml/gba1.shtml#two)

Chapter 2 The Role of Marketing in the Business
References
1. PA Consulting Group *Survey on Managing for Shareholder Value*, 2002
2. Welch, Jack *Winning*, 1999
3. Walton, Sam *Sam Walton: Made in America*, 1993
4. Adapted from Aaker, David *Building Strong Brands*, 1995
Recommended Reading
1. Thomas, Mark *The Complete CEO – The Executive's Guide to Consistent Peak Performance*, 2006

Chapter 3 Strategy Development
References
1. Kay, John *Strategy and the Delusion of Grand Designs*, Financial Times, 1999
2. McKinsey and Co *Quarterly Survey*, January 2005
3. Henderson, Bruce, Boston Consulting Group *Perspectives on Strategy*, 1996
4. Porras, Jerry I and Collins, James C *Built to Last*, 1997
5. Igor Ansoff's Matrix was first published in the *Harvard Business Review* in 1957
Recommended Reading
1. Barrow, Colin; Barrow, Paul and Brown, Robert *The Business Plan Workbook – The Definitive Guide to Researching, Writing Up and Presenting a Winning Plan*, 2008
2. Lake, Neville *The Strategic Planning Workbook*, 2006

Chapter 4 Competitive Analysis
Recommended Reading
1. Fleisher, Craig S and Bensoussan, Babette *Strategic and Competitive Analysis: Methods and Techniques for Analyzing Business Competition*, 2002

Chapter 5 Setting Objectives and Measuring Marketing Performance
References
1. The CMO Council *Assessing Marketing's Value and Impact*, 2004
2. Drucker, Peter F *The Practice of Management*, 1955
3. Armstrong, M *A Handbook of Human Resource Management Practice*, 2006
4. Pareto, Vilfredo *Pareto's Principle*, 1906 (also known as the 80/20 rule and the rule of the vital few. Named after the Italian philosopher Vilfredo Pareto (b. 1848, d 1923)). Wikipedia website (en.wikipedia.org/wiki/Pareto_principle)

Recommended Reading
1. Eechambadi, Naras *Chapter 4 – The Measure of Marketing, High Performance Marketing*, 2005
2. Odiorne, George S *Management by Objectives*, 1970

Chapter 6 Customer Strategy
References and Acknowledgements
1. Maslow, Abraham H *A Theory of Human Motivation*. Psychological Review, 50, 370–396, 1943
2. Maslow, Abraham H *Motivation and Personality*, 2nd ed, New York, Harper & Row, 1970
3. Reproduced with kind permission from BBC Gardeners' World at BBC Worldwide
4. Doyle, Professor Peter *Marketing Management and Strategy, 1996 Industrial Markets* , 1996

Chapter 7 Product Strategy
References
1. Morita, Akio *Sony History (chapters 17 and 18)*, Sony website (www.sony.net)
2. Lavidge, Robert J and Steiner Gary. A *A Model of Predictive Measurements of Advertising Effectiveness:* Journal of Marketing, vol. 25, no 6, 1961
3. Hertzberg, Frederik *The Motivation to Work*, 1959
4. Peters, Tom *The Pursuit of Excellence*, 1994
5. MacDonald, Professor Malcolm, Cranfield School of Management, Paper on *Key Elements of World Class Marketing*, 2002

Chapter 8 From Strategy to Delivery
References
1. Daft, RL *Essentials of Organisation Structure and Design*, 2001
Recommended Reading
1. Champy, James *Reengineering Management: the Mandate for New Leadership*, 1995
2. Dibb, Sally; Simkin, Lyndon; Pride, Willima M and Ferrell, O.C *Marketing: Concepts and Strategies*, 2005
3. Drucker, Peter F *Managing in Time of Great Change*, 1995
4. Fill, Chris *Marketing Communications: Engagement, Strategies and Practice: Enhanced Media Edition*, 2007
5. Smith, Paul *Marketing Communications: An Integrated Approach*, 1998

Chapter 9 Financial Management

References
1. Case, Karl E and Fair, Ray C *Principles of Economics*, 1999
2. Box, George and Jenkins, Gwilym *Time series analysis: Forecasting and control*, 1990
3. Simon, Hermann; Bilstein, Frank F; Luby, Frank *Manage for Profit not for Market Share*, 2006

Recommended Reading
1. Ambler, Tim *Marketing and the Bottom Line,* 2003
2. McDonald, Malcolm; Ward, Keith and Smith, Brian *Marketing Due Diligence: Reconnecting Strategy to Share Price,* 2007

Chapter 10 Structuring the Function

References
1. Kim, Peter *Reinventing the Marketing Organization,* Forrester Research Inc, 2006

Recommended Reading
1. Weick, Karl E *The Social Psychology of Organizing*, 1980

Chapter 11 Day to Day Management

References
1. Blanchard, Kenneth H and Johnson, Spencer *The One Minute Manager,* 1999

Recommended Reading
1. Covey, Stephen R *7 Habits of Highly Effective People*, 1999
2. Acas website (www.acas.org.uk/media/pdf/n/m/G03_1.pdf)

Chapter 12 Team Motivation and Development

References
1. Hertzberg, F; Mausner, B; & Snyderman, B.B *The Motivation to Work,* 1959
2. Steers, Richard M and Porte, Lyman W *Motivation and Work Behavior*, 1975

Chapter 13 Managing the Board and Business as a Whole

References
1. Dorn, Robert *The Center for Creative Leadership*, 1988
2. Campbell, David *If I'm in Charge Here Why is Everybody Laughing*, 1980

Recommended Reading
1. Bain, Neville *The Effective Director – Building Individual and Board Success,* 2007
2. Bass, Bernard M *Handbook of Leadership*, Stodgill's, 1981
3. Blanchard, Kenneth *The One Minute Manager Builds High Performing Teams,* 1994
4. Dunne, Patrick *Running Board Meetings,* 2007
5. Institute of Directors *The Director's Handbook – Institute of Directors The Director's Handbook – Your Duties, Responsibilities and Liabilities,* 2007
6. McCormack, Mark H *What they don't teach you at Harvard Business School,* 1984
7. Mills, Geoffrey *On the Board*, 1985

Chapter 14 Managing Market or Customer Research

References
1. ESOMAR (European Society for Opinion and Marketing Research) 2002

2. *The Market Research Handbook* (www.mrs.org.uk), *The Association of Qualitative Research Handbook* (www.aqr.org.uk) and *ESOMAR Handbook* (www.esomar.org), The Marketing Society (www.marketing-society.org.uk)
3. Professional Research Consultants Inc (www.prconline.com/tools-ssc) and Statpac Inc (www.statpac.com/statistics-calculator)
4. Woods, Richard *Changing How to Look at Brands*, Brand Strategy, March 2000

Recommended Reading
1. Birn, Robin *The Effective Use of Market Research*, 2004
2. Gordon, Wendy and Langmuir, Ray *Qualitative Research*, 1988
3. Miriampolski, Hy *Qualitative Market Research*, 2001

Chapter 15 Managing Agencies

Recommended Reading
1. ISBA Agency Brief (www.isba.org.uk)
2. Katz, Helen E *The Media Handbook*, 2003
3. Lewis, Harold *Choosing and Using Consultants and Advisers*, 2006
4. Ogilvy, David *Ogilvy on Advertising*, 1985
5. Percy, Larry and Elliot, Richard *Strategic Advertising Management*, 2005
6. Steel, Jon *Truth, Lies, and Advertising: The Art of Account Planning*, 1998

Chapter16 Brand Management

References and Acknowledgements
1. Aaker, David A *Managing Brand Equity*, 1991
2. Davidson, Hugh *Even More Offensive Marketing*, 1997
3. Interbrand website (www.brandchannel.com)
4. Global Vantage, Standard and Poor's and McKinsey as featured in an article by Bryan, Lowell L and Zanini, Michele *Strategy in an era of Global Giants, McKinsey Quarterly 2005* Number 4, 2005
5. All logos are registered trademarks and are reproduced with kind permission from their respective owners: 'Nike swoosh' – Nike, Inc., 'Coca-Cola' - The Coca-Cola Company
6. Lucozade website (www.lucozade.co.uk)
7. Tesco website (www.tesco.com)
8. All logos are registered trademarks and are reproduced with kind permission from their respective owners: Tesco Stores Ltd., BT plc, the British Broadcasting Corporation, The Ford Motor Company and Green & Black's (Cadbury plc)
9. Oando Energy Group website (www.oandoplc.com)
10. Reproduced with kind permission from Agatha Christie Ltd (a Chorion company)
11. Bullmore, Jeremy WPP, quoted in the *Financial Times*, July 2002
12. Harvard Business Online

Recommended Reading
1. Aaker, David A *Building Strong Brands*, 1996
2. Miller Jon, and Muir David, *The Business of Brands*, 2004
3. Taylor, David *The Brand Gym*, 2002

Chapter 17 Optimising Customer Communications
References
1. Peppers, Don and Rogers, Martha *The One to One Future: Building Relationships One Customer at a Time,* 1998
2. Internetworldstats website (www.internetworldstats.com)
3. Packard, Vance *The Hidden Persuaders,* 1957
Recommended Reading
2. Kimmel, Allan J *Marketing Communication: New Approaches, Technologies, and Styles,* 2005

Chapter 18 Customer Relationship Marketing
References
1. Stevens, Mark *Extreme Management,* 2001
Recommended Reading
1. Bird, Drayton *Commonsense Direct and Digital Marketing,* 2007
2. Chakravorti, Samit *Customer Relationship Management (CRM),* 2007
3. Godin, Seth *Permission Marketing: Turning Strangers into Friends and Friends into Customers,* 2007
4. Newell, Frederick *Why CRM Doesn't Work: How to Win by Letting Customers Manage the Relationship,* 2003
5. Rapp, Stan and Collins, Thomas L *Maxi Marketing,* 1987

Chapter 19 Customer Channel Management
Recommended Reading
1. Arikan, Akin *Multichannel Marketing: Metrics and Methods for On and Offline Success,* 2008

Chapter 20 Project Management
References
1. Wikipedia website (en.wikipedia.org/wiki/Critical_path_method)
2. Gantt, H. L *Work, Wages and Profit,* The Engineering Magazine, 1910
Recommended Reading
2. Poole M. S and Van de Ven, A. H *Central issues in the study of change and innovation,* 2004
3. Westland, Jason *The Project Management Lifecycle,* 2007

Chapter 21 Creativity and Problem Solving
References
1. de Bono, Edward *I am Right, You are Wrong,* 1992
2. de Bono, Edward *Six Thinking Hats,* 1985
3. Parnes, Dr Sidney *Source Book for Creative Problem Solving,* 1992
4. Olsen, Robert W *The Art of Creative Thinking,* 1980
5. Capodagli, Bill and Jackson, Lynn *The Disney Way – Harnessing the Management Secrets of Disney in Your Company,* 1999
6. Gordon, W J J *Goodthinking,* 1999
7. Shell International Ltd (www.shell.com) *Shell Global Scenarios, 2005*
8. Capodagli, Bill and Jackson, Lynn *The Disney Way – Harnessing the Management Secrets of Disney in Your Company,* 1999

Recommended Reading
1. Allan, Dave; Kingdon, Matt; Murrin, Kris and Rudkin, Daz *?What If? How to Start a Creative Revolution at Work*, 1999
2. Dru, Jean Marie *Beyond Disruption, Changing the Rules of the Marketplace*, 2002

Chapter 22 Restoring Growth
Recommended Reading
1. Thomas, Mark *Chapter 3, Dealing with Underperforming Businesses, The Complete CEO*, 2006

Chapter 23 Product Development
References
1. Product Development and Management Association (www.pdma.org), 2004
2. Kuczmarski, Thomas *Innovation Leadership Strategies for the Competitive Edge*, 1996
3. Cooper, Robert G *Winning at New Products*, 1993
4. Wikipedia website (en.wikipedia.org/wiki/Abbie_Hoffman)
5. Rich, Ben; Janos, Leo *Skunk Works*, 1996 (www.skunkworks.net)
6. Tomlinson, Guy *Views, The Journal of the Qualitative Research Consultants Association*, spring 2005
7. Bases website (www.bases.com)
8. Acupoll website (www.acupoll.com)
Recommended Reading
1. Bennis Warren G and Biederman, Patricia W *Organizing Genius: the Secrets of Creative Collaboration*, 1998
2. Kahn, Kenneth B *The PDMA Handbook of New Product Development*, 2004

Chapter 24 Marketing and Digital Technology
References
1. Moore, Gordon E *Cramming More Components Onto Integrated Circuits*, Electronics, 1965
2. Moore, Gordon E *No Exponential is Forever...But We Can Delay 'Forever'*, presentation at International Solid State Circuits Conference (ISSCC), 2003
3. MarketingProfs website (www. marketingprofs.com)
Recommended Reading
1. Bocij, Paul; Chaffey, Dave; Greaseley Andrew and Hickie, Simon *Business Information Systems: Technology, Development and Management in E-business*, 2005
2. Kline, Stephen; Dyer-Witheford, Nick and de Peuter, Greig *Digital Play: The Interaction of Technology, Culture and Marketing*, 2003

Chapter 25 Mergers and Acquisitions
References
1. Frost and Sullivan Research, 2006
2. O'Sullivan, Kate *Secrets of the M&A Masters, CFO Magazine*, September 2005
3. Porter, Michael E *Competitive Strategy*, 1990
4. Wilson, Richard M and Gilligan, Colin *Strategic Marketing Management: Planning Implementation and Control*, 1997
5. Kaplan, Robert S and Norton, David P *The Balanced Scorecard: Translating Strategy Into Action*, 1996

Recommended Reading
1. Hanna, David and Walker, Paul *What makes a successful merger?* Strategic Finance, April 1999
2. Sudarsanam, Sudi *Creating Value Through Merger and Acquisitions: The Challenges, an Integrated and International Perspective*, 2003

Chapter 26 Rationalisation or Downsizing
References
1. Hamel, G and Prahalad, C K *Competing for the future*, Harvard Business Review, 1994
2. Cameron, K S *Investigating organizational downsizing-fundamental issues*, Human Resources Management, 1994
3. Hickok, Thomas A *Downsizing and Organisation Culture*, Public Administration and Management: An Interactive Journal, Volume Three, Number 3 1998 (www.pamij.com)
4. Kearns, D and Nadler, D *Prophets in the dark: How Xerox reinvented itself and beat back the Japanese*, 1992
5. Acas website (www.acas.org.uk/index.aspx?articleid=777)
6. Downs, Alan *Corporate Executions*, 1995
Recommended Reading
1. Department for Business Enterprise and Regulatory Reform website *Redundancy consultation and notification: guidance* (www.berr.gov.uk/employment/employment-legislation/employment-guidance)
2. Downs, Alan *Corporate Executions*, AMACOM, 1995
3. Hickok, Thomas A *Workforce Reductions: An Annotated Bibliography*, 2004

Chapter 27 Culture Change and Brand Delivery
References
1. Kotter, John P and Heskett, James L *Corporate Culture & Performance*, 1992
2. Daft R L *Essentials of Organisation Structure and Design*, 2001
3. Tomlinson, Guy – research paper presented at New Solutions event, *Winning Strategies for Building a Distinctive and Appealing Brand Experience*, 2003
4. Rucci, Kirn and Quinn *Employee-Customer Profit Model*, Harvard Business Review, Jan-Feb 1998
5. Adapted from Pine, James and Gilmore, James *The Experience Economy*, 1999
6. Lewin, Kurt *Frontiers in Group Dynamics*, 1946
7. Argyris, Chris *Empowerment: the Emperor's New Clothes*, Harvard Business Review, May-June 1998
8. Pascale, R; Millemann, M and Gioia, L *Changing the Way We Change*, Harvard Business Review, November-December 1997
Recommended Reading
1. Gilmore, Fiona et al *Brand Warriors: Corporate Leaders Share Their Winning Strategies*, 1998
2. Senge, Peter M et al *The Fifth Discipline, The Art and Practice of the Learning Organization*, 1990
3. Schein, Edgar H *Organisation Culture and Leadership*, 1992

Chapter 28 Crisis Planning and Management
Recommended Reading
1. Gustin, Joseph F *Disaster & Recovery Planning: A Guide for Facility Managers,* 2004
2. Coombs, W. Timothy *Ongoing Crisis Communication: Planning, Managing, and Responding,* 2007

Chapter 29 Communicating with Other Audiences
Recommended Reading
1. UK government gateway to corporate social responsibility (www.csr.gov.uk)
2. Blowfield, Michael and Murray, Alan *Corporate Responsibility: A Critical Introduction,* 2008
3. Haywood, Roger *Corporate Reputation – the Brand and the Bottom Line,* 2005
4. Schmitt, Bernd H *Experiential Marketing,* 2000
5. Wheeler, David and Sillanpaa, Maria *The Stakeholder Corporation,* 1997

Chapter 30 Marketing and the Law
References
1. The Chartered Institute of Marketing, *Trends Survey,* November 2007
Recommended Reading
1. UK Statute Law Database (www.statutelaw.gov.uk)
2. UK Intellectual Property Office website (www.ipo.gov.uk)

Appendix 2   Acronyms

AIDA	attention, interest, desire, action
AMV	Abbott Mead Vickers
B2B	business to business
CED	customer experience director
CEO	chief executive officer
CFO	chief financial officer
CIM	Chartered Institute of Marketing
CLV	Customer Lifetime Value
CSR	corporate social responsibility
DAM	digital asset management
EDLP	everyday low pricing
EMM	electronic marketing management
EP	economic profit
ESOMAR	European Society for Opinion and Marketing Research
EU	European Union
FD	financial director
FMCG	fast-moving consumer goods
FOS	Financial Ombudsman Service
FSA	full service agency
GDP	gross domestic product
GRPS	gross rating points
HR	human resources
Idis	in-depth interviews
IDM	Institute of Direct Marketing
IP	intellectual property
IPTV	Internet Protocol TV
ISP	Institute of Sales Promotion
IT	Information Technology
JIT	just in time
KVI	Known Value Item
KPI	key performance indicator
M&A	mergers and acquisitions

MBO	Management by Objectives
MD	managing director
MMC	Monopolies and Mergers Commission
MPM	marketing performance measurement
NPV	net present value
OFT	Office of Fair Trading
PAF	postcode address file
PBT	profit before tax
PDMA	Product Development and Management Association
PEST	political, economic, social and technological
PLC	Public Limited Company
PP	payback period
PPC	pay-per-click
RFM	recency, frequency, monetary
ROI	return on investment
SEO	search engine optimisation
SLA	service level agreement
SMART	specific, measurable, actionable or agreed to, realistic, time specific
SWOT	strengths, weaknesses, opportunities, threats
TLA	three letter acronym
TQM	total quality management
TSR	total shareholders' return
TVRS	television ratings
VOIP	Voice Over Internet Protocol

The Marketing Directors' Forum

Our aim in writing this book is to help you be a superior and successful marketer. Given the rapidly changing world about us, the skills, expertise and tools needed tomorrow may be very different to today. So to help us make additions or improvements to future editions of the handbook, please send us any insights or ideas to do this as well as any stories that you think evidence best practice or superior marketing.

You can get in touch by writing to The Marketing Director's Handbook, The Old Barrel Store, Brewery Courtyard, Draymans Lane, Marlow, Buckinghamshire, SL7 2FF, UK, by e-mail to <handbook@themarketingdirectors.co.uk>, or by joining in our discussion forum at <http://www.themarketingdirectorshandbook.co.uk>.

We'll assume we can acknowledge your contribution unless you tell us otherwise.

Our on-line discussion forum is also a place where you can pose questions and discuss your marketing challenges and experiences with fellow marketing directors and readers of this book.

Index